D0573553

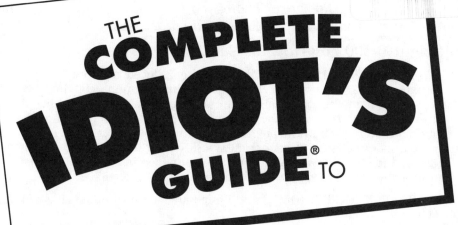

THE

COMPLETE IDIOT'S GUIDE® TO

Starting Your Own Restaurant

by Howard Cannon with Brian Tarcy

ALPHA

A Pearson Education Company

I dedicate this book to all the restaurant operators out in the trenches each and every day providing a heaping helping of hospitality, quality, service, and cleanliness at a fair price. Thank you for your continued dedication to your customers, your employees, and your craft.

Copyright © 2002 by Howard Cannon

International Standard Book Number: 0-02-864168-X
Library of Congress Catalog Card Number: 2001095862

04   03   02   8   7   6   5   4   3   2   1

Interpretation of the printing code: The rightmost number of the first series of numbers is the year of the book's printing; the rightmost number of the second series of numbers is the number of the book's printing. For example, a printing code of 02-1 shows that the first printing occurred in 2002.

Printed in the United States of America

Publisher
Marie Butler-Knight

Product Manager
Phil Kitchel

Managing Editor
Jennifer Chisholm

Senior Acquisitions Editor
Renee Wilmeth

Development Editor
Michael Thomas

Production Editor
Billy Fields

Copy Editor
Heather Stith

Illustrator
Jody Schaeffer

Cover Designers
Mike Freeland
Kevin Spear

Book Designers
Scott Cook and Amy Adams of DesignLab

Indexer
Angie Bess

Layout/Proofreading
Svetlana Dominguez
Ayanna Lacey

Contents at a Glance

Contents

Appendixes

Foreword

Close your eyes. Now picture yourself, a sleek and sophisticated restaurateur, flitting from table to table in your understated yet elegant dining room, which is packed with satisfied diners.

"How is everything this evening?" you ask.

"Oh, it's just wonderful," they gush. "Are you the owner?"

"Why yes," you reply, beaming. "Yes, I am."

Now, WAKE UP!

You share your fantasy with many. The perceived glamour of the restaurant industry lures people from all walks of life. Movie stars, real estate tycoons, sports figures—it seems that everyone's opening a restaurant these days. After all, all you need is a name people recognize and guests will flock to your door, right?

Wrong. Even celebrities are learning the hard way that a name might bring people in once, but it takes a commitment to delivering quality food, quality drinks, and quality service every time to keep them coming back.

Getting from square one, where you probably now stand, to the fantastic scenario described above, requires many months, if not years, of long, hard work. And along the way, your bank account might disappear, your family might forget what you look like, and your friends might recommend that you "get help."

Still interested? Great—you've come to the right place!

There are a lot of difficult truths in the restaurant industry, and while no one can claim to know them all, Howard Cannon comes darn close. A 20-year veteran of the industry, Cannon has owned restaurants, managed hundreds of units for national chains, and consulted for some of the foremost restaurant companies in the country. Lots of people claim to know how to run a restaurant, but few can explain it with the wit, sincerity, and experience-based expertise Cannon offers.

Cannon takes you step-by-step, from creating your concept to opening your second store. From business plans to site selection, purchasing to hiring, promoting to serving—and everything in between—Cannon gives you a crash course in the reality of starting a restaurant. For everything you've already thought of, he knows 10 more challenges that probably never occurred to you.

The restaurant industry is highly competitive, fast-paced, and dynamic. As soon as the trade press identifies a trend, it changes. As soon as you've analyzed your market research, your demographics shift. Just when you've trained the perfect chef, your headwaiter quits. But that's okay, because restaurant people know how to handle it. Restaurant professionals are some of the most intelligent, dedicated, and truly enthusiastic people I've ever seen. The successful ones are so passionate about what they do that they excite everyone they meet. They're educated, quick-witted, and voracious seekers of knowledge. They're just like you.

Restaurants do succeed. And they all start just like yours, so your chances are as good as anyone's. Better—because you're starting here. Good luck!

Jennifer Kramer Williams
Editor, *Restaurant Marketing* magazine

Jennifer Kramer Williams has covered the food and beverage industry for four years with Oxford Publishing Inc., publishers of *Restaurant Marketing, Nightclub & Bar,* and *Beverage Retailer* magazines, and producers of the Food & Beverage Convention and Trade Show. You can contact her at jwilliams@oxpub.com, or visit www.restaurant-marketing.net.

Introduction

You are excited about someday opening and operating your own restaurant. Maybe it will happen next week, maybe next year, or maybe a few years from now, but the dream is vivid, and the passion is as hot as a bowl of French onion soup. I understand. Owning and operating restaurants is in my blood, and I am proud to say it is a part of me. For the past 14 years, I have been living the dream.

Business ownership is a big part of the all-American dream, and restaurants have been, and continue to be, the largest entrepreneurial opportunity in the land. America has more than 844,000 restaurants already, and thousands more are built each year. The restaurant industry boasts the second largest workforce in the United States with more than 11.3 million people working in restaurants. Restaurant sales are pushing the $400 billion threshold, and that number continues to climb.

From national chains to single restaurants in your hometown, all restaurants started as an individual idea, a concept, a dream. Some dreams have turned into bigger realities than the founders could have ever imagined. Who would have thought a kiosk serving hamburgers would turn into a competitive fast-food marketplace where thousands of restaurants compete for your business every day? Or that pizza made in a garage would turn into today's pizza wars? What's next? Maybe your concept!

But this restaurant business is not an industry for the timid, the uncommitted, or the undereducated. My intent in this book is to give you a view of the industry from every conceivable angle. When you finish this book, you will more clearly see through the eyes of the customer, as well as the employee. You will understand more about handling food, as well as serving customers. You will become a journeymen accountant, human resources director, lawyer, and purchasing agent. That is part of the beauty about owning and operating a restaurant—the angles are far and wide. To be successful, you must be multitasking and multitalented.

I want you to understand the restaurant business inside and out. With this understanding, you will more likely make the first of a long line of decisions that will be right for you. By the time you finish this book, you will have gained in-depth knowledge about your own motivations, the inner workings of any restaurant, and a solid idea about what it's going to take to make the restaurant of your dreams a reality. The rest is up to you.

Let's begin to build your restaurant legacy. It starts now.

How to Use This Book

This book is divided into five parts.

Part 1, "What You Don't Know Can Hurt You," challenges you to think about the many aspects of starting your own restaurant. With a good, solid gut check or two, you will know whether this business is for you.

Part 2, "Building a Solid Foundation," walks you through the many stages of putting together a restaurant concept.

Part 3, "The Restaurant Operator: A Jack of Many Trades," helps you recognize the importance that the support functions play in building a successful restaurant. In fact, you can't build a successful restaurant concept without them.

Part 4, "Open for Business: The Basics of Operating," provides step-by-step instructions on operating the business effectively and efficiently.

Part 5, "Now What? Growing and Optimizing," shows you how to unleash top-notch performance and growth. Sure, one successful restaurant is nice, but the chapters in this part will help you make even more dough.

The appendixes provide additional resources and reference material that you may find helpful in your quest to operate profitable restaurants.

Extras

A visual reference is provided throughout the book in the form of various tips, warnings, thoughts, and definitions that pertain to the topic under immediate discussion.

Wet Floor!

These boxes give you warnings about situations you may face and advice on how to handle them.

Food for Thought

These boxes include interesting facts from the restaurant business that will help you understand how it all works.

Recipes Revealed

These boxes define common restaurant terms.

Tip Jar

These boxes give you ideas on how to make starting or running a restaurant easier.

Acknowledgements

From Howard Cannon:

I want to thank the academy (oh, wrong thank-you speech). Let me reorganize my speeches. I should be serious. This is a serious thing. The completion of a book is a time to reflect and recognize those who got me where I am today: sitting in a lonely office typing away to hit a dubious deadline with nothing more than my unique little ideas of how to run restaurants wanting to escape my strange little mind.

I don't want to turn these acknowledgements into a three-hour awards show special, so I will keep this list to people who have impacted me both personally and professionally for ages and those who were directly involved with this book.

Many of the companies (from small to large and from east to west) who have used my services and the services of my company, Restaurant Operations Institute, Inc., expect and demand anonymity. Many others have no qualms about their privacy. Either way, it is easiest to just say thanks without listing names. Thank you all so very much.

I also want to thank the many people who have worked with me both in my own company and in my time in corporate restaurant America. It was a pleasure working with and for each one of you.

Thank you Alpha Books for seeing the value of this book and fostering the continued success of *The Complete Idiot's Guide* series. Also, a special thank you goes to the entire CIG team for your hard work and dedication on this entire project.

Thank you to Brian Tarcy for making my writing smoother and to Michael Snell for walking me through this book business. Thank you to Chris Goldschmidt, Christi Marlin, and Jeff Hayes for believing in me and assisting me in far too many ways to list. And a special thanks to all of you for simply listening when I needed you to.

Finally, I want to acknowledge you, the reader, the dreamer, the restaurateur. I thank you for your willingness to grow on both a personal and professional level. This book is for you.

Special thanks …

To my wife Ronda and my sons, KC and Payton, for their everlasting love and support.

To my Mom, June, and Dad, Merlyn. To my brothers and sisters, Bob, Frank, Cathy, Shelley, Stuart, and Damon, and all the rest of the gang. Without the closeness of my family, I would be nothing.

To my buddies and partners in business and life, you know who you are. Thank you for always being there for me. If any of you need me for anything, I will deliver.

To my Grandma Kate Tyler, may her wonderful soul rest in peace. You have forever left your mark on me, and I love you so very much for it. The entire Tyler family tree is proud to say we will always be connected to each other because of you.

From Brian Tarcy:

I thank Howard Cannon for teaching me so much and for your professional approach to this project. I understand fully why you are so successful. It is always amazing to me, the things I learn. So yes, thank you. Someday I hope to eat at one of your restaurants. From your work on this project, my taste buds imagine the experience would be pure bliss. For now, simply, cheers.

Thanks to the staff at the Parrot Restaurant for providing the sustenance of life: cheeseburgers and beer.

I thank my previous co-authors for also teaching me so much and especially Hap Klopp, who first believed in me. Yes, I must pinch myself—the things I have learned since then. Thanks Hap, you were right about so much. And thanks to Mike Snell, who started this craziness a lifetime ago.

I have a very long list of great friends, and no list can include everybody. I'm sure lots of people make me rich, but I'm positive about Paul Sigler, Paul and Heidi Perekrests, Bob Vander Pyl and Sandy Sutherland, Stan Ingram, Gretchen Klaasen, Dan Ring, Gregg Alexander, and Vaughn Sterling. Four others also make me proud: Jason Rutledge, and Miles, Morgan, and Tristan Anders. To all of you: thanks.

I thank my children, Denim, Derek, Kayli, and Marissa for every meal that I ever enjoyed with you, from bagels to hot dogs to pizza or steak. Whenever you smile no matter the meal or the occasion, for that moment, my life is perfect. Thank you can never be enough. My wish, simply, is that you always find good food and someone to share it with.

As this is a book about restaurants, I thank the person who has cooked the best food I have ever tasted. You are the best friend I could ever imagine. I say "Yum!" I say "Wow!" I am lucky as pie to love Maureen Anders.

Finally, I thank my parents, Paul and Dorothy, and my brothers Gary and Dave. When I think of food, I think of family. When I think of family and food, I go back to the great Hungarian and Bohemian cuisine of my Cleveland childhood. I loved it all, especially the mouth-watering pig's feet. Now, on Cape Cod, the reward from my backyard Atlantic Ocean is too real to be a dream, but I still miss the famous harvest of Buckeye Road. And, of course, when I think of food I think of Grandma's cookies. God bless her, always.

Trademarks

All terms mentioned in this book that are known to be or are suspected of being trademarks or service marks have been appropriately capitalized. Alpha Books and Pearson Education, Inc., cannot attest to the accuracy of this information. Use of a term in this book should not be regarded as affecting the validity of any trademark or service mark.

Part 1

What You Don't Know
Can Hurt You

All great recipes are the result of the acquisition of vast amounts of knowledge. It may seem easy now, but somebody once figured out how much, at what temperature, and for how long. Creating a successful restaurant requires a lot of knowledge as well.

Part 1 explains exactly what is involved in running a restaurant, what the state of the industry is, what to consider when choosing your restaurant, and where, how, and why to get lots of professional advice. So come on in. It's time to start putting together your own recipe for success.

Table for One: Is This for Me?

Welcome to my book. Today's special is your dream. Yes, it seems everybody knows somebody who has the dream. If you're reading this then you have entertained thoughts of opening a restaurant with visions of raking in piles of cash and entertaining friends and neighbors, all while getting compliments for your delicious food and fabulous service. It's perhaps the most popular *entrepreneurial* dream of all—to own a restaurant. After all, restaurants are in nearly every village, town, and city in the world. Everyone eats. And besides, doesn't it look fun and easy?

Restaurant owners have owned sports teams, appeared on cooking shows on television, and led the local chamber of commerce. Restaurant success is relative, but in any town or city there are examples of those who have built thriving restaurants and wonderful lives. You've been in a restaurant. You know you can do it. Right?

Yes, you can.

But it may not be as easy as you think. Okay, the truth is that it won't be easy at all. You will certainly have to roll up your sleeves, and maybe the most important investment you'll make will be in a comfortable pair of shoes. But if you're in the restaurant business for the right reasons, all the hard work you're in for can be incredibly rewarding. Just remember, this is a different kind of life.

The best piece of advice I can offer you is to examine your passions. If you're running *from* something (a bad job, a bad boss, etc.) rather than running *to* the restaurant business, then you need to reconsider. Restaurant ownership is not for the timid. The rewards certainly can be great, but the path is arduous.

This chapter is about risks and rewards and deciding whether the restaurant business is for you. I offer a gut check of pitfalls (for example, the dishwasher skipped a shift and you're elbow deep in pans after a 14-hour day) and rewards (Ray Kroc, who eventually owned the San Diego Padres baseball team, started McDonald's on less than $1,000). Come on in and have a seat, and I'll try to help you figure it all out. What would you like to drink?

Recipes Revealed

An **entrepreneur** is a person who starts their own business. Being **entrepreneurial** is having the desire and ability to take risk, envision the future, and develop new business concepts and ideas or improve upon the business concepts of others.

Wet Floor!

Being a good cook, a great social host, or even a solid manager in a corporate environment does not guarantee your restaurant's success. Being able to point out the problems at the local restaurant is no guarantee of success either. A restaurant is your own show. Restaurants can have powerful profit-making potential if they're run extremely well, but they can also be a severe cash drain if they're run poorly.

Why a Restaurant?

Something must have attracted you to the restaurant business. Was it the money, the lifestyle, the desire to serve others? All three are certainly draws, although the first two are a bit of a stretch as attractions—at least in the beginning. The truth is there probably won't be a lot of money at first, and as for lifestyle— well, let's clear up some tee time and regular dinner date issues. If you start a restaurant, you need to reconsider your social life. Sorry, but that is a fact. You'll hardly have any leisure time at all.

First, the money issues: If you are good at what you do, the restaurant business is a great place to make a healthy and substantial living, but huge profits don't often come quickly. As with any form of entrepreneurship, a long period of time, often many years and even decades, passes before a person hits it big. Many entrepreneurs never do. There are no guarantees. Thus, you'll need lots of patience.

Still, don't stop yourself from dreaming big and don't allow anyone else to stop you either. But understand that you have to do an awful lot of work before wonderful things can happen for you. Too often I see a new owner acting like he has reached the pinnacle of success by just opening a restaurant. He forgets that opening a restaurant isn't the objective; building a profitable restaurant is.

As for lifestyle, owning a restaurant is more than a full-time job. When you start a restaurant, your free time becomes limited like never before. There is always more to do: organizing, ordering, cooking, cleaning, and on and on. And just because you have employees doesn't mean you'll be able to delegate everything. People can be unreliable. You will, at times, do every job in your restaurant, and often the times you have to do these jobs will be just when you want to leave for the day.

To be successful in the restaurant business, you have to enjoy serving people. Serving people is what a restaurant does, after all. People come to your place for food, but they won't come back if the service is bad. If serving others is something that is in your blood, then you will be passionate about the restaurant business. And your customers will notice.

Tip Jar

The 90/10 Rule is a variation of the 80/20 Rule, which states: Spend 80 percent of your time on the 20 percent most important things. The 90/10 Rule is to spend 90 percent of your time on the 10 percent most important things. Starting a restaurant takes supreme effort and focus. To do it successfully, you must clear as much of your schedule as possible and stay focused on the task at hand.

There Are No "Typical" Days

Running a restaurant involves many twists and turns: staff turnover, broken equipment, slow moments, and mad rushes. The restaurant business is full of rapid change, and the restaurant owner must be able to perform many different tasks requiring a multitude of skills. A start-up operation requires that you do tasks, such as check the previous day's receipts, prepare bank deposits, order products, do inventory, conduct operational checks, prepare food, build work schedules, greet customers, repair broken pieces of equipment, and more.

Very few fields require such a wide variety of skills and abilities as the restaurant business does. And the required skills change by the day, the hour,

Wet Floor!

As a restaurant owner, count on being "hands on." There are things you will be unable to avoid—washing dishes, mopping floors, unclogging toilets. And, oh, by the way, someone spilled a soda at table 27. Can you grab that?

and even the minute. There is no schedule except for this: You're always on the go in the restaurant business.

You can count on a few things, though. Long hours, sore feet, and intense rushes seem to go hand in hand with a booming restaurant business. The alternative of short days, sitting around, and no rushes could spell disaster. Depending on your hours of operation and restaurant concept (a topic which is covered in Chapter 3, "Choosing Your Restaurant"), you could be in for your fair share of late nights, early mornings, long weekends, and missed family gatherings.

So what is "typical" in the restaurant business? There is no typical.

Wanted: Management Skills

Somebody has to run this restaurant. Somebody has to manage these people. Somebody has to make all the decisions. Guess who that somebody is? Once you've made the decision to become a restaurant owner, you need to be prepared to manage three core things: yourself, your people, and your business.

Yourself

People who are great at leading themselves are usually great decision makers. Confidence garnered from knowledge makes it much easier to make smart decisions. Lack of data and information can cause you to make an uninformed and therefore bad decision. So use your head. Collect practical information and ask questions. Use your heart as well: See how you feel about your conclusions. Use the clock, too: Once you have the required data, don't be afraid to take a 24-hour cooling-off period to make a quality decision. If you're still torn about your decision, don't ignore your feelings. They're telling you to go back and do more research.

Another part of managing yourself is being able to assess your talents and personality honestly. Do you like risk? That's a major test of this dream of yours because your life becomes a risk when you take an entrepreneurial leap. An entrepreneur is able to endure and even enjoy risk as associated with a working business. Risk is part of the game. Winning strategies reduce risk.

Tip Jar

To learn about how a restaurant works and whether the lifestyle appeals to you, get a job on someone else's payroll. Although working for someone else is not the same as running your own place, the experience can be a great education.

Your People

The restaurant business is a people business. The number of people it takes to create one positive dining experience can be mind-boggling.

The core of building any team or relationship begins and ends with trust. The word *trust* itself is also a helpful acronym for the elements necessary to build a successful team:

➤ Truth: Be truthful to yourself, your people, and your vision. If you always tell the truth, even when it would be easier to go another route, you will never have to remember what story to tell.

➤ Respect: To be successful in any business you must respect the people who work for you, the people who work with you, and the customer who pays you.

➤ Understanding wants and needs: Understanding the perspectives of others will help you. If you know the goals, wants, and needs of others, it will help you build a more substantial and long-term business relationship.

➤ Solidifying team goals: Goals are wonderful—team goals are powerful. If the team gets the opportunity to set their own goals and build action plans to achieve them together, you will see more team spirit and significantly better performance.

➤ Touching hearts: Leading people and engendering excitement within people begins by touching their hearts. It is not enough to merely understand. You must care.

Your Business

In order to manage your business, you need plans: business plans, financial plans, marketing plans, and operational plans (for more details, see Chapter 5, "The Plan Is to Plan"). You cannot just wing it.

The Great Money and Time Questions

Two of the most popular questions that I hear from people who want to start a restaurant are: "What are the financial requirements for starting a restaurant?" and "How long will it take to open a restaurant?"

These loaded questions are impossible to answer without knowing more details about the type of restaurant you're opening. Are you taking over a pre-existing establishment or opening a new one from scratch? Is the structure free-standing or is it in-line (a mall-type environment)? Do you want to lease or own the property? You get the idea. There are many questions to answer. If you pursue your dream wisely, it will be many months before you serve your first glass of water.

If you want to open a restaurant, you need to make the restaurant your passion. And if you invest the time into putting together a plan, you will find the money you need to fund that passion. If you are haphazard and vague about your goals, you will most likely struggle to find financing or be forced to fund your ill-conceived plan on your own.

If you proceed carefully and thoroughly, the financial requirements will become quite clear, and the hurdles of getting the necessary capital will be easier to navigate. Tons of capital resources are available (see Chapter 7, "Shake the Money Tree," for more information), but investors always want to know your plan and how committed you are to that plan. Risking your own money is one way to demonstrate your level of commitment to other investors. If you are reluctant to risk your own money, not many people will risk theirs on you. But if the concept and business plan, born of your passion, work, the money will follow.

Food for Thought

The one significant difference between a dream and a goal is that goals are written down. Paper and pen are still the most powerful of all tools.

Tip Jar

There are no rules about where startup money must originate. I have seen many cases where little or no money comes out of the owner's pocket, and I have seen others where the entire show was self-financed. The only rule about investing is this: The successful owner always invests all of his or her passion.

Preliminary Start-Up Costs

Starting a restaurant is clearly going to cost you lots of time doing research and planning. You will need to present to investors what you are specifically proposing and how much starting your restaurant is going to cost. Planning takes an immense amount of time, but you can keep most of the preliminary planning costs to a minimum.

A computer, which you might already have, is the tool of the trade during the planning stages. (If you don't have a computer, you can get one for a few hundred bucks or borrow one at the library for free.) Research data, which is discussed in Chapter 3, is easily accessible and mostly free. Business planning software and/or guidelines can cost you around $200 or can be accessed for free at the local library. Your office space can be your dining room table or even the food court in the mall. (Using the food court as an office is a great way to get you into the hustle and bustle of the restaurant business, not to mention the ideas it might spark during your concept design phases.)

As you can clearly see, the costs of initial planning are very small—unless you count the price of missing television.

Ask Questions

Being a restaurant owner takes an extreme amount of knowledge and interest in a wide variety of areas, so learn from the experts. Surround yourself with professional assistance every chance you get. Of course, you should take this advice with the understanding that defining who an expert is is difficult. An expert is very much in the eye of the beholder.

Engaging multiple experts with specific knowledge bases will enable you to get to the heart of many different areas quickly. Talk to bankers, lawyers, accountants, repairmen, vendors, chamber of commerce staff, teachers, professors, and more. Don't forget other entrepreneurs, especially restaurateurs. Talk to virtually anyone who has a level of expertise that may come in handy.

The best part of all this expert advice is that it does not have to come at an hourly rate. If you're great at networking and building lasting friendships, you can learn for free. The key, of course, is being prepared to pose the right questions to the right people.

Take stock of your motivation and pinpoint your focus. Make your questions specific and take notes. Then find the intestinal fortitude to pursue the answers. And consider this question: Are you asking the right questions or just getting the answers that you want to hear?

A Story About Service and Risk

I close this first chapter with one of my favorite restaurant stories. It illustrates what I believe about service, investment, planning, and risk.

During my early Mexican food days, a softball team that had never been in before came into my restaurant. They ordered 16 regular bean burritos, 1 bean burrito with no onions, and 17 sodas. My team made the 16 regular bean burritos. I personally made the bean burrito with no onions and properly marked it.

Soon after receiving his food, the guy who had ordered the no-onion burrito came up to the counter stomping, spitting, and swearing, insisting that he did not get his no-onion burrito and that all the burritos had onions on them. I knew that he had received the correct order, but I admit I was a bit intimidated by his size and the number of his equally big buddies, not to mention the scene they were making.

Tip Jar

Here are a few of the right questions to ask an expert:

➤ What are the three most important keys to becoming a successful restaurant owner?

➤ What are some of the best educational resources for learning more about _____?

➤ Who is the best person you know at _____? Can you introduce me to him/her?

➤ How did you get started in your field?

➤ Would you mind if I called on you once in a while to ask for advice?

I decided that for simplicity's sake and in the interest of avoiding bodily harm, I would not recognize the fact that they were either wrong, confused, or trying to cheat me (which I truly thought was the case). Instinctively, I asked him, "What can I do to make it right?" Immediately, I could sense that his desire to fight went away, and he said, "I want a bean burrito with no onions for me and 16 more bean burritos for the rest of my team."

I immediately said, "Yes, sir. We are on it!" I then profusely apologized, handed him the entire order remade, smiled sheepishly, and thanked him for the opportunity to satisfy him and his team.

He, of course, strutted back to his table with his newfound wealth of burritos and the envy of all his teammates. I was simply happy to have all the commotion dissipate. Then a lady walked up to me and whispered that she had overheard the team jesting about "getting one over" on me regarding this whole burrito issue. I thanked her for her concerns, but told her that I wasn't worried about it and just wanted to make sure that each and every customer of mine was satisfied to the best of my team's ability. She was shocked and in awe of my commitment to customer satisfaction.

When I did my follow-up visit with the ball players to ensure that they were happy, they admitted that they had taken advantage of me and that there really was no burrito issue. They thought it was hilarious that they each got two burritos for the price of one. I laughed along with them and praised them on their creativity and negotiating skills. They became even friendlier. Interestingly enough, the whole team eventually became regulars and stopped in after every softball game.

The whole bean burrito story, as I now fondly call it, became legendary conversation and a cornerstone of my restaurant career. Those 17 extra bean burritos cost me about $4 in *food cost*, but they netted me thousands of dollars of sales. That's the restaurant business in a nutshell. You never know what kind of risk you may face, but if you do the right thing you've always got a good chance to reap tremendous rewards.

Tip Jar

Don't worry about the very small percentage of people who may take advantage of you. Concentrate instead on the huge wins you can have by sticking to your business ideas and turning all situations into ways to build and/or start loyalty.

Recipes Revealed

Food cost is one of the more important expenses to control if you are in the restaurant business. It is the cost of the ingredients that the restaurant pays. If you pay $1.25 for the ingredients that go into your Chicken Noodle Casserole and you sell it for $3.99, your food cost is $1.25, or 31.3 percent.

The Least You Need to Know

➤ The restaurant business is a different kind of life: long hours, long weeks, a fast pace one minute, a slow and relaxed pace the next. Expect to be on your feet all day and have lots of customer interaction.

➤ No two days in the restaurant business are exactly alike. Restaurant owners need to have a variety of skills, do many different tasks, and be able to adapt quickly.

➤ A good plan will go a long way in helping you find money and avoid pitfalls. Take the time to think it through.

➤ Being in charge means making lots of decisions.

➤ Your biggest investment will be your time.

➤ Risk brings reward.

Everybody Eats: The State of the Industry

It all started, as you might expect, in Paris.

A chef named Boulanger opened Champ d'Oiseau in Paris, France, in 1765. This was the first restaurant on record, and it came about because Boulanger had the audacity to try something new in the business world—serving food for profit at an outside establishment. Until then, chefs had worked for the wealthy, and everyone else cooked their own meals. But the concept of restaurants started to spread around 1789 when more chefs who were employed by the wealthy found themselves out of work and took to the idea of feeding the public for a price per meal. The French Revolution, it seems, spurred a revolution in how people ate.

By 1826, Union Oyster House was founded in Boston, and Delmonico's was founded in New York City in 1827. After World War I, the changing lifestyles of the American people (spurred especially by the invention of the automobile) prompted sweeping growth changes to the restaurant industry.

In recent decades, many concept and industry changes have occurred as a result of the increasing importance of convenience in the mobile society. This chapter describes the current state of the restaurant industry, including the risks and threats to the restaurant business and the many opportunities that exist.

Some Recent History

By the mid-1980s, there was a variety of restaurants to cover every taste imaginable and a concept to fit within every budget. Every corner had a restaurant, or so it seemed. That growth trend continues today. Approximately 13,000 to 17,000 new restaurants open in this country every year, and the concept designs and table fare continue to blossom.

People no longer go to restaurants simply to eat. They go to be entertained, to meet with clients, to build social relationships, to relax and unwind, and yes, to save time.

The restaurant consumer has grown to have very high standards. Because of the large influx of unique and varied cuisine, the American palate has become both educated and critical. Our desire for great products and services at a fair price has become intense, and our loyalty to any one restaurant is liable to change. Restaurant owners and chefs have come to realize that they are no better than the last meal they served. There are too many dining choices for them to be complacent.

An Abundance of Opportunity

Whether you're planning to start a restaurant in New York City or Teardrop, Wyoming, you'll find plenty of opportunities. All of the great ideas have not been done quite yet. Even if your idea has been done before, you can always compete by outperforming the competition.

There are many ways to break into the restaurant business. A variety of options allows you to choose something that fits your lifestyle and excites your passion. You need to believe in your idea, or you may as well burn your money. Each type of restaurant has its own client base and requires a unique set of skills to be successful. (We discuss how to develop a restaurant concept in Chapter 3, "Choosing Your Restaurant.")

Wet Floor!

Eighty percent of new restaurants fail within three to five years.

Restaurants are typified by the kind of food they serve, their style of presentation, their atmosphere, and their price range. Some restaurants focus on a particular meal, such as breakfast or dinner, or offer only a portion of a meal, such as desserts or snack foods. Other restaurants specialize in a certain kind of food. The following list provides some common examples:

➤ Ethnic food (Mexican, Chinese, Italian, and so on)

➤ Chicken

➤ Barbeque

➤ Pizza

➤ Hamburgers

➤ Seafood

➤ Ice cream

➤ Sandwiches

➤ Hot dogs

Restaurants also differ in the way they serve the food. For example, a deli or a diner probably offers counter service. A pizza place may provide only take-out or delivery service. Steak house servers come to the customers' tables, and buffet restaurants let customers serve themselves.

Atmosphere differs greatly from restaurant to restaurant. A fast-food place is worlds away from a fine-dining establishment. A themed restaurant doesn't look the same as a truck stop. A restaurant's atmosphere attracts certain types of customers and affects the food prices. Coffee shop customers expect to pay less for their food than customers at a casual-dining restaurant, for example.

Evaluate your options. Do you want to be the hot dog king of your world, or would you be more content with a deli or a formal dinner place serving seafood? Remember, it's your dream.

Strategies for Success

The restaurant industry is thriving like never before. The reasons for this growth include the following:

➤ The concept of franchising (see Chapter 3 for more on franchising)

➤ The cultural changes of the American society (for example, more air travel, longer commutes, more women in the work force, and more entertainment opportunities)

➤ The growth of fast food or the quick service restaurant (QSR) *segment*

Recipes Revealed

By **segment,** I mean the "style" of a restaurant based on its prices, service, presentation, and atmosphere. Restaurant segments include casual dining, fast food, fine dining, concept dining, and many others. Each of these is considered its own segment in the restaurant industry.

➤ Easily accessible capital—more people are getting more money to open more businesses, especially restaurants, than ever before

➤ The American love affair with food, entertainment, and convenience

In America, we are surrounded by the abundance of opportunity that we call free enterprise, and the restaurant business is no exception. An early-morning person can choose a breakfast-oriented business. A late-night type can choose a dinner house with or without a bar. A chef can be a caterer. The choices are open to your imagination. You can invent a category. Go ahead, I dare you. The opportunities to do what you want are great.

Food for Thought

Here are the four big reasons restaurants fail:

➤ Lack of knowledge

➤ Poor planning

➤ Poor execution

➤ Undercapitalization

Tip Jar

The restaurant business changes at the speed of light. Just when you think you know everything, something new comes into the picture. To be successful in this business, you must always continue to learn about it.

The flip side to this wealth of opportunity is that restaurants close down every day. The numbers are astonishing and rather sad because all of these owners thought they had a great idea. How can you avoid joining the statistics? Read on.

Get Past the Curse of Ignorance

What you don't know *can* hurt you. Every day that you don't learn means that there is more you don't know, and a lack of specific industry knowledge and/or a lack of general business knowledge can quickly kill a restaurant. Complacency about the business will allow other, more aggressive owners to take advantage of what they know and exploit your weaknesses.

Learning is a required part of this job. Spend the necessary time gaining the required technical skills and absorbing as much information as you can about the industry. Then you can be comfortable knowing that you have approached your decision to enter this arena armed with a knowledge base and current information. Do the following to increase your restaurant knowledge:

➤ Conduct personal research on the restaurant industry. The National Restaurant Association, *Nations Restaurant News (NRN)*, and your state Restaurant Association (you should become a member) are all wonderful places to conduct research.

➤ Read trade magazines and books. *Nations Restaurant News (NRN), QSR Magazine, Restaurants and Institutions, Chain Leader,*

Restaurant Marketing Magazine, and many others are helpful resources as are restaurant-specific books like this one and others that cover more broad-based concepts, such as accounting and marketing (check out *The Complete Idiot's Guide to Accounting* and *The Complete Idiot's Guide to Marketing*). My company's Web site (www.roiontheweb.com) offers our listing of books that will provide your restaurant all kinds of educational resources.

➤ Attend industry seminars. There are multiple industry-specific trade shows and seminars every week somewhere across the country. Spend a few bucks and attend some of them. Many are free. Dates, location, and subject matter are listed in many of the industry magazines.

➤ Get information from vendors and suppliers. Pick up the phone book and call a few in your area. They have a vested interest in helping you be successful. You are the potential customer.

➤ Take useful industry-specific and general business classes. Register at the local college or university or sign up for some of the traveling classes listed in the newspaper.

➤ Know all you can about your customers and your competitor's customers. It is a people business, and knowing more about the people you deal with is critical.

➤ Conduct a *feasibility study* before buying or building a restaurant. Will your idea work?

➤ Seek guidance from reputable lawyers, accountants, and restaurant industry experts. It's back to the potential customer point. If they want your business, they will help you get started.

➤ Join local associations and network with other business owners and restaurant operators. Every city has many networking opportunities sponsored by the local chamber of commerce or other civic groups.

➤ Compare your performance to industry and segment averages and educate yourself on how others optimize performance.

Recipes Revealed

A **feasibility study** tests the many components of your business concept to see if it will work. There are plenty of great ideas out there, but getting them to actually work can be a different story. A feasibility study is something that you hire outside help to conduct. It can run you a few to many thousands of dollars, but is worth it if you aren't sure your concept will be a go for the consumer. (In Chapter 4, "Is This Legal?" we talk about feasibility a bit more.)

Once you dig into all of these resources, you will see all kinds of industry information pouring out. Look at it and compare, compare, and compare some more.

Don't Plan to Fail

People don't go into business planning to fail. However, plenty of people go into business failing to plan. A well-conceived and thought-out business plan is essential to making your business work and is a key ingredient to determining your restaurant's success or failure.

A business plan takes time, effort, analytical ability, and commitment. Your business plan will help you think through your ideas and refine areas of concern, as well as areas of strength, quickly and easily without the large cost of making a mistake later on. Your plan is meant to be a working document, which means that it is subject to change as your circumstances change. But it should still be solid enough to be used as a guide to business success and a refocusing tool when you get off your planned path. It will also help you immensely with your restaurant and business educational processes. (See Chapter 5, "The Plan Is to Plan," for more information about creating a business plan.)

Get It Done

Poor execution is a bad meal, an unhappy employee, or a misplaced order. It is lost focus or what I facetiously call "that loving feeling."

Lost focus allows things to slide. For some reason or another, maybe personal issues, ego issues, forgetfulness, or who knows what, the simple tasks of running a restaurant move down the priority scale. Lost focus also happens when the owner becomes bored, disinterested, or unexcited by the prospect of owning a restaurant once all the work of the job is discovered. The owner forgets that running a restaurant is a career and comes to treat it like a hobby he or she is tired of.

At this point, the competition starts sniffing around. The complacent restaurant owner suddenly finds that the well of black ink has gone red while no one was watching. I have seen it happen many times.

Tip Jar

Competition can come in many forms, from a similar restaurant to a candy machine.

Find Some Money with Grit, Goals, and Guts

People say it takes money to make money. I say it takes money to buy forks, fire insurance, and cheese. Money is the blood of any business, and in the restaurant business lack of money can destroy your options and cause you to make bad decisions. Many poor decisions in the restaurant business come from being undercapitalized. Lack of money might tempt you to …

➤ Select the cheaper of two sites.

➤ Skip legal and regulatory steps.

➤ Buy lower quality products.

Plenty of other poor decisions are made in the restaurant world every day because of undercapitalization.

Investors are always looking for good ideas, but getting money for a business venture can be challenging. To be successful, you need grit, goals, and guts.

Grit is what keeps you asking for capital even when you have been rejected 37 times in a row like I was the first 37 times I asked for a business loan. Goals become more clearly defined when you write your business and financing plans because, without such planning, you can kiss virtually every capital resource good-bye. Guts are the intestinal fortitude to trust in your idea, your plan, and yourself.

Restaurant Industry Challenges

Lions, and tigers, and bears, oh my! Well, maybe not, but even if you don't stray off of the yellow brick road (your business plan), there are plenty of challenges in the restaurant business.

Turnover

About 11 million people work in the restaurant industry in the United States, which makes the industry the second largest employer in the country behind the federal government. As you'll learn when you start your restaurant, these folks have a tendency to change jobs.

Turnover in the restaurant business has become a disease of astronomical proportions. Industry turnover averages run in excess of 200 percent for hourly employees and exceed 100 percent for salaried management. To put these numbers into perspective, if you have a projected staff level of 35 employees and a projected turnover of 200 percent, you will need to hire 70 employees in the next year

Wet Floor!

Restaurants on average are running 15 to 30 percent understaffed. It is the way of the restaurant world.

Wet Floor!

Hasty decisions about site selection have caused much pain for many restaurant companies, including Boston Market. Bad site decisions put a significant long-term strain on restaurant profitability, causing restaurants to raise prices to pay for overpriced property. These overpriced menus then resulted in declining customer bases and declining customer frequency which resulted in lower sales. The effects of those decisions are still being felt today by many other restaurant owners and operators who followed their lead by selecting less than wonderful sites at significantly higher prices than the sites should have demanded.

to stay at 35. In this example, the average tenure of one of your restaurant employees is six months.

In addition, the shortage of qualified applicants is growing. Turnover has affected every segment of the industry and continues to be a driving force behind rising compensation levels, poor operations, and profit erosion. (Chapter 20, "Retaining the People You Have," talks more about how to control the turnover beast.)

Minimum Wage Laws

Minimum wage laws always affect the restaurant business. Where state and federal minimum wage levels are not the same, the higher of the two wage rates prevails. States such as Oregon, Washington, and California are leading the charge to increase the minimum wage well above the federal guidelines, and cities such as San Francisco, are providing city-mandated living wage rates that increase the minimum allowable wage inside that city's limits even more. An increase of 50¢ in minimum wage can cost the average restaurant tens of thousands of dollars in lost profitability in a given year. This loss results in either a decrease in profits or an increase in menu prices to make up for the shortfall.

Recipes Revealed

Saturation is having more restaurants in a particular locale than the available customer base can support. Inexperienced restaurateurs open up poorly planned restaurants and customers spread their dollars around to try out the new dining experiences. For a short while—until the customer realizes a dining experience is not worthy of their repeat business (usually a six-month process)—the pieces of the consumer spending pie get split more ways. This causes the good restaurants to take a financial hit until the poor-running restaurants go out of business.

Legal Issues

The restaurant industry has become a legal minefield. Without the proper protection and knowledge, any restaurant owner can be destroyed both professionally and personally. (See Chapter 4 for more information.)

Site Selection

Site selection changed forever in the early 1990s. Back then, the economy was strong, the restaurant industry was booming, cash was easy to get, and growth was running wild. Companies like Boston Market came along and scooped up sites at alarming rates and unbelievably high prices and forever changed the restaurant site selection landscape. Today, because of those past poor decisions when companies did not care about paying 30–100 percent more for a site than it was worth, finding a quality site at a fair price is much more challenging.

Saturation

Saturation of any one market or specialty threatens the industry. The marketplace became inundated with restaurants that were poorly planned and restaurateurs who were inexperienced. In some parts of the country, the restaurant business became oversaturated and same-store sales started to decline.

If You Are Great, You Will Succeed

In a sense, however, the state of the restaurant industry is the same as it has always been. Change is always in the air, but the business is still serving food and catering to the American love of quality.

American restaurant owners know what customers expect. They do not expect a New York strip or a kung pao chicken dinner from McDonald's, so McDonald's doesn't try to deliver that. Customers want all-beef hamburgers, and McDonald's gives the customers what they want. Its success is tough to argue with. A customer who orders a filet mignon at a Morton's Famous Steakhouse wants a top of the line piece of meat and is willing to pay for it.

Regardless of your restaurant's menu, category, or concept, if you are competing near the top of your segment with great products and services, you will always have a chance. Customers will frequent the restaurant that delivers the best products and services at the right price in a given market area. If Bill's restaurant is all that's available, that's the place people will spend their money. If they have two or three choices, they will spend their money at the place providing the best food and service at the fairest price. The restaurant business is a fun, competitive environment—if you're great.

The marketplace has plenty of room for new and innovative concepts as well. Our society has shown great interest in making a dining experience like a short vacation. If you have new products or services to bring to the market, you may very well find consumers who will buy. If you bring old products

Food for Thought

Does McDonald's serve high-quality products? This is not a trick question. The answer is absolutely, undeniably, yes! McDonald's purchases the best products money can buy and has the corner on many of the beef and potato markets because of the volume of purchases it secures. Product quality is a segment-oriented thing.

Food for Thought

The restaurant industry has grown at record levels for 10 straight years. In 1999, 844,000 restaurants were operating in the United States. Sales projections for 2001 are forecast to exceed $399 billion. Yes, people like to eat out, and they will spend money to do so.

and services to the market, but deliver them in a new way, you may find a niche in today's competitive restaurant environment as well.

Although the restaurant business is difficult, new people are always stepping into the industry wanting to compete. Some want to compete with the big boys, some want to compete with the mom-and-pop places, some want to compete with new concepts, and some want to compete by improving on what has always been done, but they come in busloads ready to compete. The question that you must answer for yourself is, do you have what it takes to stand out from the crowd and succeed?

The Least You Need to Know

➤ New restaurant concepts continue to blossom.

➤ Eighty percent of new restaurants fail in three to five years.

➤ Success comes with having the necessary knowledge, a good plan, the ability to execute well, and an ample supply of money.

➤ The best strategy is to be great at what you do.

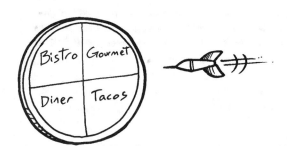

Chapter 3

Choosing Your Restaurant

In This Chapter

➤ Buying an existing restaurant versus starting fresh

➤ The facts about franchising

➤ Places to find information

➤ Why you should hire a concept design team

➤ Menu, price, and service questions

Guess what? Opening a restaurant means actually opening a restaurant. This means opening in a building with a concept and a menu and a staff. We're talking real stuff now. No more dreams.

In the last two chapters, we concentrated on the big picture. Now it's time to focus. It is astonishing but true that, like America itself, the restaurant business offers a chance at a great life in a million ways. What do you want to be? That, in life and in the restaurant business, is always is your best option. Find a passion and go for it.

Of course, at least in the restaurant business, it helps to find an opening.

This is a chapter about options and how to measure your passions against the opportunities available. There are many types of restaurant opportunities—franchising, buying an existing business, creating a new business in an existing building, or building a new creation. Location is also a consideration. Opening a restaurant means actually making decisions. So, if you decide to, read on.

Start from Scratch or Buy an Existing Business?

Starting a restaurant from scratch takes a lot more planning, designing, and developing than buying an existing restaurant does. A new restaurant requires you to do everything that has already been done in an established restaurant. You must establish the business licensing and structure, find and analyze the location, develop and design the concept, purchase the equipment, develop the systems, hire and train your staff, set up your vendors, and more. You will also be entering the world of the unknown. Will anyone know you are open? Will your location and signage be visible? Will you be able to compete? Will the consumer like your menu?

The big advantage to starting from scratch is that you can do things your own way with your own unique flair. You don't have to live with past transgressions, poor decisions, and past customer opinions.

Buying a pre-existing restaurant requires a significantly different approach than starting one from scratch. To buy a pre-existing restaurant, you must be a sort of private investigator. You must take care to ensure that you do not make a poor choice. If you buy a restaurant with a tarnished reputation, you are buying the reputation. If the restaurant has, for one reason or another, an incompetent staff, a poor lease, an abused appearance, nonworking equipment, or even inaccurate bookkeeping, those problems become yours also. So do some investigating and find out exactly what you are buying.

Buying an existing restaurant can have a ton of upside. This upside can include immediate cash flow, well-trained and motivated staff, effective and efficient product and service formulas in place, and reduced start-up costs.

Both building a restaurant from scratch and buying an existing restaurant have advantages and disadvantages. Yet with hard work and focus, either way could be a road to success.

Wet Floor!

Beware of inaccurate bookkeeping (sometimes called "cooked books") if you're considering buying an existing restaurant. Discovering too late that there is a lot of debt or no real equity can quickly turn a dream into a nightmare.

Wet Floor!

If you're buying an existing business, insist that your accountant receive all the necessary information to thoroughly investigate the official books for the business. Ask to see past tax statements and determine whether all tax obligations are in order and current.

Going It Alone Versus Franchising

Franchising works. It has made a long and lasting positive impact on the restaurant industry, providing an opportunity to operate a business under a recognized brand name. But it's not for everybody.

So what exactly is *franchising?* A franchise is born when a business (the franchisor) licenses its trade name and brand (like McDonald's or Pizza Hut) to a person (the franchisee) who agrees to operate the restaurant according to the terms of a contract (the franchise agreement) and within the guidelines of company policies and procedures (the operations manual). In exchange for these rights, as well as a certain amount of support and even training and expertise, the franchisee usually pays the franchisor an initial entry fee (franchise fee) and an ongoing fee, usually based on sales volume (known as a royalty fee).

Ideally, the concept of franchising reduces your financial risk by providing you a clear road map to follow toward success. But it also limits your unique concepts and designs and provides less in the way of total creativity and flexibility. You buy a franchise to get a canned process to buying, building, designing, and even operating a restaurant. You are a part of a greater company.

Recipes Revealed

Franchising is a system for expanding a business and distributing goods and services.

All franchisors are not created equal. They provide significantly different services and have significantly different guidelines and support structures. Study what you're getting into before jumping into a franchise.

We have probably all heard war stories from people who purchased a franchise expecting more of a support structure than what they got. This usually happens when the franchise agreements are not read thoroughly by the potential franchisee. In today's legal and franchising community there is so little room left for misinterpretation that most everything is spelled out to the umpteenth degree; however, these things are not as simple to read as the books in *The Complete Idiot's Guide* series, so employing the services of reputable legal council is prudent.

I've seen franchise systems where you purchase only the name and concept rights and everything else is up to you—purchasing, marketing, site selection, and so on. Yet there are other franchises that use what is referred to as a "turn-key" system. The franchisor does virtually everything for you. You get a key to the building and you operate the place per their preset system. They do the site selection and the marketing and set up all the purchasing guidelines. All you do is "turn the key" to the front door and operate. Of course, there is every combination in between as well. The true "key" is to read and reread your franchise agreement, so you know what you're getting into.

Research Is Your Friend: Determining Your Concept

The best decisions are informed ones. Research can take a lot of time and effort and can cost a bit of money, but great research can and does save many times its original cost and is the best way to determine your concept.

Sources of information come in many forms and in many places. Most cities in the United States have restaurant associations and business associations. These associations provide weekly and monthly meetings with people who share your interest in restaurants or business in general. They are a good place to meet smart people who may be able to help you find information.

But the person who will be the most help in reaching your dream is in the mirror every day. You will have to decide where to look for information and what information to look for. The millions of pages of available restaurant-based concept information include surveys, data, and opinions on to how choose a restaurant, and the more you look the more you can find. So where do you begin?

You need three pieces of critical information to help you choose your concept:

➤ **Demographic surveys:** Demographic surveys determine and analyze such characteristics as age, gender, income levels, lifestyles, consumer habits, and more. Restaurant start-ups frequently conduct demographic surveys to collect this type of data to help determine locations, concept types, menu offerings, prices, and so on. A demographic survey helps a restaurateur pinpoint a market that is appropriate for a concept.

➤ **Target market analysis:** Who is your main projected customer? What does he or she look like in terms of age, income level, lifestyle, and so on? This information is critical to know because it will be a determining factor in site selection, the marketing plan and execution, menu design, and more. This target market affects virtually every aspect of your restaurant.

Tip Jar

The Standard Periodical Directory, 24th Edition, lists 187 trade publications for the restaurant industry. Each of these publications has lots of information about very specific subjects in the restaurant industry, ranging from site selection to product knowledge and from human resources management to menu design.

Food for Thought

The best place in the world to study your restaurant reading material is in a restaurant. Sit down in a mall food court, a coffee shop, or a sports bar. Absorb some atmosphere, ask some questions, and study.

➤ **Competitive analysis:** A competitive analysis helps you understand and predict who your competition will be, what your competition provides in the way of products, services, and benefits to the customer, and how well you will be able to compete against the competition. Ultimately, the customer decides whether to give you money or give that same money to someone else. You need to know how they make that decision.

The Concept Design Team

The overall concept design of your restaurant is your most important decision. As you try to figure out exactly what kind of restaurant you want to own, you should understand that this decision entails more than you think. It entails *everything*. Consider this partial list of things that will be affected by your initial decision on concept:

➤ The equipment you order

➤ The plateware and silverware

➤ The amount of kitchen space you will need

➤ The amount of freezer, cooler, and dry storage space needed

➤ The dining room decor

➤ The building signage and exterior

➤ The size and ability of your staff

➤ Employee dress codes and uniforms

You can design everything yourself and trust your ability to juggle a million things at once and understand how it all fits together, or you can find some help. The choice is yours. But unless you are an expert in all of the areas of restaurant concept design, your best bet is to hire, partner, or network with a restaurant concept design firm.

Tip Jar

By using a demographic survey and a target market analysis together, you can clearly determine where you want to build a particular restaurant. For example, once you know where a large concentration of college kids live, work, and party, it becomes much easier to pinpoint where to build a restaurant that produces large pizzas at low prices.

Wet Floor!

If your target market is females between 19 and 35, an all-you-can-eat buffet concept may not be the best idea. This conclusion may seem obvious to you, but I have met restaurant owners who spend bags of money on marketing with no clue about their target market. They might as well have thrown their money away.

The amount of money you spend on hiring professionals to help you will be small compared to the money and time they will save you. These professionals usually work in teams of two or three and guide you toward wise decisions. A good team will provide help in five areas:

➤ Clearing away obstacles

➤ Growing ideas

➤ Determining feasibility

➤ Determining restaurant flow

➤ Making everything work together

Clearing Away Obstacles

Stuff happens. Especially in the early days of preparing a restaurant, the unexpected can shake you up. Expert restaurant design and concept people have been through it all many times before and can add a solid dose of confidence to your efforts. They have experience in dealing with vendors, manufacturing companies, designers, and marketing firms and can deal with nearly any obstacles you may encounter to the concept design process.

Tip Jar

You can find restaurant concept design professionals by locating their advertisements in the back of trade magazines. You can even contact my firm:

Restaurant Operations Institute, Inc.
65 Woodbury Drive
Sterrett, AL 35147
Phone: 205–323–5559
E-mail: roi3434@aol.com

Growing Ideas

Brainstorming with experts can be very beneficial. When you bring your passion into a world of experienced people who share your passion, great ideas are born. Sometimes, the best investment you make is in brain cells.

Determining Feasibility

Will it work? A restaurant concept design team can determine how to make the new idea or concept work and to project potential obstacles and expenses. A good team can also determine how customers will respond to your product. Because of the vast experience the concept design experts bring, they can also determine customer and employee perception as well as perceived value (see "How Much for a Cheeseburger?" later in this chapter for more on perceived value).

Determining Restaurant Flow

People move all over restaurants. They exit and enter through the doors, travel to and from the bathrooms, wander in and out of the bar, and walk back and forth from the kitchen. A restaurant concept design team can make your restaurant run more smoothly by anticipating traffic flow issues you may not have imagined.

Making Everything Work Together

Everything that a customer feels, sees, hears, and smells in a restaurant is an impression. From the moment customers pull into the parking lot to the very last view of your facility out the rear view mirror, they inhale atmosphere, good or bad. Colors, sizes, sounds, shapes, textures, forms, smells, uniforms, and noise level all combine to make an impact that should be remembered in a good way.

A restaurant concept design team ensures that all pieces of the puzzle fit together. The concept, site, staff, uniforms, and equipment all function as parts of a working whole. This kind of structure is known as a congruent organization.

I often see restaurant owners determining the menu and restaurant concept mere weeks before opening for business. By then, it's too late. Nearly everything you purchase or design must be in place early on. Don't assume that you can adapt or adjust a restaurant kitchen to nearly any menu or concept. It's not that easy and can be quite expensive. A design team can help you avoid such costly last-minute changes.

The Concept Decision

What kind of restaurant do you want to own? Don't just sell food. Instead, sell something you are passionate about because your passion could make all the difference.

Kee Chan opened his Heat restaurant in Chicago because he wanted to give the customer a whole different level of sushi. Unlike most Japanese restaurants, Heat displays live fish in saltwater tanks for the customers to select. Heat is trying to deliver an authentic Japanese dining experience. You can see and feel the passion as the restaurant workers secure your personally selected fish, prepare it behind the sushi bar (sliced thin), and serve it.

Recipes Revealed

The **core menu concept** is the main product line of your menu, and you define it: Italian, Mexican, American, Japanese, or even hamburgers, chicken, or pizza. Traditionally, the owner has a preliminary feel for what kind of food he/she wants to serve: "My goal is to open an Italian restaurant" or "I have this great chili recipe that I want to open a restaurant with." The rest of the menu (beverages, appetizers, desserts) is usually secondary and is added to the core menu concept.

Of course, you don't have to have such a noble reason to open a restaurant as to provide an authentic ethnic meal or experience. Frank Carney once stated that he simply loved eating pizza, so he founded Pizza Hut. Tom Moghnahan wanted pizza delivered to his home and saw an untapped marketable concept and service. His desire and observations led him to found Domino's Pizza. Passion can come through in a variety of ways. So what is your passion? And what isn't?

A vegetarian probably should not own a steak house. If you don't like seafood, stay away from a crab shack. This observation is simple, but true: If the owner doesn't love the restaurant, why would the employees? And if the employees don't love the restaurant, the customers are not likely to fall head over heels for it either.

The Core Menu Concept

So what will your restaurant be? At the heart of your answer to this question is the *core menu concept*, which will more clearly define what your decor, ambience, style of dining service, and overall concept should look like.

Don't try to be everything to everybody. Instead, try to be something great to specific people. Too often in the restaurant business, the quest for more sales leads to the creation of large, unmanageable menus that cause operational glitches and profitability strain. Not everyone will eat at your restaurant anyway, so why not concentrate on those who will? Finding these customers is first about finding yourself and your passion.

The more things you try, the more difficult it is to be great at one of them. What, for instance, would make a pizza place think they should serve breakfast or a taco joint serve gourmet coffee? Surveys show that consumers pigeonhole most restaurants in one or two core concepts, and unless you have a marketing budget that rivals McDonald's, that perception is quite difficult to change. Even McDonald's has thrown away big dollars in different parts of the country trying to add *day-parts* and be something they are not to the consumer.

Recipes Revealed

A **day-part** is the time of day when a specific type of meal is served. Breakfast, lunch, and dinner are all separate day-parts. A day-part add-on is when a restaurant, such as Hardee's, which is clearly a lunch and dinner sandwich chain, decides to add a breakfast menu to try to garner some early-morning traffic. Many restaurants have begun adding day-parts to try to generate additional sales when they normally wouldn't even be open.

Your Menu Needs Professional Help

As a restaurant owner, you must appreciate the menu as the important document it is: It is your Magna Carta, your Declaration of Independence. From the menu flows the story of a great restaurant.

A restaurant's menu has an influence on everything about the restaurant. Thus, the planning of a menu should be taken seriously and should always be a team effort between an owner and a chef. Yes, planning a menu involves a chef. Even if you are selling hamburgers and french fries, you should employ a chef to develop the menu. A well-educated chef knows the availability and cost of food ingredients, is an expert when it comes to kitchen staff and equipment capabilities, and understands the total picture when it comes to food handling and preparation. The owner/operator will most likely bring a fair share of food knowledge as well, but usually not the level of knowledge that a certified chef would have. The owner brings a different perspective and, with a good chef, can develop a vision in a great document called the menu.

How Much for a Cheeseburger?

A key element of the menu is the price listed for each menu item. Everything costs something. First it costs you, and then it costs your customer. So how do you determine how much to charge for whatever you decide to sell?

You can determine the price range of your menu in many different ways, and all of them can be reasonably justified depending on your concept, menu, and location. But the most important factor to consider is the *perceived value* for any meal.

Two of the bigger errors that I see restaurants make are underpricing their menu when the customer will gladly pay more and overpricing their menu when the poor products and services they deliver don't justify the prices. Both are major mistakes.

The prices that you charge will influence the type of clientele your restaurant attracts, the sales volume and profitability of the restaurant, and the frequency with which your customers return. People of lower incomes tend to frequent restaurants with lower pricing while people with higher incomes tend to patronize restaurants with higher prices. Customers tend to be more forgiving of poor service in restaurants that have lower menu prices and less forgiving if the menu prices are high.

Tip Jar

When pricing your menu items, you must estimate costs and sales volumes. To stay in the restaurant game for very long, you need to be able to balance making a profit with customer satisfaction and frequency. Pricing your menu appropriately will have a significant impact on whether this balance happens.

Recipes Revealed

Perceived value is a fair price, determined by the customer. It is based on a mixture of what a customer receives in the way of products, services, environment, and so on and what the customer pays for that overall feeling. If the customer is happy with the overall experience, then the perceived value is good.

You must try to determine these two extremes of pricing any product:

➤ The highest price the market will bear and still continue to retain the customer.

➤ The lowest possible price you can charge and still realize a fair profit.

The price you charge the customer on every menu item will need to fall somewhere between these two extremes.

What Type of Service Will You Offer?

How will people get their food at your restaurant? Consider the choices:

➤ Dine in

➤ Delivery

➤ Carryout

Tip Jar

After your restaurant is open, you should test prices frequently (I suggest every third month) to assure that they are competitive and appropriate for your style of service and concept. To get started, check with the National Restaurant Association for comparable pricing in your segment and conduct a survey of your potential competitors close by to compare like products, as well as check averages. (The National restaurant Association can be contacted at www.restaurant.org or by calling 202-331-5900.)

Dine In

Dine-in restaurants provide one of three major styles of service: quick service, casual dining, and full service. Quick service is distinguished by the following characteristics:

➤ Customers order at a counter by looking at menu board signage.

➤ The emphasis is on speed of service and convenience.

➤ The cost of a meal is at the lower end of a check average, below $7.

➤ The decor is simple and practical.

➤ Customers want their food fast.

Casual dining is characterized by the following:

➤ Customers order at a table by looking at a menu.

➤ The emphasis is on providing a fun yet relaxing environment. The food is of a good quality, yet unlike full service establishments, not every detail is attended to.

➤ The cost of meal is in the middle portion of the check average: $6 to $15.

➤ The decor may provide a theme or some fun features.

➤ Customers want close to the full dining experience without feeling that they have to dress up or act in any given social manner.

Full service is characterized by the following:

➤ The customer orders at a table by looking at a menu.

➤ The emphasis is on excellent service, high-quality food, and the overall dining experience.

➤ The cost of a meal is at the higher end of the check average, normally above $15.

➤ The decor is tasteful and more upscale in nature.

➤ The customer wants the full dining experience.

These three styles are the main umbrellas, but many more specific styles have become known in the restaurant industry, including quick casual, modified service, cafeteria dining, home meal replacement, and banquet dining.

Delivery and Carryout

Some of the more important things to consider regarding a delivery service are the size of your delivery area—in other words, how far from your restaurant are you willing to deliver to, what type of food you will be delivering, and how well, quality wise, it will hold up. Poor quality food delivered 25 miles from your restaurant does no one any good.

Carry-out concepts, on the other hand, are more about convenience and price. The customer wants a quick and easy meal at a reasonable price.

Who Are You? Picking a Name

The name of your restaurant means a lot, more than you probably think. This simple choice will be one of the most important business decisions you make, so take some time and make the name fit with your vision. You want your name to convey a message to your target market. You want your name to have sweeping implications from culture to style of menu to theme and decor.

Pick a name and then test it on family, friends, and others you know. Don't settle for the first name you think of. Instead, search out the perfect name. A good name will absolutely help you sell food. Check the phone book to be sure the name you pick is not taken or to look for inspiration from the other restaurant names. (See Chapter 4, "Is This Legal?" for more information on researching your restaurant's name.) Also, ask your restaurant design team or marketing experts to help with suggestions.

The Least You Need To Know

➤ The big early decisions, such as buying a franchise or an existing restaurant or starting from scratch, will affect you for the life of your restaurant.

➤ Do lots of research to determine a workable concept and pinpoint a target market.

➤ Hiring a concept design team helps ensure that everything comes together just right.

➤ Your menu is the heart of your restaurant.

➤ Pricing is part of everything your restaurant does, and it must fit in with the rest of the finely tuned machine that is your restaurant.

➤ Your restaurant's name is a major decision, so treat it as such.

Is This Legal?

The restaurant business involves more than cooking, cleaning, and serving. Sure, those tasks are a big part of the business, but you will also need to be a mixture of a real estate agent, banker, lawyer, insurance agent, college student, accountant, human resources specialist, purchasing director, and much more if you expect to make your restaurant work. In addition to learning these skills yourself, you will most likely need to hire others. You will need advice on a myriad of things, especially at first when you negotiate your way through the wonderful world of regulation.

Beyond the fun of the kitchen is a full day's worth of paperwork for you every day. And when you first start your restaurant, you have even more to do. New restaurants need to have permits, licenses, and forms and need to meet certain requirements. The restaurant business is full of specific rules that you must obey.

This chapter deals with the legal paperwork of restaurant ownership. Here you will learn the types of business structures to choose from, the maze of agencies you must get through, the types of professionals you should hire, and what to do with your permits when they arrive.

Business Structure

Every company operates under one of four broad legal classifications:

➤ **Sole proprietorship:** This kind of business is owned and run by one person and is a common form for small businesses. Although this legal structure is the simplest and cheapest to set up, it can cost you tons in lost tax advantages and increased personal liability.

➤ **Partnership:** In this business relationship, two or more people agree to share their talents, profits, and losses in specific portions. This structure is more complex than the sole proprietorship and has some advantages, but like the sole proprietorship many restaurant owners have abandoned the partnership structure due to tax and liability issues.

➤ **Corporation (C-Corp):** This legal entity exists separately from the restaurant owners. A corporation is legally like a person in that it can be sued, own property, or acquire debts. Setting up a corporation is expensive in the beginning, but it is usually well worth the expense if you plan to be in business for a while. Corporations come in many forms and offer better tax advantages and liability reduction than either sole proprietorships or partnerships.

➤ **Limited Liability Company (LLC):** This structure is becoming more popular and combines the best of many structures, but check with your local advisors to see if and how this structure would benefit you. An LLC combines some of the benefits of a partnership with some of the benefits of a corporation.

The legal form your restaurant takes is a very important decision that should not be made lightly. It's a tax-related decision, and the tax codes in the United States are many thousands of pages long. The ramifications of making the wrong decision can be quite costly, so don't make this decision on your own and don't use a do-it-yourself corporate set-up kit. Find an attorney and an accountant that you can trust with your dream.

Tip Jar

Find an advisor you trust and work through these six questions before deciding on your restaurant's legal structure:

➤ Who will the owners of the company be?

➤ What level of liability protection do you require?

➤ How do you intend to distribute the company's earnings?

➤ What are your financing plans?

➤ What are the opening requirements and costs?

➤ How will the legal structure you choose affect your tax strategy?

Uncle Sam's Rules

Federal laws and guidelines apply evenly across the country. The federal agencies you will deal with are the Internal Revenue Service (IRS), the Department of Labor, and the Bureau of Alcohol, Tobacco, and Firearms (BATF).

The IRS

The IRS will collect taxes from you, your business, and your employees. You need to obtain an Employer Identification Number (EIN) by filing form SS-4. Also, you are required to pay estimated federal income taxes quarterly as well as withhold federal income taxes, Social Security taxes (FICA), and Medicare taxes from all of your employees' paychecks. This experience can be taxing (pardon the pun), but the IRS does provide an assortment of pamphlets and circulars that spell out all the guidelines. You should contact a tax or accounting professional also. Do this step right. You do not want tax trouble.

The Department of Labor

The Department of Labor, sometimes called the Labor Board, administers the Fair Labor Standards Act. It ensures compliance with and adherence to the rules and regulations surrounding the federal minimum wage and the managing of the Equal Employment Opportunities Commission (EEOC), which deals with discrimination complaints. To understand the rules covered by EEOC, I suggest you study all the government's pamphlets carefully.

Food for Thought

Most daily licensing and legal needs are dealt with on a state or local level, not a federal level. State laws vary, and becoming informed on your given state's guidelines is critical to your success. Local guidelines vary even more than state laws; because of zoning, guidelines can be different between restaurants that are merely blocks apart. The state and local agencies are typically focused on adherence to the liquor laws, the health codes, and the safety guidelines.

The Bureau of Alcohol, Tobacco, and Firearms

BATF is a division of the United States Treasury Department and is the entity you go through if you're planning to serve alcoholic beverages in your restaurant. You will need to obtain a Special Occupational Tax Stamp, which is in essence a receipt for payment and not a federal license. Without this stamp, you will not be allowed to serve alcohol. However, your state and local governments have control over the liquor license itself. This federal stamp needs to be renewed every year before July 1. For more details on federal liquor laws, contact your local BATF office and request a free booklet, ATF P 5170.2.

Local Laws

All local laws are in place to ensure that you run a safe and fair restaurant, but the enforcement and specific rules restaurants must follow differ widely from state to state and city to city. Every state, every city, every county, and even every township has its own set of procedures and regulations that can cause delays if you fail to do the paperwork correctly, and delays cost money. The instructions for dealing with this issue are simple: Know the local rules.

Contact your local attorney and knock on the doors of your local government agencies. Pick up the phone book and find out where they are located and set up a time to chat.

If you don't know the local rules, you live and you learn as I did in 1985 when I opened an ice cream restaurant in Colorado. Just prior to opening, I thought my team had done a great job pulling it all together. I was impressed, and my team was very confident. So there we were for the final step, and the health inspector, after giving us passing grades on everything that he examined, asked to see our Dairy Use Permit. No one on my team had ever heard of such a permit. "You are required to have a Dairy Use Permit to serve ice cream in this part of Colorado," the inspector said. Getting the permit created a delay that could have been avoided.

Just like the federal government, local governments have several departments that restaurant owners deal with on a regular basis. These departments include the health department, the fire department, and the building department.

The Health Department

The health department makes sure that what you eat is safe. It exists in local government to ensure that food service establishments operate in a sanitary manner that complies with food safety and sanitation guidelines. Without a permit from the health department, you are not allowed to sell food of any kind to the public. These permits are issued for one year at a time and can be revoked at any time due to poor execution or failure to comply with specific guidelines. State and local health departments often work together to administer inspections, issue licensing, and offer educational materials.

The Fire Department

The fire department issues fire permits, and a restaurant cannot open without a fire permit. Generally, the state fire marshal's office and the local fire department work hand in hand to administer a set of guidelines and regulations that closely resemble that of the National Fire Protection Code. The local fire department usually performs the required inspections and sets up your restaurant's specific guidelines, as well as issues the permit itself. Obviously, you want to protect your restaurant against a fire.

The Building Department

The building department issues building permits and performs inspections. From community to community, the building codes differ greatly. If you build more than one restaurant, make sure you know that rules change depending on your location. In many places, you have to check with several agencies before applying for and receiving a building permit and a certificate of occupancy.

A Typical Legal Process for Building a Restaurant

The process for building a restaurant usually includes these steps:

➤ Check with the zoning board to ensure that the zoning at your proposed location allows a restaurant. If it doesn't, don't panic. Zoning restrictions can sometimes be changed. Contact your lawyer or real estate business broker for assistance.

➤ Obtain a site approval from the planning board or commission.

➤ A public hearing takes place at which time people can and sometimes do voice their objections concerning your business and plan, especially if you're serving alcoholic beverages. Try to find out about any possible objections before the meeting so that you can address them appropriately during the meeting. At the hearing, the board considers environmental impact, traffic impact, community impact, and more.

➤ A plan review meeting is held with a building department official and a fire department official present. They review the plans in detail for structural integrity, fire code compliance, occupancy capacity, and more.

➤ Make a formal application for a building permit. After a building permit is issued, construction may begin.

Tip Jar

Hire the best lawyers and accountants you can afford. They are worth it.

➤ The building inspector makes periodic announced and unannounced inspections of the construction or renovation to ensure its compliance with codes.

➤ When the construction is complete, both the fire inspector and the health inspector make a final inspection.

➤ When everything meets the required codes and guidelines, a certificate of occupancy (C of O) is issued to the owner of the business.

Other Agencies

Depending on the locality of your restaurant, you may need to contact a few other agencies and offices and find out specific details of what their responsibilities are with regard to your restaurant:

➤ The signage commission controls all aspects of signage and usually requires a permit to be obtained before a sign is installed.

➤ The Americans with Disabilities Act (ADA) Commission determines all disability guidelines and wheelchair accessibility requirements.

➤ The water and sewer commission determines water supply and septic system guidelines.

➤ Dairy commissions are more common today than they were when they surprised me years ago. Many times they are combined with the health department.

Wet Floor!

On more than one occasion I have had an agency lose my paperwork. Thank goodness I had copied all forms because without those copies my restaurant would have opened late. Don't find yourself filing paperwork again because someone else has lost your forms.

You Have Your Permits, Now What?

Once you have all your permits, you must perform these essential tasks:

➤ Copy them for your records

➤ File them or post them per the requirements

➤ Get ready to conduct business

Some agencies require you to post the permit or license while others have you file them. Again, this requirement is specific to the state, county, and city that your restaurant is in. Usually building permits, health permits, and fire permits are posted in an easily visible and accessible area. Follow your given agencies' directions exactly. You may want to post the licenses under a piece of plastic for safekeeping and easy readability.

Your Legal Name

Once you've selected your business name, you must get it approved and registered with the secretary of state's office in your restaurant's home state. You should do some research to ensure that your restaurant's name hasn't already been taken. A good lawyer can do this research for you, or you can do it yourself at your local library. Just tell the librarian what you are searching for and he or she will direct you through the business name search process. Or you can contact your secretary of state's office and request a search. The business name you select will be put into a computer and screened through the database to see if anyone else has previously registered it. If it has not been previously registered and you want it, you can register it.

Registering a business name is simple. The secretary of state's office (usually in your state capital) can send you the appropriate forms. Fill out the forms by following the easy instructions and make sure to include a check for the requested fee. Then the restaurant name is legally yours.

Tip Jar

Registering a trademark (which is a symbol, word, or design used to identify a business) is more difficult than registering a name. Owning a trademark gives you the right to prevent others from using a confusingly similar mark, name, logo, or symbol. Not every business has or needs to have their logo trademarked. That can be determined based on your growth objectives. Consult a business attorney to determine if a trademark is necessary for your business.

The Least You Need to Know

➤ The restaurant business is about more than food and service. It's about being an amateur lawyer and private investigator, knowing where to go for help, and playing by the rules.

➤ Your business structure will affect you in many ways, not the least of which is taxes, funding flexibility, and personal liability, so get some good advice about how to set it up.

➤ Federal laws, from taxes to labor laws, are enforceable across the United States.

➤ Local laws vary from place to place.

➤ Professional advice will help you avoid costly mistakes.

Part 2

Building a Solid Foundation

Building a solid foundation for your restaurant requires more than bricks and mortar. (You are not quite ready for that part yet anyway.) The foundation of your business may not be as heavy as the materials holding up your building, but it is no less formidable. This part gives you help in building your business foundation through planning, site selection, funding, and preparing the preopening calendar.

Chapter 5

The Plan Is to Plan

In This Chapter

➤ Reasons to build a business plan

➤ The business plan audience

➤ The basic components of a business plan

➤ The specific requirements of the financial plan

The journey from your wonderful and exciting restaurant idea to serving your first customer is a trek that requires commitment, stamina, willpower, and creativity. It also requires a plan.

This journey can be one of the greatest learning experiences of your life, and it can also be difficult. If you don't have a plan, it will painful as well. Many aspiring entrepreneurs have great ideas and set out on their journey without a road map. They open up shop without preparing themselves for the many aspects of business ownership. And then something they didn't expect destroys them, and they close shop. Those with a plan end up in much better shape. This chapter will help you develop a business plan so that you don't get lost on the way to achieving your dream.

Why Build a Business Plan?

Building the restaurant of your dreams requires a sound plan, but creating a business plan is not an easy task. The best way to approach it is to write down everything you want to accomplish with your restaurant and proceed from there. Treat the business plan as a road map to your business.

By writing down your intentions, you will know what you expect of yourself and your business, and you will make decisions accordingly. If your plan is well done, you will be able to use it to make the right decisions for your business.

Your attitude has plenty to do with the effectiveness and efficiency of your business plan. If you understand why you need a plan, you will have a better chance of making it work. If you don't understand why you need a plan, keep studying until you do.

Who Reads the Plan?

A business plan is not the great American novel. You are writing a plan to run your business, so the audience is small and specific. In addition, different parts of your business plan are geared toward different people:

➤ Potential investors tend to be more interested in the quality of the founding management team and the potential for growth than nearly any other factors. They want to feel comfortable that they are investing their money in a team that has a track record of success and in a concept that is going to return handsome profits.

➤ Bankers tend to require more data to give themselves the comfort level that you will repay the loan. Bankers tend to look at your qualifications as well, but many times they rely more on your personal creditworthiness and may ask you to personally guarantee the loan repayment no matter how well financed the new business is and regardless of your background and expertise.

➤ New management or potential partners can be recruited with a strong business plan. A solid plan may give people more confidence in leaving the security of their current situations to come on board with your team. Potential key players are most interested in your operational and organizational plans and want to be able to clearly see where they fit into your needs.

➤ You and your team can use the plan to establish and build your *company culture.*

➤ Vendors or service providers may also be interested in your business plan. Usually their interest lies in your potential for growth and how their company can benefit by doing business with yours. Clearly, if your business is growing and they are suppliers, their businesses are growing as well.

Recipes Revealed

The **company culture** is the environment you build to surround every decision that is made inside your restaurant. This environment includes how you treat employees and customers, how you make decisions, how you take care of business, and how you deal with success and failure.

You do not need to share every component of your business plan with everyone. Depending on who the reader is, you can determine which pieces of the plan to share. Nevertheless, having all of the needed information available in one document is important. If you're trying to secure some form of funding, which is probably the case, the money folks will want to see a comprehensive version of the plan.

The Basic Business Plan Components

There are a lot of different ways to write a business plan, but most business plans have similar components. If you look at a business plan for Krystal, a fast-food hamburger chain throughout the South, and Ferreira Café, a fine-dining establishment in Montreal, you will see significantly different looking business plans. Upon closer inspection, you will realize that the basic elements have stayed reasonably the same. The following sections describe those basic elements.

A Cover Page and a Table of Contents

Your cover page and table of contents are just like any book report cover and contents page. They don't do anything other than make your plan nice and pretty and more accessible. These qualities are more important than you may think, especially if the person reading your plan has 30 others to read. The cover page should include the business name, your name, the date, your contact information, and perhaps your new restaurant logo or signage design. The table of contents is just a listing by page number of everything in your plan.

An Executive Summary

An executive summary is a one- to six-page section that tells the reader the bare essentials of the business. This section is a sales tool for your business and your plan. People usually read this section of the plan to determine whether they have enough interest in the overall concept to even continue to read the rest of the plan. The executive summary should discuss the key aspects about your restaurant concept, the potential customer base, the benefits to this customer base, the talent level of the executive team, and your main objectives. The content of this section is up to you, but this section is not the place to spell out too many of the details. Many times this section is more like a visionary piece filled with bells and whistles and just enough data to keep the reader hungry and interested.

The Business Concept

The business concept is a one- or two-page detailed and visionary explanation of the purpose of the business, the products and services provided, the core values, the unique and distinctive features, the benefits, and the primary customers. The business concept is an important tool; you will need to be able to give a verbal description of your restaurant concept many times going forward, so it's important for you to be comfortable pitching the concept. The background of the concept, the proposed restaurant location, the menu, and the unique features of the restaurant all need to be a part of this section.

Tip Jar

Consider writing the executive summary after you have detailed the facts of the business. Having all the facts at hand makes it easier to pick out your concept and business strengths and display them appropriately in your executive summary.

Recipes Revealed

A company must try to clearly define its **competitive advantage** over its competition. Simply stated, a competetive advantage is what makes a customer choose to do business with you versus doing business with your competitor. Once you know this, it becomes easier for you to market to your potential customer base.

The Management Team

The management team section is a glorified resumé of you and your founding management team. In one to two pages for each person, write out what each of you is responsible for and what each of you has accomplished in the past. This section is a great place to have complete resumés on each of the founding key players as well. Also, mention what expertise each of you plans to continue to develop in any given area.

The Market Analysis

The market analysis pinpoints your industry description and trends, your target market, your key competitors, your pricing, your *competitive advantage,* and your available market size and customer base. These facts are important for determining whether your business concept has any legs. The length of this section can be anywhere from 2 to 12 pages, and it should include specific data regarding your projected clientele, attractions in your area that will drive customers your way, the benefits you will provide to the consumer, and all kinds of research regarding your competitors and where they may or may not be missing the mark. This section should also be full of industry and segment data and information and should clearly outline industry, geographic, concept, and consumer trends.

The Process Analysis

The process analysis is the technical description of your products and services, your distribution channels, and your concept designs. This section is much more detailed than your business concept section and provides more in the way of data, facts, and figures. The business concept section is more visionary. This section is for the technically driven, data-hungry executive who may ask, "Can this team really make this concept happen?" Not everyone will be interested in reading this section, but you should include it for those who want to be in the know. The length of this analysis depends on the technical nature of your concept. A simple concept can be covered in a page or two; a technically driven concept may require 20 pages or more.

The Organizational Plan

The organizational plan is where you lay out your management philosophy, company culture, legal structure, organizational chart, and guidelines for doing business. This section is technical in nature and not real sexy or fun to create, but it is pertinent information that needs to be shared. The philosophy and culture devised by the management team need to be more than pie-in-the-sky stuff. This section should show that your method of conducting business is as important as the type of business you conduct. This section is usually two to six pages long.

The Marketing Plan

This three- to six-page section is where you explain how your target customer will see or hear of your business. This section should include your marketing strategy, media budget, and miscellaneous marketing and public relations tools. As your business evolves so will the marketing plan and vice versa. In this section, list your marketing strategies by month, quarter, and even year.

The Financial Plan

The financial plan should include start-up requirements, estimated sales and profits, capital needs and requirements, *break-even analysis*, payback periods, funding plans, sources and uses of funds, *projected proforma* and financial statements, and other pertinent projected financial data that may be requested based on your individual circumstances. The length of the financial plan does not matter. It

Food for Thought

The section on the management team is a good place to mention the members of your support team: accountant, attorney, contractors, vendors, consultants, insurance agent, bankers, mentors, concept designers, and so on. Add anyone who seems relevant and who strengthens the overall picture of your team. Lenders like to know that the level of talent is stacked in your team's favor before they cough up any cash.

Tip Jar

You must build your brand for the long haul. To do that, your marketing plan must be more than a bunch of singular disconnected ploys. Instead, it should focus on a congruent marketing approach with many little concepts and programs that are interrelated in order to drive brand awareness.

Recipes Revealed

A **break-even analysis** is used to determine when the company will break even. In essence, you will need to complete a projected proforma to determine in what month will the revenues and expenses be equal? Many times this is illustrated in a neat little line graph that shows the point where revenues and expenses meet.

A **projected proforma** is a guess of your revenues and your expenses. Put them on paper and you have a projected proforma. I advise you to be overly conservative and lean toward underestimating revenues and overestimating expenses. This gives you wiggle room just in case things don't go as planned.

Food for Thought

Estimating start-up costs is a work in progress. The more items you guess at and research, the better your projections will be.

must be full of pertinent data, and it will be scrutinized whether it takes 3 pages or 20.

The financial plan is traditionally the most highly scrutinized section of your business plan. And just like the core of the business plan, the financial section of your overall business plan can have many different forms and structures. The two most basic and important aspects of any new restaurant's plans are start-up cost projections and the proforma or income statement. In addition to these basic parts, you need to include three more things in the financial plan: the timeline and growth plan, the contingency plan, and your supporting documents.

Start-Up Cost Projections

Estimating your start-up cost is much easier than it sounds. You just need to think one step at a time. The key is your ability to guess prices and then do research. First pick a reasonable cost for each item. Then contact some people who know prices, such as vendors, suppliers, and other restaurant people, and ask for their more educated guesses.

As you think about costs, remember to include everything. For example, paying your crew is a big expense. Also, you cannot do the entire electrical work on the facility by yourself even if you are a certified electrician and you want to save a few bucks. As you continue this tallying of start-up costs, you must continue to ask yourself, "Can I afford this?" That is a normal reaction, and it is a good question. In some cases, you will need to reevaluate and make the necessary adjustments.

The Proforma or Income Statement

The proforma or income statement section tries to answer the question of whether your restaurant can make money. There are six numbers that potential investors want to see. Of course, there are plenty of other numbers to look at, but with these six numbers the investors can calculate the rest on their own:

➤ Projected sales

➤ Projected food cost

➤ Projected labor cost

➤ Projected controllable expenses

➤ Projected facility costs

➤ Projected profitability

At this stage the only help you'll need in estimating these numbers is your own thoughts after checking on other restaurants in your segment. You can get these numbers from a variety of industry and affiliate sources.

Don't be afraid to forecast great results. But you must include a clear explanation of what you are going to do differently and better than your competitors.

The Timeline and Growth Plan

What's going to happen, and when will it happen? The timeline and growth plan is your calendar for getting the location open, a tactical approach to making the restaurant a success, and your vision of the business for the next three, five, and seven years. This plan usually is a two- to three-page section that provides the investor with a description of what could be. The future is fun to imagine, but remember to stay realistic. Growth takes hard work, strategic steps, and time.

The Contingency Plan

The contingency plan is your plan B, just in case plan A doesn't work. This plan is not negative thinking; it's realistic. Things happen, so be honest. Point out risks and threats to your business and the overall industry. Investors like to know that you are aware of potential problems.

A contingency plan is also necessary when you don't know what to expect. A few years ago, I built a restaurant for a client in Utah. At the time, the city was still debating whether or not the new street in front of our site was going to be a one-way heading south or a one-way heading north, or even possibly a two-way going in both directions.

We knew the site was going to be a great one and we wanted to get ahead of the competition, but our concept was dependent on the city's decision.

Wet Floor!

Your numbers must be reasonable. If, for instance, you are opening a lunch buffet restaurant that seats 100, it is unreasonable to suggest that you can do $3 million in sales. A number cruncher will realize this. The lunch buffet concept traditionally has a lower check average, the length of the average lunch period is short, and 100 seats is not that many.

We took our completed concept design and added in three different contingency plans to accommodate whichever route the city decided to go.

Extra work? Yes. Was it worth it? Big time!

We opened many months before any of our competition. When the city decided to go with two-way traffic, which we were hoping for, the place was a giant success for all three day-parts. But we were ready with other options. If they had decided on a northerly flow of traffic we would have served only breakfast and lunch. If they had decided on a southerly flow of traffic we would have served dinner and cocktails. Instead they went both ways, and so did we.

The Supporting Documents

Support your cause with all you can. If you have anything to support your plan, put it in the supporting documents section. This section is for all the legal and professional documents, as well as any other applicable forms and papers, that make your plan even more complete. This section has plenty of room to put in forms, appendixes, pictures of sites and concepts, or whatever else you think fits.

Your Business Plan Is a Living Document

Even as you go through the planning process, personal and business circumstances can change. Fuel prices, for instance, could go up. Labor costs could go up. Keep the fluidity of the world in mind as you write your plan and revisit it often.

The Least You Need to Know

➤ Writing down your intentions makes it easier for you to make them come true.

➤ Investors, bankers, management, partners, yourself, your team, and vendors will read your business plan, so gear it to everyone.

➤ There are many ways to write a business plan, but all business plans contain many of the same essential elements.

➤ The financial plan part of your business plan is the key component of your proposal.

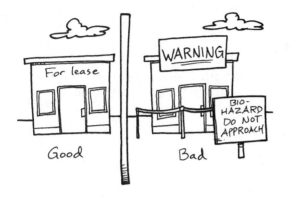

Chapter 6

Choosing the Right Site

In This Chapter

➤ Understanding the requirements behind site selection

➤ Determining accessibility and traffic

➤ Determining preliminary space requirements

➤ Choosing and securing the site that's right for you

➤ Sealing the deal

Where is your restaurant? Your answer to this question may be the single most important factor in your restaurant's success. To be a success in the restaurant business, you need more than a great concept. Plenty of great concept ideas are failing miserably because of poor sites. The opposite is also true. Plenty of mediocre concepts with grade-A sites are making money hand over fist.

Look around you. Fast-food joints populate the interstate and small coffee shops have sprung up inside bookstores. Maybe you've noticed the sandwich shops and dessert kiosks inside department stores. Or possibly you've visited the fine-dining establishment at the top of the Space Needle in Seattle, Washington. If you've been to a ball game recently, you may have noticed that many stadiums have moved beyond the typical hot dog vendor to offer a great variety of restaurants. From a gas station that offers Chinese food to a fine-dining restaurant by a racetrack, the options for combining concept and location seem endless.

When your dream comes clearly into focus, you must concentrate on the critical matter of site selection. This chapter covers the restaurant site search and selection game. Here you will find out how to search for your new home away from home. This chapter is about finding opportunities and then cutting a deal.

What Makes a Site Work?

The big question is, why do some sites work and others don't? The simple answer is that some locations are money machines, and others will never make money, no matter what kind of establishment you put up.

So what makes a site work? It comes down to five things:

➤ Concept and location fitting together

➤ Traffic

➤ Visibility

➤ Accessibility

➤ Size of space

Food for Thought

To the Oceana restaurant in New York, image is everything. The customer base is predominantly a corporate clientele being served an outstanding menu of signature dishes. Put this highly successful restaurant in a rural community in South Dakota in a strip mall, and you may be looking at a mountain of debt and a dining room of empty tables.

Make Sure Your Concept and Location Fit Together

Your location and concept should be intertwined. The wrong location for the given concept can destroy a perfectly good business opportunity. So take some time to think through what you are planning as you look for a place to put your restaurant. Asking the following important questions can help you figure out a good match between the location and concept:

➤ Who is your target market and how do you want this market to perceive your restaurant? How important is image?

➤ Who is your competition? Where are they located and why?

➤ Will your business depend on walk-in traffic, overflow from other restaurants, or customers coming specifically to your restaurant (commonly called destination traffic)?

➤ Is the location consistent with the image? Building a fast-food restaurant in a senior living residential area may not be the appropriate decision.

If the concept and location don't fit together, you may be doing the equivalent of opening a college pizza concept in a retirement community. A bad location choice may be the only mistake you make in your business start-up, but the ramifications of that decision will last until you close shop.

Consider the Traffic

Traffic matters. If cars are driving past your restaurant, drivers may notice it and decide to stop for some food. If cars are driving past someone else's restaurant, chances are the folks in them are not thinking of your establishment.

Your goal should be to open where a lot of people can see your restaurant at the times you are most likely to be busy. However, following this simple advice can become a bit complicated. It involves specific types of *traffic counts* pinpointed to the times of day that you are planning to serve.

Traffic counts are very important numbers. For instance, you would not want to put a breakfast-focused restaurant in an area that has no morning traffic. You would also not want to put a bar in an area that has little traffic after four in the afternoon.

Sadly, many new restaurants make location decisions based upon traffic count alone. They fail to realize that *when* the traffic occurs is more important than *how much* traffic occurs. Therefore, traffic count data on an hourly basis is significantly more important than daily counts.

Traffic flow is also crucial information. Understanding the traffic, its origin, and its destination is very important. For example, traffic could be huge going to a sports arena during certain dates and times, but that doesn't mean any of the people who are going to the game are inclined to stop at your hot dog stand along the way.

What is a good traffic number and what is a bad traffic number? Depending on your state, region, and community, traffic numbers vary greatly, so you must do some research.

Examine your area in great depth and detail. Get as much input from as many people and sources as

Recipes Revealed

Traffic counts are derived from a traffic survey that can be conducted by a real estate firm, demographic firm, planning commission, highway department, or you. Traffic counts are figures that indicate the average daily number of cars or pedestrians passing a particular location within a 12- or 24-hour period. Generally, these numbers are calculated by placing a black rubber hose connected to a digital counter across a traffic artery.

Food for Thought

I have heard operators say, "I will not buy any restaurant unless it has a traffic count of (fill in the blank)." Such a blanket statement has no logic. Too many other variables are important.

you can. Remember, information is power. Compare, compare, and then compare some more. Then do some thinking. What is right for your particular needs? You can figure this one out.

Talk to real estate agents about traffic counts throughout your city or area and contact the city planning commission to find out which intersections have the highest and lowest traffic counts and which roadways are the most and least used. Stop in at the city and county road-works building and ask them for traffic data. They will have it readily accessible or will know where to send you to get it.

Before long you will get a feel for what is a high, low, or mediocre traffic count number for your community. Then lean towards the higher numbers if everything else is equal.

Make It Visible

Visibility is more than simply being seen. It is being seen by the right people at the right time. Visibility is therefore connected to traffic. You want your target market (see Chapter 3, "Choosing Your Restaurant") to see your establishment when you are most likely to be serving them. Owning an ice cream treat and dessert restaurant that is seen mainly by morning rush hour traffic doesn't help, does it?

The greatest visibility happens when you have chosen a site that is on a heavy traffic pattern at the right time of day by people who fit your target market. These sites, re-ferred to as grade-A sites, can be expensive, but they are well worth the price. You can also improve your restaurant's visibility by using directional signage, marquee sign-age, neon lights, DOT (department of transportation) highway signage, and more.

Accessibility: Can Customers Get There?

Customers have to be able to get to your restaurant. How easy do you make it for them? Do they have to take a train or a bus or a boat or walk down the alley? What are the surrounding streets like? Is there a parking lot nearby?

Recipes Revealed

Ingress and **egress** are words that denote ease of entrance (ingress) to and ease of exit (egress) from the restaurant.

Usually, when a restaurant operator talks about acces-sibility, he or she is talking about *ingress* and *egress*. Ingress and egress should be analyzed for both present and future sales opportunities, as well as customer flow. The reality is that even if access to the commu-nity and trade areas is excellent, traffic to your specific restaurant may be limited.

In fact, I often get called by a restaurant owner who says to me, "We have a great location, right in the heart of a wonderful trade area, but we have no sales coming in. Can you help us?" I gladly make the trip to see what I can find out and a mere two minutes into my analysis I can clearly see the restaurant has poor ingress, egress, or both.

One sandwich operation in Georgia didn't do any research regarding accessibility. Then, the city planning commission decided to change a major intersection right in front of their restaurant—literally six months after they opened. By the time they called me for assistance the road crew was already at work.

Customers couldn't even get to them any longer during the construction phase and after the work was completed the consumer was not willing to fight traffic to get in and out of the restaurant at all. I advised them to cut their losses quickly—which they did.

Sadly, this project had been planned by the city for two years prior to this restaurant's opening. If the owners had done some research they would have known about the intersection change prior to taking the site.

Sometimes, traffic barriers cause a potential patron to slow down. And because our society is very much driven by convenience, a small traffic barrier can cause a big problem for you. The following common traffic barriers can affect your customer traffic flow in various ways:

➤ **Rivers and bridges:** Many times people prefer to do business on their side of the river due to the delays that often happen as a result of a bridge crossing, especially drawbridges.

➤ **Railroad crossings:** Railroad usage has declined over the last decade or two, but trains still have an effect on traffic. People who live on the opposite side of the tracks from your restaurant may be reluctant to use your establishment because they don't want to wait for trains to pass.

➤ **Traffic congestion:** Naturally, people avoid heavy traffic arteries if they can. Sometimes, time-for-travel is a more important number than the distance in blocks or miles.

➤ **High-crime areas:** If people feel unsafe driving to or through your restaurant's neighborhood, they won't stop. Traffic counts in such areas may be high because many people drive through them, but these people are unlikely to leave the security of their cars for your restaurant's food. Ask your local law enforcement office for some insight.

Tip Jar

Consider breaking some site selection rules. A decade ago, most restaurant real estate people would have recommended against putting a fine-dining restaurant inside a corporate tower. But the fine-dining restaurant in the United Technologies Corporate Gold building in Hartford, Connecticut has been an overwhelming success. So have many other corporate fine-dining facilities across the country.

➤ **Road construction:** This barrier can impact a business for both the short and long haul. Short term, people will find alternate routes to go where they need to go. And this will kill your sales. Long term, people may build a new set of habits.

➤ **Median strips:** Avoid median strips! They are location killers. Fifty percent of your traffic will look for easier access points on their side of the road. Medians that prohibit a convenient left-hand turn are especially bad because few people will do an illegal U-turn to grab a meal from you.

Accessibility involves other issues as well, such as the type of road you are on. Most high-volume restaurants need to be on primary traffic arteries rather than off the beaten path. In addition, consider the number of lanes of traffic in front of your restaurant. The more free-flowing traffic is, the more easily a driver can turn, slow down, enter, or exit.

How about curb cuts? Curb cuts are the driveway entrance points to and from your restaurant. Curb cuts are critical to a restaurant's ease of access. If your zoning board permits them, curb cuts on the roads leading to and from your restaurant can help you take a mediocre site and make it great.

Finally, consider pedestrian traffic. In a shopping mall, for instance, restaurant location is determined by foot traffic. Foot traffic is also a factor for many downtown locations. Foot traffic can make a huge impact on certain concepts in certain locations. Much like vehicle traffic, you must consider factors such as the time of day, type of concept, and target audience to determine whether the foot traffic is of value.

Tip Jar

If you are buying an existing restaurant, the business will be worth somewhere between two and a half and six times the profit plus any owners distributions, salary, bonus, benefits, etc. This is commonly called earnings. If you are buying or leasing property, then the site is worth basically what the market will bear.

Is Size Important?

How much space do you need? Would you rather have a huge dining room half full or a small dining room with people waiting to be seated? Do you have enough parking? Do you even need a dining room? How much space is allocated to the kitchen?

All of these questions will be answered differently based on your concept design and business model. But consider the size of the restaurant as part of the site selection process.

How Do You Know Whether the Site Is Right?

No matter what you do, you will not know for sure if your site is right until you open the restaurant. You can take every precaution, and you will still have the jitters on opening night. As of the writing of this book,

I have opened 108 restaurants in my career and each one made me nervous. That's part of the game. In fact, it's part of why you play.

Your best bet is to make an educated guess about which site is right for your restaurant. Do your research and talk to bankers, suppliers, repairmen, lawyers, accountants, marketing experts, possible patrons, neighbors, or anyone else who may be able to provide some insight into site selection. Even competitors can give you a wealth of knowledge, especially if they don't realize you are a soon-to-be competitor. Ask questions and you will get answers. Chapter 24, "Restaurant Forms," has a "Restaurant Site Analysis Worksheet" for you to copy and use.

What Should I Pay?

How much should you pay for your site? The answer to this simple question involves a lot of factors. Putting a value or a price on any site is difficult. The seller and the seller's broker usually ask more for the property than it is worth. On the other hand, the buyer and the banker want to pay less than the property is worth. Somewhere in between the two camps find common ground and make a deal.

Property valuation can be a very challenging game. You do not want to get caught on the expensive side of a bad deal. However, shorting the seller is not in your best interest either because the only way to really win is if both sides are happy.

How much should I pay for an existing restaurant? How much should I pay for rent? Both are great questions that have no single right answer. Site cost is a key component to your site selection process, as are the terms of the arrangement. Market demand, regional economics, and competition for space all play major roles in this process as well.

Ultimately, buying a restaurant site is much like buying anything else. The two primary factors are …

> ➤ What does the seller want for it?
> ➤ What are you willing to pay for it?

Wet Floor!

Be sure to compare apples to apples. The earnings calculation for a restaurant can vary greatly based on accounting method and the legal structure of the business. Also, current trends of both the business and the economy play a major role; past performance may not be a solid indicator of future performance. Earnings, just like all other forms of valuation, should be just one measure that you look at to determine what you are willing to pay for a business.

Recipes Revealed

Small wares include many things, such as can-openers, scales, kitchen and bar utensils, serving trays, and so on.

Recipes Revealed

The Internal Revenue Service defines **goodwill** as any amount paid for a business that exceeds the fair market value of hard assets. The law allows goodwill to be apportioned to such items as trademarks, patents, copyrights, customer lists, name recognition, concept attributes, the community image, and public perception.

Recipes Revealed

A **triple net lease** is when the leasee pays expenses, such as property taxes, insurance, and maintenance.

The following four methods are commonly used to determine the high and low end of an acceptable price range:

➤ **Comparable values:** What have similar restaurants sold for in the area?

➤ **Earnings approach:** What are the annual earnings of the business? Once this yearly earnings value is determined, a multiple is used to establish a theoretical value of the business. This multiple ranges from two and a half to six times the annual earnings.

➤ **Replacement value:** What would it cost to replace everything in the restaurant with the same business scenario, equipment and *small wares* needs, and start-up costs? This valuation method is most commonly used when you are interested in purchasing the assets of a restaurant, but you can use it to give you a feel of how much the seller has invested as well.

➤ **The adjusted book value:** This number is arrived at by subtracting total liabilities from total assets and coming up with a book value. This data is based upon the establishment's most recent balance sheet. Then an adjustment is made for *goodwill*.

If a lease is your preferred way of securing a site, consider the length of the lease. Traditionally, the shorter the lease, the higher the monthly rent.

Location and traffic again play critical roles in determining rent levels, as do the age and desirability of the building. Amenities such as heat, light, water, parking, cooling, cleaning, and so on also affect rent levels and must all be considered when comparing like properties. If you have a *triple net lease,* you must also factor in the extra costs of such a lease in the equation. Traditionally, occupancy costs (which include rent, insurance, and property taxes) should run 4 to 10 percent of your total yearly sales range, depending on region of the country and competition level for sites.

Ask questions and do some research. Use these questions to get started:

➤ What is my rent versus projected sales?

➤ How much will I need to spend in marketing to get this site noticed?

➤ What will happen to this area, community, or region over the next 3, 5, 10, and 20 years that could affect this site location either positively or negatively?

➤ Will the lower rent cause me to spend more in upkeep and advertising to maintain the business? Am I better off going with a higher rent situation where the facility needs less maintenance?

Let's Make a Deal

Once you finally settle on a site, have your lawyer and accountant look over every aspect of the deal before signing on the dotted line. Don't play amateur lawyer and accountant. Hire professionals who are familiar with the restaurant industry and have all documents reviewed before you sign them to ensure all line items of any paperwork are on the up and up.

Finally, be sure to make your agreement contingent upon your being able to acquire the necessary licenses and permits. Without permits and licenses, you cannot open. The inability to secure licenses and permits after signing a contract is more common than you may think, due to ongoing rezoning and new legislation.

Food for Thought

Talk to 20 different restaurant owners and operators and you will get twenty different opinions on leasing vs. buying space. I have done both many times and will continue to do both. If I want a site for a particular concept, the monthly expense for that space is more important to me than whether it is a lease or a purchase. Also, the amount of upfront money I need to put into it for improvements is a major determining factor.

The Least You Need to Know

➤ Making your site and your concept fit together is critical to your success.

➤ Traffic counts are important, but no specific number can determine likelihood of success or failure.

➤ Investigating all traffic barriers to a site can be a daunting task, but it is crucial to picking the right site.

➤ No site is a 100 percent sure thing.

➤ Ultimately, the price of a site comes down to what you are willing to pay and what the seller is willing to accept.

Chapter 7

Shake the Money Tree

In This Chapter

➤ The three stages of funding your restaurant

➤ How to handle the word *no*

➤ What you need to find money

➤ How to ask for money

➤ Where to look for money

Imagine that you need $250,000 to begin building your restaurant, and you can just whip out your ATM card and withdraw that amount from your account. Later on you can withdraw the additional $750,000 or so that is required to finish the project. Go on—imagine. It sure is easy, isn't it?

Back in the real world, the darn ATM machine turns you down, way down because the $170.12 in your account won't cover a quarter of a million dollars. (If you are able to withdraw $250,000, you should probably be reading an investment book and eating in my restaurant.) Now what?

Keep your chin up. All is not lost. You have achieved a wonderful milestone in the entrepreneurial life. You have just received your first bank turndown. How wonderful! You are now one step closer to securing your first bank approval. This chapter helps you unlock the vault to get the cash you will so desperately need to start your restaurant.

The Three Stages to Financing Your Restaurant

Funding a restaurant is a systematic process, not a one-time thing. Financing is a three-stage process, and each stage requires you to find money:

➤ **Seed capital stage:** You need to obtain start-up funds to finish preparing the business for launch and then to start operating it.

➤ **Growth capital stage:** Your restaurant has proven it is a viable concept and is ready to grow.

➤ **Harvest cash stage:** This stage is usually brought on by one of the investors or possibly even the owner wanting his wealth out of the business, or possibly wanting to exit, or wanting to bring on other investors.

How Do You Get Money?

Money is always available, and you can get money for your good idea. But some money people really like to say no. Get ready for it. Resilience is the theme of this chapter.

When you hear no (and you will, several times), just pick yourself up and move on. In business, you cannot let a turndown deter you. Almost everyone in business has heard no more times than they ever heard yes. But if the plan is solid, the concept is viable, and you are passionate about the project, in time you will hear that magic word *yes* from your local banker, a venture capital firm, or even Aunt Emma.

Food for Thought

Colonel Sanders spent seven years traveling the country selling his chicken out of the back of his station wagon before he found someone to fund his secret recipe. He didn't care who said no. He knew the only right answer was yes!

The problem for some businesses, though, is that they don't know how to get the capital they need. Those businesses fail. So how do you get money? In addition to having a great restaurant concept (see Chapter 3, "Choosing Your Restaurant"), a complete and well-conceived business plan (see Chapter 5, "The Plan Is to Plan"), and the right site (see Chapter 6, "Choosing the Right Site"), you have to do the following tasks to unlock capital resources:

➤ Develop a funding plan

➤ Put together a strong start-up team

➤ Know how to ask for the money

Develop a Funding Plan

The funding plan, called the money plan by some, is a set of strategies for targeting the right amount of money from the right sources, at the right time, for the right price. Be sure to examine all the sources you can and then you can build your money plan.

First, figure out how much money you need. Don't ask for less than you need because you think you can't get more, and don't ask for a lot more just because you think you can get it. Falling short later can be more painful than not getting anything now, and greedily overreaching is just bad karma.

Also, define the points in your business plan when you will most likely need an injection of cash. Knowing ahead of time what you need and when is much better than trying to take all your money at once or, worse, going to the money well too many times.

It is best to have money in place about six months before you need it, and a safety net equal to at least two months of projected revenues. Look at your projected proforma and projected cash flow and plan on infusing capital at times when your financial plan shows a shortage of cash.

For instance, if I project the restaurant to do $70,000 per month in sales, I want to plan on having $140,000 in additional cash available at all times during the start-up stages. Many times I get this by getting a line of credit from my friendly neighborhood banker that is equal to $140,000 that I can tap if I need it and won't tap if I don't need to.

Wet Floor!

Asking for too little money is asking for trouble. This is commonly called being undercapitalized. A business that is undercapitalized is akin to a fish being out of water.

Put Together a Strong Start-Up Team

Can your team get the job done? Often, a loan is decided based on the level of experience, professional appearance and attitude, and the personal track record of the members of your team, as well as your ability to engender confidence.

If you want money for your restaurant, you need to be able to prove your team's capability to an investor. Surround yourself with people who cover any deficiencies you may have, whether it be leadership, accounting, or marketing.

Once you have assembled your team, ask yourself, "Would I loan money to these guys?" If you don't

Tip Jar

Carefully consider what the use of someone else's money will cost you. What are you willing to give up in ownership? How much are you willing to pay in interest?

believe in your own team, it will show. On the other hand, if you have a team you believe in, that confidence will shine through to a smart investor.

Know How to Ask for the Money

You can beg and grovel for money, or you can skip the begging and play hard to get. It depends on your situation. But strategy and logic always help when you ask for money.

Lenders and investors need you just as badly as you need them. Without people to lend money to they don't make money either, so you are important to them.

You want to give them the impression that you will not take any money they give you at any interest rate. Let them know that you know you have other options—you have thousands of lending institutions and investors to choose from.

There is an art to asking for money: Always be professional. Don't be afraid to hear no. Work smart. Build contacts. Don't be afraid to hear no. Smile. Shake hands with confidence. Don't be afraid to hear no. Come prepared. Be on time for meetings. Don't be afraid to hear no. The key to knowing how to ask for money is to just keep asking.

Different lenders and investors all want different things, so understanding that you cannot be everything to all of them is important to remember. Your next meeting could end with someone uttering the word *yes*. The only way you will find out is if you are not afraid to hear no.

Finding Cash by Looking

The flow of cash into a restaurant is essential. When you are not serving up any soup or enchiladas, you are not making money to support your restaurant. Thus, you need to look around for money to keep the restaurant going.

Food for Thought

In the business world, the need for money is hunger, breathlessness, and thirst combined. Money is life in business, and the need for it cannot be ignored.

You can find money wherever there's a piggy bank. Although a piggy bank is not the first place you should look for funding, no place should be ignored. You may find cash in your old guitars or in a banker's signature. But you have to examine all possible sources in order to find it.

It All Starts with You

More than 70 percent of entrepreneurs start their businesses by tapping personal resources, including personal savings, IRA accounts, credit cards, second and third home mortgages, personal assets, and money from friends and family.

Why do so many entrepreneurs need to dig into their own pockets when so many financial resources are available? The reason is quite simple: A new business is a big risk. It is unproven. Investing your own money in the business demonstrates to investors that you believe in your vision and concept. If you won't invest in the business, it can be difficult to get anyone else to.

Begging, Borrowing, and Bartering

The world runs on deals, but not all deals are the same. Sometimes, especially for the aspiring entrepreneur, bartering, borrowing, or even begging is helpful. Don't be embarrassed. Try these strategies:

➤ Borrow office space and office equipment from an established company. I have done this on more than one occasion and find it not only a frugal alternative, but it helps me network with new people each and every time I do it.

➤ Use the library computers for free and copy everything on a diskette.

➤ Trade professional services for your hard work. I once mowed a neighbor's lawn for a summer in exchange for free legal advice.

➤ Use your network of friends, family, and associates for advice, input, and even concept designs in exchange for a small piece of ownership.

➤ Ask vendors and suppliers for favorable payment terms and credit limits.

➤ Borrow from friends and family at your own risk. The only fair way is to make it clear that this loan is a business loan and risks are involved. Specify that only people who can bear to lose their investment should take this risk. Then in exchange for the loan, you should repay your friend or family member with interest like anyone else.

Angels with Money

After personal assets, a private investor, also known as an angel investor, is the most common source of capital for starting or growing any business. Angel investors typically ask for a business plan, goals and objectives, and a significant equity stake in the business in exchange for their cash infusion.

Angel investors are the largest pool of capital in the United States and are traditionally very low profile, making them difficult to find. Typically, entrepreneurs find angel investors through networking with people across the industry. Many

Tip Jar

Forget the perks and be frugal. All your money should be spent on getting you closer to opening your restaurant. You don't need the nicest office furniture yet. You need dependable stoves.

times people build a strong network across the corporate restaurant scene, and in time it leads them to angel investors who work within the corporate sector as well as the private sector. Also, meeting people who support restaurant companies, such as vendors, suppliers, bankers, lawyers, accountants, and the like, will lead you to people who invest in the industry.

Tip Jar

An angel investor who provides more than just money can help immeasurably. An angel investor who aligns with your goals, clearly sees your vision, is reputable (don't be afraid to do a background check on these investors), has many contacts throughout the industry, and acts as a mentor can be a godsend.

Food for Thought

RTM Restaurant Group, the largest Arby's franchise with nearly a thousand restaurants total, started as a partnership between three men named Russ, Tom, and Mike (hence RTM). But now RTM stands for Results Through Motivation and has become one of the most successful restaurant companies in America. Only Russ Umphenour stuck around for the long haul and the big bucks.

The Wonderful World of Venture Capital

A venture capital firm is a professionally managed pool of funds that comes from multiple investors, including individuals and institutional resources. It is usually set up as a limited partnership, and the money is invested on behalf of the firm.

Venture capitalists (VCs) and angel investors are different, yet they have very similar ways of securing funding and dealing with parameters:

➤ VCs typically invest at the second or third stage of funding but not always. They tend to be looking for very fast growth and even quicker turnaround of their investment.

➤ Finding VCs is similar to finding angel investors: You must use your network. The difference is that venture capitalists tend to be a bit more accessible.

➤ As with angel investors, make sure you know what you're getting into and with whom you're conducting business.

The Pluses and Minuses of Partnerships

How about finding a partner, maybe two? Partnerships have been the backbone of many great restaurant companies. Some of the biggest names in the business started as partnerships.

Like most everything in business, building a partnership has some upsides and downsides. The upsides include the following:

➤ Shared responsibilities and more idea generation

➤ More financial and credit resources

➤ More networking opportunities

➤ Friendship and a shared experience

A partnership could have some downsides as well:

➤ The wrong partner with a different vision can make the relationship uncomfortable and fraught with conflict.

➤ Split control and decision-making can lead to power struggles. I have seen this on more than one occasion, so new partnerships beware.

➤ A partnership agreement can become cumbersome and intimidating.

Partnerships do not need to be set up with equal ownership, and each partner does not have to share equally in the profits or losses. Also, each partner can have a different level of decision-making authority and responsibilities.

Partnerships range from limited partnerships to silent partnerships and general partnerships. A reputable attorney can walk you through the finer points of building any partnership, including the construction of a partnership agreement.

Bankers Really Do Loan Money

Who gets money from banks? You know the old joke: only the people who already have money! Traditionally banks have avoided providing money during start-up funding stages. Banks become more interested during stages two and three of funding.

So how do banks make loan decisions? Most banks make loans to restaurant entrepreneurs based on the 10 Cs:

➤ Character of entrepreneur: Are you well known and well respected?

➤ Capacity to repay the loan: Do you have the money to cover the monthly loan repayment?

➤ Collateral to secure the loan: Do you have something they can secure the loan with like a home or investments? In other words, if you don't pay them, what can they take from you?

➤ Credit report of the entrepreneur: Do you have a good track record of paying off your bills?

➤ Concept design and feasibility: How solid are your concept plans and can the idea work?

➤ Competitive environment: How competitive is the community around where you want to build this restaurant and are other restaurants finding succes in your area?

➤ Capital needed to make it happen: Have you carefully figured out your capital needs?

➤ Cash flow projections: Is the business projected to make money and are the projections reasonable?

➤ Common sense business plans: Is the entire plan well thought out and does it make sense and seem achievable?

➤ Commitment level of the entrepreneur: Are you committed to making the thing work and are you passionate about the concept?

Bankers are looking for a high level of commitment from entrepreneurs. Ask yourself: Are you fully invested both financially and emotionally in the restaurant?

Recipes Revealed

The **prime interest rate** is the interest rate a bank charges to customers who have the best credit. It is a reference point for other loan rates given by the bank.

Commercial Finance Companies

Commercial finance companies can have high rates of interest, but they are more likely than a bank to lend money to a start-up. Commercial finance companies typically charge 3 to 7 percent above the *prime interest rate*.

Lines of Credit

Lines of credit come in a variety of forms and tend to be much easier to secure than a cold hard cash loan. Credit cards are one type of credit line, but house accounts, account payable terms from suppliers and vendors, and even a verbal financial commitment in case of emergency from your best friend are all forms of credit lines. Your personal banker may give you a line of credit as well if you have been a good, well-respected customer.

More than one entrepreneur has opened a restaurant using lines of credit. Besides, what else would you do with all those credit card solicitations? Using credit cards is an expensive proposition, but if the other sources aren't lining up to give you money, it's an option.

Equipment Leasing

Equipment leasing is a popular source of funding in the restaurant industry. Leasing equipment in the restaurant industry is as common as making the morning prep list. Whether you own one restaurant or 100, leasing equipment is not unusual. There are many competing equipment-leasing firms and many different equipment and financing packages. Shop around. (See Chapter 14, "Get It Right on the Back End: The Back of the House," for more on leasing equipment.)

It is quite easy to secure an approval for an equipment lease, and many times these firms will help you find other sources of capital because they know that you will be leasing equipment from them once you secure the appropriate funding.

Small Business Administration Loans

The Small Business Administration (SBA) guarantees loans up to 90 percent and works with commercial lenders to execute and deliver these loans. The success rate for businesses that decide to use SBA-funded loans tends to be significantly higher than the average business, and with the 90 percent guarantee, lenders enjoy working with the SBA. However, the SBA regards restaurants as a high risk.

The SBA will look upon you favorably if you can impress it with your experience and a good plan. For more on SBA loans and SBA loan guidelines, contact your local SBA-approved commercial lender. Look in your local Yellow Pages to find an SBA-approved commercial lender, which could be virtually any type of lending institution.

Knowledge Is Your Friend

Running a restaurant is a profession. If you dedicate your mental energies as well as your physical energies to your profession, you will be better at it. Searching for money follows the same rules. If, with your mental energy, you find the right information, you can avoid wasting a lot of physical energy on stress.

Finding money is not as hard as it seems. You can save yourself a lot of trouble by taking the time now to find the right amount of money to get your business going right. Listen. Somewhere out there money is calling you.

The Least You Need to Know

➤ Finding money is not a one-time thing. Financing a restaurant involves three stages: the seed capital stage, the growth capital stage, and the harvest cash stage.

➤ Keep asking for money. You will hear no a lot, but if you have a good idea, someone will eventually say yes.

➤ Create a solid business plan and assemble a strong management team to win over investors.

➤ Your own savings and assets, angel investors, venture capital firms, partners, banks, commercial finance companies, lines of credit, and SBA loans are all potential sources of money.

Chapter 8

The Preopening Calendar

In This Chapter

➤ Accomplishing your goals on time

➤ The best way to organize your lists

➤ All the checklists you'll need, from one year before opening to one night before opening

Can you remember 1,000,000 things in 3,000 categories? Can you remember them in order? Starting a restaurant is not quite this kind of intelligence test, but the tasks you will juggle are too numerous to leave to mental energy alone. Instead, I recommend the two greatest tools known to the modern restaurant owner: pencil and paper.

When you're opening a restaurant, it's not the time to test some new Zen strategy or some memory techniques you learned on late-night television. This is business. Your restaurant opening needs to go off without a hitch. Turn on the tactical and systematic part of your brain and develop your way of doing things.

For years, I have been helping restaurants open. And in that time, I have developed checklists to help the owners accomplish their goals on time. This chapter presents a series of checklists that will take you from idea to opening. Copy these lists and use them to build specific steps to make your dream go smoothly.

The Organizational System

A three-ring binder system that has matching paper files and a matching computer folder will become your best friend. With such a binder, you can keep everything neat and organized and easy to access at a moment's notice.

Try these eight categories. They cover everything the beginning restaurateur needs to get him or her on the path to owning and operating their own restaurant. Everything in this entire book will fit nicely into one of them. Use them—you'll be glad you did.

➤ Concept development

➤ Competition and research

➤ Financial information

➤ Operations

➤ Legal

➤ Personnel

➤ Contacts and vendors

➤ Business plan

Food for Thought

In the early 1990s, I overheard the chef, manager, and wine director of New York City's Tribeca Grill just before the restaurant was to open. They calmly discussed how they had executed their preopening plan. They had it all under control and were sure they were set up for success. They were right. The Tribeca Grill is a giant success, and all three leaders are still in place.

One Year Before Opening

➤ Begin preliminary research of types of restaurants, the competitive environment, the number of restaurants in your area, voids in the marketplace, and the general choosing of your restaurant concept. (See Chapter 3, "Choosing Your Restaurant.")

➤ Visit other restaurants and write down ideas you like and ideas you don't. Make notes about menu, pricing, decor, and service style.

➤ Determine which restaurants are thriving and which ones are failing and spend time analyzing why.

➤ Network with restaurant owners and operators, lawyers, accountants, bankers, marketing firms, and for that matter anyone else who will give you the time of day. Build your support structure and find a mentor or two. Ask tons of questions and search for answers (see Chapter 1, "Table for One: Is This for Me?").

➤ Conduct your preliminary site selection and site analysis process. Become familiar with the community and traffic patterns. (See Chapter 6, "Choosing the Right Site," for more information.)

➤ Put together rough financial statements and projections. Don't worry about overanalyzing the numbers at this point. Pick a number and go with it.

➤ Investigate potential ways to secure future funding. (See Chapter 7, "Shake the Money Tree.")

➤ Get a feel for potential costs of buying, leasing, construction, start-up, and so on. (See Chapter 5, "The Plan Is to Plan.")

➤ Build preliminary Profit and Loss forms and guidelines. (See Chapter 11, "Basic Accounting: It's More Than Just Counting the Beans.")

➤ Start observing your competition's operational parameters and developing your own. Begin to eat at other establishments, looking for how they operate the restaurant. Spend time pinpointing things you like and things you don't. The following sentences should be filled in many, many times: "When I open my restaurant I wouldn't _____" (fill in the blank). Or "When I open my restaurant, I'm going to _____" (fill in the blank).

➤ Build operational "like" and "don't like" sets of lists. For instance, *I like that they frost the beer mugs,* and *I don't like the thin unfrozen French fries that come with the grilled cheeseburger.*

➤ Try to determine minimum, maximum, and optimum square footage requirements for your facility. These numbers are determined by adding up kitchen needs, dining room needs, and storage needs. (See Chapter 15, "Upfront Effort: Setting Up for Service.")

➤ Start building your recipes file and begin to put in place the most important of all concept decisions: your menu (see Chapter 3).

➤ Build a network with the many new and used restaurant equipment dealers and get a feel for the cost of equipment. (See Chapter 14, "Get It Right on the Back End: The Back of the House.")

➤ Interview restaurateurs and government agency and legal people to determine the legal issues and hurdles that must be considered. Start your search for lawyers, insurance agents, accountants, and more people who can be of assistance.

➤ Get information about obtaining health permits, liquor licenses, and building permits. Determine the legal entity you want to form for the business (see Chapter 4, "Is This Legal?").

➤ Discuss your restaurant idea and concept openly with friends and family who will keep it confidential and give you some honest input.

➤ Talk to restaurant owners and other entrepreneurs about their experiences as business owners.

➤ Analyze your personal strengths and weaknesses and determine a plan of action to develop your knowledge base or hire people who cover your shortcomings.

➤ Find and catalog restaurant-based Web sites, associations, trade magazines, and research material for easy access (see Appendix A, "Additional Reference Materials").

Tip Jar

Ask restaurant owners for a copy of their menu. Then use it to determine concepts and designs for your own menu.)

Recipes Revealed

Points of distinction are what make you different from your competitors. They may be your menu and decor, your prices, or a host of other things. To be successful in this business, you must be known for something.

Eight Months Before Opening

➤ Outline your business plan and mission statement and begin putting the pieces together. (See Chapter 5.)

➤ Continue to research the industry and the market.

➤ Continue to design and develop the restaurant concept and menu. Now is the time to hire a concept design team. They will help you flush out your preliminary ideas and concepts.

➤ Determine the target market you want to serve (see Chapter 3).

➤ Determine the style of service you will provide and the industry segment.

➤ Spend quality time determining the name of your restaurant. This decision is critical, so spend time asking for input (see Chapter 4).

➤ Determine your restaurant's *points of distinction*.

➤ Conduct a complete competitive analysis (see Chapter 3).

➤ Begin to build a site criteria checklist.

➤ Meet with real estate agents and bankers in the area you are considering and begin discussions regarding your concept, your funding needs, and your business plan progress and begin looking at sites.

➤ Get familiar with the area you are considering and its traffic count data (see Chapter 6).

➤ Begin to meet with other restaurant owners and operators in the area as well as other entrepreneurs and consumers in the area just to chat. Discussions generate ideas, questions, comments, and concerns, not to mention relationships.

➤ Continue to refine your numbers and assumptions along the way. Use industry information and averages to compare.

➤ Get a good feel for what products and services are provided in the area and at what menu prices.

➤ Continue to refine your menu and recipes.

➤ Contact several vendors and contractors to begin estimating and refining costs and time availability and requirements.

➤ Meet with all necessary government officials, legal counsel, insurance agents, and accountants to ensure you understand the process for application, the cost, the time frame, and the necessary steps to getting the appropriate licenses and permits.

➤ Join trade associations and networking forums.

Six Months Before Opening

➤ Select your advisors and support team. You will need an attorney, accountant, and insurance agent as part of your professional support. (See Chapter 7.)

➤ Complete your business plan (see Chapter 5).

➤ Set up the restaurant's name and legal entity and obtain a taxpayer ID number (see Chapter 4).

➤ Finalize the restaurant concept (the menu, the decor, the style of service, and so on). All the details should be on paper.

➤ Zero in on a site or two that matches your needs.

➤ Check with the local zoning board, planning commission, and health department to ensure the site is (or will be) approved for its intended use.

➤ Discuss plans with contractors, lawyers, mentors, aunts, uncles, brothers, sisters, friends, and family to get their input.

Wet Floor!

Choose your advisors wisely. Do a thorough interview and background check and spend the necessary time getting to know them before you give them the total picture of your concept and the green light as one of your advisors. Choosing these advisors carefully is critical to your success and the success of your restaurant. Following the advice of some snake oil salesman will cost you in the end.

Wet Floor!

Some restaurants take longer to build than others. Depending on the type and size of the restaurant you're opening, the extensiveness of the decor, and the location, it can take two years or two months. Large, expensive, and free-standing restaurants take much more time to open than small hot-dog stands inside a shopping mall. It really depends. Give yourself plenty of time. Don't rush things and don't open until you're ready. That first impression is critical.

Tip Jar

Major foodservice vendors like Sysco Foods, US Foodservice, and others can help you plan your product needs. These companies are not only experts in dealing with restaurant products, they have large staffs and an interest in your success. After all, if you succeed, you'll buy more products.

➤ Review all financial projections with your banker, accountant, contractors, vendors, and lawyers to ensure accuracy. Determine all cash needs.

➤ Continue to tweak and revise all financial projections, analyses, and needs as more information comes to light.

➤ Map out preliminary dining area, kitchen area, and storage area floor plans for your potential site (see Chapter 15).

➤ Determine preliminary equipment needs based on your potential site (see Chapter 14).

➤ Investigate all of your options for obtaining the necessary cash and line up your funding (see Chapter 7).

Five Months Before Opening

➤ Select your location and complete the deal. Make sure your advisors walk through every step of this process with you.

➤ Revise your plans where necessary to reflect your new site.

➤ Begin to schedule contractors and vendors. Plan the execution of the opening and steps needed to make it happen. Build a facility construction plan and calendar. The contractor will help you do this. You give him the planned opening date, and he will give you the facility construction plan.

➤ Apply for your health permit, liquor license, building permits, and any other licenses and permits you need.

➤ Join the local chamber of commerce, the National Restaurant Association, and any local business groups to gain more networking opportunities.

Four Months Before Opening

➤ Determine office set-up and equipment needs.

➤ Determine silverware, small wares, glassware, china, linen, and other miscellaneous dining services needs and prepare your order. (See Chapter 14.)

➤ Finalize your pricing strategy to reflect your concept and your area.

➤ Finalize customer count and sales forecasts.

➤ Finalize your food cost projections and determine the food cost of every item on your menu. (See Chapter 22, "A Restaurant Named Profit: Hit the Numbers.")

➤ Begin to write your operations manual and employee handbooks (see Chapter 10, "Managing Your Risks").

➤ Ensure that the facility construction is progressing per the construction schedule.

Three Months Before Opening

➤ Get an office facility and set up office, bookkeeping, and accounting systems.

➤ Begin feeding friends and family the menu selections from your restaurant when possible to get menu design feedback. Invite people to your house for dinner and serve them your proposed table fare.

➤ Determine ideal staffing needs. (See Chapter 9, "Whoever Gets the Best People Wins: It's a People Game.")

➤ Determine what the area demands for salary and wage guidelines.

➤ Finalize projected labor costs.

➤ Make sure you have all of your licenses in hand or have at least filed the necessary paperwork with the proper agency.

➤ Continue to revise and develop all of your financial plans.

➤ Finalize your marketing, advertising, and public relations plans. (See Chapter 13, "Restaurant Marketing 101.")

Food for Thought

Most people like the idea of a free meal, and they love feeling a part of something fun and exciting like the launch of a restaurant. But the best part is that you really don't know who you know. I have made many professional contacts by breaking bread this way. I suggest to all of my clients that they should never open a restaurant without having this kind of trial dinner.

➤ Have all of the appropriate marketing pieces designed and printed. This material includes business cards, letterhead, menu boards, signage, and promotional material.

➤ Meet with all your approved vendors to prepare orders and determine delivery schedules and terms. (See Chapter 12, "Purchasing: It's More Than Buying a Can of Corn.")

➤ Order all equipment, tables, chairs, cash registers, and small wares to be delivered at an appropriate time closer to opening. Ordering ahead of time prevents back-orders from affecting you.

➤ Make changes to your plans if you deem them to be necessary and prudent. However, keep in mind that things should be just about finalized at this point.

➤ Build a sourcing, selecting, hiring, training, and an overall people plan.

➤ Ensure that the facility construction is progressing per the construction schedule.

Two Months Before Opening

➤ Put in all orders for food and beverage products to arrive three to four days before your open date (see Chapter 12).

➤ Determine the hours of operation of the restaurant.

Food for Thought

Operating hours have more to do with your concept design, local traffic, and ability to generate sales than they do with your desire for early nights, late-morning snoozes, and fun and exciting weekends. Common sense says that traffic should determine your appropriate hours of operation.

➤ Design all cash-handling procedures, inventory procedures, checklists, forms, and control processes. (See Chapter 11.)

➤ Finalize the menu. Get the menu designed and printed based on your concept design.

➤ Arrange for the acceptance of credit cards (Chapter 11) and order the necessary equipment and supplies (see Chapter 12).

➤ Finalize written job descriptions and all manuals, systems, and employee policies and procedures.

➤ Have all required and suggested insurance coverage put in place to take effect at the predetermined time. Meet with your insurance agent to discuss and plan the schedule (see Chapter 10).

➤ Finalize your entire operating statement, cash flow statement, balance sheet, and all projections and review them with your accountant, banker, and lawyer. (See Chapter 11.)

➤ Begin executing your people plan. Place ads, conduct interviews, offer positions, and determine start dates (see Chapter 9).

➤ Ensure that the facility construction is progressing per the construction schedule.

➤ Set up all services, such as electricity, telephones, garbage removal, water, and sewer services.

➤ Check on the status of any and all outstanding permits, licenses, and insurance policies.

➤ Begin your preopening promotional plans, especially the preopening countdown campaign (see Chapter 13).

➤ Keep to a minimum any changes to the core concept from this point on. Making changes this late in the game becomes significantly more expensive and risky. Changes do sometimes occur at this point, but if you prepared properly early on, you can avoid them.

Thirty Days Before Opening

➤ Ensure that the facility construction is progressing per the construction schedule.

➤ Finalize all operating systems, financial tracking and reporting systems, control systems, information and management systems, and ordering systems and test them to ensure they work properly.

➤ Finalize all arrangements with vendors (see Chapter 12).

➤ Hire staff (see Chapter 9) and begin the training process (see Chapter 20, "Retaining the People You Have").

➤ Send out *VIP party* invitations to community leaders, friends, family, and civic organizations.

The Final Two Weeks Before Opening

➤ Ensure that the facility construction is progressing per the construction schedule.

Recipes Revealed

A **VIP party,** often held the night before the opening, is when you invite community leaders, business associates, neighboring business employees, family, friends, the mayor, and whomever else you want to invite to your restaurant for a private party. This party builds momentum and a word-of-mouth buzz about your business being open. Fancy invitations, festive decorations and music, and free trinkets with the restaurant's logo are staples of the affair. Inviting the local media is always smart. Some free press always helps.

➤ Test all equipment to make sure it is in working order.

➤ Prepare for small wares arriving.

➤ Begin to clean up. The place will be quite dusty and disorganized from all the construction.

➤ Aim to be completely ready one week ahead of time.

➤ Ensure that your complete order of small wares has arrived per your order.

➤ Make sure you have menus and other promotional materials.

➤ Set up the entire facility.

➤ Follow up to ensure all necessary licenses, permits, insurance policies, and tax ID numbers are obtained and properly displayed.

➤ Walk through every inch of the facility with the construction manager and ensure that everything is up to snuff. This process is called a construction punch-list.

➤ Make a plan with the construction manager to address anything that is out of order or unsatisfactory.

➤ Ensure that your food, beverage, and supplies orders have arrived.

➤ Begin dress rehearsals with friends, family, neighbors, and associates as nonpaying customers.

➤ Prepare for your VIP party.

➤ Ensure that all construction punch-list concerns have been addressed and sign off on the construction as meeting your standards and expectations.

Tip Jar

Don't be afraid to let all pieces of equipment run for three to four hours. This is not the time to worry about the $17 of wasted electricity and gas on your utility bill. You want to work out any and all kinks before you open, so crank 'em up and let 'em run.

The Night Before Opening

This checklist is the most important one. This is the night before the biggest night of your dream, so you have to be sure to follow this checklist with precision.

➤ Make sure all items on previous checklists are complete.

➤ Relax and enjoy yourself. This will be your last night to relax in a while.

➤ Get some sleep.

The Least You Need to Know

➤ Don't leave all the necessary details to memory. Work from checklists.

➤ You need to do certain things at certain times in the preopening calendar. So you need lists for what to do every month for up to six months before opening.

➤ You will develop your own specific plans and lists as you learn the restaurant business.

➤ On the final day before you open, relax. It may be your last chance for a while!

Part 3

The Restaurant Operator: A Jack of Many Trades

You would think that restaurants are about food, and you, of course, would be right. But running a restaurant is more than cooking beans, mopping floors, and filling water glasses. Part 3 addresses the big responsibilities of restaurant ownership and management: human resources, risk management, legal compliance, accounting, purchasing, and marketing.

Chapter 9

Whoever Gets the Best People Wins: It's a People Game

In This Chapter

➤ Figuring out your staffing needs

➤ Creating an ideal staffing chart

➤ Recruiting the best staff

➤ Interviewing successfully

➤ Handling the hiring (and not hiring) right

NOW HIRING: APPLY WITHIN

You see this sign outside of a restaurant and what do you think? Does the restaurant have the right number of people to serve me my meal? How desperate is the restaurant management? Why does the restaurant always need people? Is the environment so unfriendly that the management can't keep people? Do I really want a trainee spilling soup all over me?

If you are just gearing up to open the business, these signs are wonderful, but once you're open, they are questionable at best. These signs may cause you to lose customers before they even give you a try.

Yet all restaurants need people. It is a business with high turnover, so you will inevitably need to hire more than once. But a good restaurant is adept at finding the right people and, just as important, retaining them (see Chapter 20, "Retaining the People You Have," for more on retaining your employees).

Tip Jar

Not everyone is going to like working for you. Some employees will move out of the area, and others won't work out the way you thought. In other words, you will lose employees, a process known as attrition. When opening a restaurant, I always hire 20 percent more staff than I need to allow for attrition. For example, if my restaurant needs 35 employees, I hire 42.

Tip Jar

For your first two to three weeks, go with your ideal staffing chart for each particular day-part every day. Staffing your restaurant this way allows for additional training, operational execution, and simple team cohesiveness. Those first weeks are critical to building a staff.

This chapter is about putting your team together. In it, you learn how to determine your staffing needs, how to chart which employees work when, and how to determine what to pay your people. You also learn some insider recruiting tips as well as a good tool to help you evaluate people.

Determining Your Staffing Needs

How many people should work in your new restaurant? The answer to this question is a source of much confusion. Many restaurant owners don't have a clue about how many people it takes to execute the restaurant concept properly. They may know how many people they need to hit some labor hours or labor percentage target, but they do not understand that managing a restaurant staff means executing the concept and serving the customer by delivering hospitality, quality, cleanliness, and accuracy.

How many does it take to get everything done right? That is the real question. You must determine exactly how many people you need. You also must figure out which times of the day you think you are going to need them.

The process of hiring the right people can be challenging and time consuming, but it is worth it. If you are unsuccessful in hiring good people, you either fail as a business, or you have to do it all over again anyway to find someone good. So why not do it right in the beginning?

Determining what your staffing needs are comes down to these four steps:

➤ Building your ideal staffing chart

➤ Determining which positions are critical components

➤ Designing and managing your wage guidelines

➤ Building an effective starting calendar

Building Your Ideal Staffing Chart

A staffing chart shows what positions you need to fill during every hour of every day throughout the week. It is similar to a lineup card in baseball except with baseball you always have nine players. In your restaurant you may have three people during one low volume hour and thirteen during a peak period. The staffing chart is designed to ensure you have all your bases covered during the busiest times of each day of the week and that you are not wasting labor dollars by having people stand around during slow periods.

To make a staffing chart, you begin by projecting your busiest days of the week. In addition, I like to build a chart for each peak period that the restaurant is open. In a breakfast, lunch, and dinner restaurant concept, for example, I would build three separate charts.

For the sake of this discussion, suppose Friday night between 5:00 and 7:00 is your busiest time. You begin making your staffing chart by writing down each and every person you think you will need on the shift to execute your concept to your standards: Chef, Bartender 1, Bartender 2, Line Cook 1, Line Cook 2, and so on. When you are done listing these positions, you will have a complete rundown of every position you need to have filled during your busiest two hours of the given daypart on your busiest day.

But how do you know how many people you need at every hour? Try this scientific technique that has been proven through years of research: guess. You are opening a new restaurant, so there are a ton of unknowns. Guess and then adjust. An ideal staffing chart, just like a schedule, is a work in constant progress. As you become more familiar with the ebbs and flows of your food sales, you will become a better guesser.

Once you have an idea of how many people you want in each day-part, use what is commonly referred to as *stair-stepping*. This stair-stepping process is built by using your common sense and, in time, your gut feel of when the business is most likely in need of more staff. Everyone knows that noon in a lunch restaurant is busy, and 10:15 A.M. and 2:45 P.M. are not. Your schedule should reflect that fact.

Recipes Revealed

Stair-stepping is using intervals to bring people into and out of the shift. In basketball, a coach rarely substitutes all five players into the game at the same time. The same holds true with restaurants. Scheduling one person to come in at 9:00 A.M., the second at 9:30 A.M., the third at 10:15 A.M., and so on or sending them home in the same manner (for example 2:00 P.M., 2:30 P.M., 2:45 P.M., and so on) provides for a smoother transition, higher productivity, and improved labor cost.

An example of a dinner day-part staffing chart. As you can see, the greatest number of employees are scheduled when there is the greatest potential for customers to frequent your restaurant.

	Position	3PM	4PM	5PM	6PM	7PM	8PM	9PM	10PM	11PM
Bill	Shift Mgr.	X	X	X	X	X	X	X	X	X
Joe	Cook	X	X	X	X	X	X	X	X	
Jill	Cook			X	X	X	X	X		
Kim	Hostess				X	X				
Mike	Server	X	X	X	X	X	X	X		
Sara	Server		X	X	X	X	X	X	X	X
Bob	Server				X	X	X	X	X	
Sue	Bar	X	X	X	X	X	X	X	X	X
Rob	Bus				X	X	X			
Total Employees		4	5	6	9	9	8	6	5	3

The process is called stair-stepping because if you looked at this in terms of flow of employees, it would look like stair steps.

Time-	3PM	4PM	5PM	6PM	7PM	8PM	9PM	10PM	11PM
Number of Employees									
10									
9									
8									
7									
6									
5									
4									
3									
2									
1									

Determining Which Positions Are Critical Components

Depending on your concept, certain positions are more critical to your restaurant's success than others. For example, a chef and sous chef are important in a fine-dining establishment, a drive-thru order taker and expediter are important in a fast-food drive-thru concept, and a bartender is essential in a restaurant with an upscale cocktail lounge.

However, regardless of concept, the management people are the key to a successful restaurant. This group of people includes you (the owner) or your manager and the assistant manager or shift manager. This group also includes your category managers.

Managers call the shots and are experts in their respective areas of responsibility. They are responsible for training the staff, building employee morale, improving operational performance, and more.

Most good restaurants have an individual who is in charge of each of the different areas of the restaurant: a dining room manager (sometimes called a host or head waitress), a bar manager, and a kitchen manager or chef, for example. These people are critical components to the successful operation and execution of your restaurant. Without this hands-on leadership, your staff will have a difficult time staying focused on what is and isn't important and will approach their responsibilities in an uninspired and undirected manner.

Paying Folks Fairly: Developing a Competitive Wage Guideline

Coming up with a competitive wage is more than just pulling an hourly wage offer out of a hat. To compete for quality employees, you must pay what the market will bear. The reality is that in some parts of the country paying a chef $8 per hour is perfectly acceptable, and in others you wouldn't get a chance to talk to an entry-level dishwasher for that. So how do you know what to pay? You look around, ask questions, and use surveys.

Every time I begin to put my start-up team together, I conduct surveys regarding pay ranges for each particular position. I do this by checking with local chamber of commerce data and unemployment job service offices. I also read classified advertisements for restaurant help. I also ask competitors and employees of competitors. Once I get a good feel for what the market is currently bearing, I then either meet it or, if necessary, exceed it. I always find myself in the game of competing for employees.

Building a Starting Calendar

When do you want your staff to begin work? Of course, it would be nice to find sharp people and have them start immediately even though you don't open for another three or four months. But that is not reasonable or affordable.

Some people you will hire weeks before the restaurant opens; others you will hire just days before. You can't afford to carry a full payroll three weeks before you open. You have no sales. You cannot pay for it. On the other hand, you do need help setting up equipment, cleaning up after construction, putting away product orders, and more. Also, some necessary training pieces must be put in place before you open.

Every restaurant and restaurant owner has different wants and needs. Depending on what those are and what you can afford, you should be able to determine a preopening labor budget that will get the necessary work done without costing you an arm and a leg. Only you know your concept. Only you know what it will take to train your crew and get the restaurant up and running. But remember, wasting labor dollars can kill your business and profitability.

When I open fine-dining establishments, I hire the chef and sous chef very early in the process. A well educated and trained chef and sous chef will lead the show and help make many of the concept design and layout decisions. I also want to get the leader of my wait-staff in position early for the same reasons. Plus, they all like to hire their own staffs.

When I open a fast-food place, I first want people who have a lot of drive-thru experience and register experience. The fact is, fast-food kitchens are easy to operate because of prepackaged and prepared foods. The bigger challenge is with the volume of customers, so I first find people who can handle that volume without getting frazzled.

Each situation is different. The timing will depend on how much you need to train them, how much previous knowledge they bring with them, how difficult your concept is, and their level of retention. Hire smart people. They retain information more quickly and lower your training costs.

Food for Thought

The main issue is not getting a restaurant staffed; the issue is keeping the people you hire. But if you are good, retaining employees won't be an issue. Great restaurant operators have no problem with staffing. They hire the right people and keep them happy (see Chapter 20 for more information).

Even if you have a large preopening labor budget, there may not be enough for a full staff to do before the restaurant opens, and you don't want people to get in the habit of resting for pay. Labor is best managed by keeping people productive at all times. If something needs to be done, get it done. If there isn't anything to do, don't have someone sitting around wasting payroll dollars.

How to Find Good Employees

Now you have a good idea of the number of people that you need to run the restaurant successfully. But how exactly do you find these people? Most people will tell you that finding good people is difficult, but it isn't. There are lots of ways to do it.

The restaurant industry employs 11.3 million people, making it the second largest workforce segment in America. Of these, you only need 25, 50, or maybe 75 or so.

Everyone knows about putting advertisements in the local newspaper. Other common ways to find people include searching Internet resumé boards, contacting the unemployment or chamber of commerce offices, and using recruiting firms. (Recruiting firms can be very expensive and ineffective if you choose the wrong recruiter.) You can even put up Help Wanted signs while you are under construction. All these methods will drive some resumés your way and may even provide you with a fair amount of people to choose from.

But I have used two other recruiting methods that are by themselves worth hundreds of times the cost of this book. I can't believe I'm going to let them out. Stop me! This information is too valuable. All joking aside, the value of these strategies is immense and will turn you from one of the people who complain about not being able to find people to one who many will come to for help when they are struggling to find people. I call these strategies relationship recruiting and reference list recruiting.

Relationship Recruiting

Every time I meet someone who is sharp, whether it be at a conference, at the grocery store, or in an elevator, I introduce myself, my company, and drop in the following recruiting line: "I must tell you, you are very sharp. You wouldn't by chance know of anyone just like you who would possibly be looking for a new career opportunity, would you?"

I wait for the person's reply, and then hand him or her my business card. I finish with, "If you come across someone who is sharp, I would love to have the opportunity to speak with that person. Maybe I will get a chance to see you around my restaurant. Take care." This strategy works. I get responses both from the person I gave the card to and from people that person has referred to me.

People love being respected, revered, and appreciated. With this technique not only have I built a great relationship that could bring me potential employees, but I have also built goodwill with someone who could become a customer of my restaurant.

Don't be embarrassed to approach people. Be nice. Offer a compliment or maybe even a great career opportunity. If you can't establish relationships this way outside your restaurant, you will probably struggle to do it inside your restaurant. Open up your personality and have some fun while you help your business.

Tip Jar

If you place an advertisement in the newspaper, make it simple. Why include statements like "fun work environment"? If it is so much fun to work there, asks the reader, why do you have an ad in this paper every week looking for people? Cut to the chase: List the available position, salary, benefits, and where or how to apply. That's all. Anything else complicates things.

Food for Thought

Relationship recruiting takes time, but it is good for business. I have had people call me a year later. People remembered that nice guy who told them they were sharp. Compliments usually stick in people's minds.

Reference List Recruiting

I ask every person I interview (either face to face or over the phone) for a list of five to seven references of people who work in the restaurant industry. I want the personal contact information of high-caliber individuals who can give me some idea of what this person is like to work with. I make it clear that these references do not necessarily have to be managers. With this simple request, I turn one resumé into five to seven possible candidates.

The next step is to call the people on the reference list. If you are interested in the individual who gave you the list of references, do the reference checks and make your decision on that individual before you begin to recruit from his or her reference list. If you are not interested in the person who gave you the list of references, don't bother with the reference check. Just recruit people from the person's reference list.

The conversation goes something like this: "Hi, my name is Howard Cannon, I was speaking with someone the other day who mentioned that you were one of the best people in the restaurant industry. I happen to own a restaurant company, and I am looking for the best people money can buy. I wanted to know if you would be interested in meeting me at my office to discuss the career opportunities I have available." If the reply is yes, set up a meeting time. If the answer is no, thank the person for his or her time and move on.

Food for Thought

Many people think recruiting is about finding a person to hire, but recruiting is really about finding a person to interview. You cannot determine whether you want to hire someone until you have done a through interview and reference check.

This strategy has the potential to get you staffed quickly and cost-effectively. Again, people love being complimented. Thus, you should have no problem finding people to speak with you.

Determining Whether They Are Right

"Are you a good employee?" "Yes."

"How many days of work have you missed in the last year?" "None."

"Why do you want to work with us?" "Because you have a great company and I enjoy your food."

"When can you start?" "Today."

"You're hired."

Welcome to a traditional interview in the restaurant business. Sad, isn't it? I hear interviews conducted like this all the time, but I am not sure what the interviewer gets out of this line of questioning and answers.

An interview needs to be meatier and have more of a conversational approach. Spend time getting to know the person rather than asking a bunch of useless questions. Use the "Interview Guide" in Chapter 24, "Restaurant Checklists, Forms, and Guidelines," to help you conduct better, more efficient, and effective interviews.

Interviewing is a skill. This skill is developed over years and is improved upon nearly every time you conduct an interview. But by following a few simple guidelines you can and will become a better interviewer, and your restaurant will become a better place to work for your employees. Best of all, it will become a better place to dine for your customers. So remember these tips:

Tip Jar

Every applicant is a potential customer, so consider offering every person who interviews a free meal coupon. This action builds goodwill and turns the interview into another way to build new customers.

➤ Know what you're looking for.

➤ Ask questions that get the applicant to talk about important things.

➤ Get the applicant to ask you questions.

➤ Check references.

Knowing What You're Looking For

When you interview for restaurant workers, the quality of the person is more important than the person's technical skills. If you have the right person, you can teach him or her almost all the technical requirements in the restaurant industry. Certainly, when you need a certified professional chef, technical skills are critical to your decision-making process, but that position tends to be an exception to the rule.

For the most part, the purpose of an interview is to find out more about the person being interviewed. I use a system I call S.I.D.E. +1+1 to determine whether I want this applicant on my side or on the side of my competitors:

➤ **S = Smart:** Does the person have common sense and intellectual smarts? Without it, I can't teach the person much. With it, I can teach him or her nearly anything if he or she is willing.

➤ **I = Integrity:** In my restaurants, honesty is not only the best policy, it's also a requirement for continued employment.

➤ **D = Drive:** Does the person have the desire and will to do a good job and work hard? Does he or she have a "fire in the belly" to succeed?

➤ **E = Enthusiasm:** Is the person happy, positive, and enthusiastic? Is he or she willing to learn and excited about the opportunity?

➤ **+1 = Image:** Does the person take care of himself or herself? Does the person dress nicely, respect others, project a professional demeanor and attitude, and speak with eye contact and confidence?

➤ **+1 = Service Orientation:** Will the person gladly serve others and provide an environment where service is revered? Is he or she people-oriented and does he or she look comfortable working with and for others?

Ask Questions That Get the Applicant to Talk About Important Things

People say an interview is supposed to be 80 percent of the applicant talking and 20 percent of the interviewer talking. This 80/20 rule seems fine, but getting an applicant to talk about things of value is even more important. When you get an applicant to talk about things of value you learn things that will help you determine his or her standing with regard to the S.I.D.E. +1+1 formula.

Tip Jar

Take a lighthearted, nonstressful approach to the interview. Make it more like two old friends becoming reacquainted rather than an interview. This approach will put the applicant at ease and encourage the person to be more like the person you will be working with.

Getting the applicant to truly talk is not as easy as it sounds. You may be thinking, "How tough is it? I ask the person a question, and he or she answers it by talking." The thing is you want the applicant to tell you what kind of person he or she is, and this information can be difficult to get. After I put the applicant at ease with small talk, I begin with the following: "Tell me about yourself. Give me the five-minute life story." This request starts the person talking, and I get to know him or her as a person. If the person can't talk about himself or herself, the interview is over, and I know this would not be someone I would be interested in hiring. Just have a conversation with the applicant so that the two of you can get to know each other. Then answer in your own mind whether the applicant has those six S.I.D.E. +1+1 components. If he or she does, you probably have a winner.

Finally, be aware of certain questions you can't ask by law. Contact your local labor board office and EEOC (Equal Employment Opportunities Commission) office to get any and all employment rules and regulations pamphlets and a chart of questions you can't ask during an interview.

Get the Applicant to Ask You Questions

It's just as important for the applicant to ask you questions as it is for you to ask questions. A good applicant should get answers he or she needs to make a job decision. Your prospective relationship needs to be a positive one for both sides. During the interview, ask three or four times if the applicant has any questions.

Applicant questions not only provide applicants an opportunity to take a break from being on the stage, but also can help you determine their interest level and intellect based on the questions they ask. Intelligent questions tell you that this applicant is an intelligent individual. No questions at all suggest the opposite.

Check References

Ask applicants for five to seven references and check them. But go a step further. No one is stupid enough to give you the name of someone who doesn't like him or her, so check with other people in the company as well. Yes, call and ask for people who aren't on the list. Ask the person who answers the phone about your applicant and even go into the company voice mail and pick a person or two at random. Use the "Reference Check Form" in Chapter 24 to conduct an effective and efficient reference check.

Wet Floor!

You cannot ask questions that are considered inappropriate and illegal by the EEOC. Anything questioning a person's age, race, religion, disabilities, marital status, and sexual orientation are not permissible and can get you fined and for that matter in a big bowl of legal hot water. First, these things have nothing to do with a person's ability to perform a job, and second, it's none of your business. I want to state again: Contact your local labor board and EEOC office and get familiar with the laws.

Remember, not every reference you talk to will think the applicant is great. Not everyone likes everyone, and that must be taken into account. Instead, use references to look for more of a pattern of comments rather than worry about one isolated negative comment or situation.

Finish the Job Right

Hiring someone is a big decision. Don't make it lightly. I recommend interviewing people on two or three separate occasions before offering them a job. Also, have your whole team participate in an interview. Ask your experienced employees to chat with a potential new hire for 30 minutes or so.

Multiple interviews give you the opportunity to see whether the applicant is putting on a show and if the stories stay the same or if the person is pitching a line. Getting the team's input is critical to ensuring that the potential employee will fit in and that the team will accept him or her.

Finally, after the interview, follow up and do what you say. More bad will is created during the week after an interview than any other point because too often the employer is busy running t⋯ ⋯nd doesn't get back to the applicant. The applicant doesn't know where the hiring process will go, causing a feeling of disrespect.

Don't leave people in the dark more than a day or two. Remember that the hiring process is part of your public relations as well. If you decide not to hire a person and don't let the person know in a timely or professional way, you'll probably lose a customer. This behavior results in bad word-of-mouth advertising.

The Least You Need to Know

➤ Plan to hire a few extra employees because you will lose employees through normal attrition.

➤ Chart out when your busiest times are and who (and how many) you will need to work during those times.

➤ Recruit through your friends and through references.

➤ Use the S.I.D.E +1+1 system to judge applicants.

➤ Interview applicants more than once.

Managing Your Risks

Things go wrong. That's life. Unfortunately, if you're in the restaurant business, you can get sued when things go wrong. After all, in the restaurant business, a hot cup of coffee can be viewed as a sort of lethal weapon. So although you may be scaling the mountain of restaurant success to its highest heights, don't forget that you are also on a slippery slope.

Restaurants face risks. Some are standard, and some, such as the dangers swirling in a hot cup of coffee, may be impossible to imagine. Nevertheless, you have to protect yourself against them all.

This chapter is about managing your risks. In it, you learn why and how a policy and procedures manual can help you, why insurance is necessary, and what the four biggest risk factors are. This chapter is about guarding yourself against the world and preserving your dream.

What's the Worst That Could Happen?

People jump from airplanes for fun, or so I've read. These skydivers are accepting a clear risk when they make the big leap, which is the possibility that their parachutes won't open.

The risk involved in the restaurant business is quite a bit murkier, but plenty of situations could send your business into the ground as fast as any desperate skydiver. Imagine getting sued because your coffee is too hot or your eggs weren't cooked right. If you are in the restaurant business, you are in the risk business.

The best way for you to know the risks for your particular restaurant is to do some heavy-duty homework. Every city, county, and state has different rules, regulations, licensing, safety guidelines, and levels of liability assumed. Available insurance options and premiums also vary from place to place.

Look around and ask some questions. Talk to your lawyer, accountant, real estate agent, insurance agent, and with other restaurant owners and operators. Spend some time at the library and ask for assistance from any and all governmental agencies. But most of all think about what could happen. Imagine the worst.

Food for Thought

When I opened my first restaurant, a pizza delivery joint, I was so focused on providing the best pizza at a price that could compete with anybody that I forgot stuff happens. On June 19, 1990, one of my drivers hit an old lady driving her new car to pick up her grandchildren. Though she wasn't injured, she sued. He didn't have insurance, and I didn't have enough to cover him. I ended up paying a lot of my own cash to cover the problem.

Risk is always present, but you can reduce your risk in three ways:

➤ Writing down your company policies and procedures

➤ Abiding by your policies and procedures

➤ Having adequate insurance coverage

Write the Book for Your Business

If you want employees to go "by the book," you must provide a book for them to go by. Although you won't get immediate rewards from writing this book, known as a policy and procedures manual, it can save your business if it is used right. Include what you think is necessary. Keep it simple, keep it clear, and put it in place on your first day.

Not only does a policy and procedures manual help your employees understand what to do and what not to do on a daily basis, it also clearly outlines your procedures for handling virtually every imaginable *what-if situation*. Such a manual helps reduce mistakes and the poor decision-making that many times leads to increased liability and responsibility on your part. A well-documented policy and procedures manual also reduces your business risk in the case of a rogue employee who makes a decision that is not in line with the company procedures.

In my early days in the pizza business, I learned the importance of building a manual with a variety of "what-if" situations. I learned because of an employee named Matt. Matt was a great pizza cook and could handle the job of four people, so on our big rushes he was quite valuable. But as soon as things slowed down, Matt went looking for ways to help me write my manual.

Matt taught me a ton. I learned that putting a pressurized aerosol can of food spray through a 475-degree conveyor oven can cause a huge commotion. I learned that a fire extinguisher isn't meant to be used to kill bugs out in the parking lot. I learned that banana peels are not the only things that will make management slip and fall. And I learned that terminating employees is not fun, but sometimes it needs to be done.

I also learned to build a "what-if" scenario for a lot of things I didn't imagine I could imagine. When people like Matt work for you, you get to develop far-fetched scenarios because "what-if" becomes "what-now?" You won't be able to list every possible scenario, but preparing for the majority of possibilities gets you thinking correctly for other situations as well.

A policy and procedures manual reduces risk by outlining the following procedures:

➤ Hiring, payroll procedures, disciplining, promoting, wage review, wage and hour policies and laws, and termination practices

➤ Safe practices and how to reduce injuries

➤ Evacuation plans

➤ Accident reporting

➤ Sexual harassment reporting and procedures for discipline

➤ Food illness complaint procedures

➤ Drug and alcohol use policies and procedures

Recipes Revealed

What-if situations are supposed to be thought out ahead of time. Having a ready response for every imaginable situation helps enormously. So put together a list of major possible issues and the appropriate way to handle each one.

Tip Jar

Staff training plays a major role in reducing your risk. The facts speak for themselves. A well-trained staff has significantly fewer workers' compensation injuries, sexual harassment claims, labor violations, and food-handling issues.

➤ Employee rules and actions taken if these rules are broken

➤ Policies, procedures, guidelines, and laws regarding the serving of alcohol

Abiding by the Rules

Rules are not made to be broken. Or else why write them? Just as important as having a policy and procedures manual is abiding by it on a consistent basis. For instance, if you state that you will not condone any form of theft and that theft will result in immediate termination of employment, then you must be capable of firing your favorite bartender when he steals $4.

I have seen many cases where a restaurant was correct in the way they handled a termination only to lose in court because it didn't handle all policy infractions and terminations consistently. Apparently the employee can assume that if Bill stole $20 and only got a reprimand, then if he or she is caught stealing a $1,300 bank deposit, a reprimand is all he or she should get as well.

Don't write your rules with any leeway. Make them clear and use them consistently, and your life will be easier.

Food for Thought

Health insurance for employees is not mandatory, but it is a powerful benefit and a strong recruiting tool you should consider. It is very expensive, but it may well be worth the cost. A restaurant that doesn't provide health insurance is left out of the competition for mature employees and is more likely to have a higher percentage of teenage employees, which in turn results in a more immature and unfocused workforce.

Protecting Your Turf with Insurance

You need to protect yourself, but you don't need to spend all of your income or anything like 20 percent on insurance. Even though there are insurance policies to cover just about any imaginable disaster, there is a limit to what you need. Basic insurance coverage packages are critical to protecting your assets.

Certain types of insurance coverage are federally mandated, which means you are legally required to obtain them. Some examples of this kind of insurance are workers' compensation insurance, unemployment insurance, and Social Security (FICA). Other kinds of insurance coverage are simply smart business, but not mandated in every state. An example of this type of insurance is general liability insurance, which should include theft, fire, accident, and so on.

Also, if you are going to serve alcohol, some states require liquor liability insurance. Other states leave that decision up to you, and others make the insurance a chore to get. The harder it is to get, the more outrageously expensive it is.

Your insurance needs depend on your individual business and locale, so select your business insurance agent carefully. Just like the relationships you have with your lawyer and accountant, you are counting on the agent's expertise with the restaurant business. Your neighborhood life insurance salesman may not be qualified. As in everything, ask a lot of questions.

Following is a chart that defines some of the many types of insurance vehicles available. The following list includes the more popular types, which may or may not be pertinent to your situation.

Type of Insurance	What It Covers
General liability	Covers claims for bodily injury and property damage due to an accident
Personal injury	Covers lawsuits due to false arrest, libel, slander, and personal injury
Auto liability	Covers damage that employees incur when driving a vehicle for company business
Liquor liability	Protects against lawsuits resulting from damages caused by a person who became intoxicated at your establishment
Property damage	Covers buildings, inventory, and fixtures against loss
Product liability	Covers against lawsuits resulting from products you serve
Fire insurance	Covers against fire damage to a neighboring building where the fire originated on your property
Workers' compensation	Covers employee injury costs for work-related injuries

With assistance from an insurance expert and from your attorney, you can build a safety net to protect you, your company, your staff, and your customers without spending a fortune. Protection just takes a plan.

The Four Biggest Risk Factors

You can never completely eliminate risk, but you can reduce it. The key to substantially reducing your risk is to focus on the four biggest risk factors:

➤ The work environment

➤ Food and beverage service

➤ Poor employee behavior

➤ Injuries

The Work Environment

The Equal Employment Opportunities Commission (EEOC) has some very clear guidelines for the work environment. Abide by them! I suggest that you contact your local employment office for not only the EEOC information, but also any local and state guidelines that apply, including minimum wage and tip credit and payroll administration laws and guides.

To paraphrase these rules, you may not make any form of employment decision based on race, color, creed, gender, age, religious beliefs, sexual orientation, disability, or national origin. Simply stated, you must treat all people equally. This is United States of America, after all.

Most people who make EEOC and labor claims charge that the boss doesn't care. After further investigation, most of these charges prove to be true. Simple caring is a good start to protecting your business against such claims. Creating the proper environment is critical to showing your staff that you care and reducing your risk. Your team members must be comfortable in coming to you and discussing any problems or concerns they may have. If you want, you can set appointments, or you can try an *open-door policy*.

Use these ideas to help you create a more caring environment and open lines of communication in your restaurant:

➤ Invite different members of your team to breakfast once a month to discuss business and life in general. Just getting to know each other improves all aspects of the relationship. I call these breakfast roundtables and invite four to five people the third Saturday of every month.

➤ Make work more of a personal experience. Remember to celebrate birthdays, give Christmas gifts, talk about family and friends, and take soup to ill team members.

➤ Spend time teaching your team goal-setting techniques and providing personal life enhancement "how to" classes, such as how to buy a home, how to go back to school, how to

Recipes Revealed

An **open-door policy** means that the boss will talk to the employees about any problems, concerns, suggestions, or questions they may have at any time. Thus, the boss's door is always open. This policy is more of a theory than actual practice in many businesses, and restaurants are no different. Usually, specific times are set up, or appointments are made. It's your preference.

Wet Floor!

If you are making employment decisions of any kind based on anything other than performance and the policies and procedures, you are doing a huge disservice to the employee, the community, the industry, and yourself. Such decisions will eventually catch up with you.

improve grades, and so on. These training sessions show that you want to help employees improve their lives. You are demonstrating that you don't just care about your restaurant. And if you do, your employees will know.

➤ Just put forth the effort to show that you care.

Food and Beverage Service

Jokes aside, who would have thought that your great chili recipe could turn into a risk? Impossible? Think again. Serving food and beverage has the potential to be a liability of major proportions. Food-borne illness, excessive alcohol consumption, foreign substances falling into the food from a chipped dish, and much more can cause you and your customers a significant amount of indigestion.

Tip Jar

Health inspections can help you improve risk management policies and procedures. Ask questions during these inspections.

In the middle of all this risk is the health department. But, believe it or not, the health department is on your side and can be a great help to reducing your risk and liability. Ask your local health department office for assistance, and you will get it. Most states and counties provide a variety of classes, tests, and educational materials, including health cards, food-handling guides, time and temperature guides, and more.

Poor Employee Behavior

Whether you are dealing with sexual harassment, excessive horseplay, swearing, or any of the dozens of other poor employee behavior issues, handle the issue as you would handle anything else pertaining to the employees: Be consistent.

Sexual harassment is a common issue. One substantiated sexual harassment claim against you or one of your employees can cost your business and your reputation. One time is all it takes to ruin you. Therefore do the right thing all the time, always. Got it?

The key to reducing your risk is to have a clear-cut sexual harassment policy in your policy and procedures manual. Providing employees the necessary training to ensure they understand what is and isn't sexual harassment is also important, as is documenting how you will handle any claims or infractions.

Sensitivity training class helps all employees understand how someone who is being sexually harassed feels. It will help give a clear set of parameters and guidelines to your entire staff. Rules are good, and training helps folks understand. You can do training in-house or hire a reputable sensitivity-training firm.

Injuries

Slips and falls, cuts and burns, lions and tigers and bears. Oh my! Injuries happen at an alarming rate in some restaurants and hardly ever in others. How is this possible?

The office of OSHA (Occupational Safety and Health Administration) states that the difference is safety awareness. Restaurant owners who are aware of and concerned about employee and customer safety have significantly fewer accidents in their businesses than their not-so-concerned brethren.

Food for Thought

Most injuries occur due to one of the following:

➤ An understaffed restaurant

➤ Poor employee training

➤ Drug or alcohol consumption

➤ Blatant disregard for company policies or procedures

➤ Not having the required safety materials or equipment

You should be concerned about the safety of your employees and customers. In fact, you should have a monthly safety meeting with all of your employees. In many states, this kind of meeting is required by law.

Finally, be sure to report injuries. Injury reports are a critical component to reducing liability and showing concern. Inform the appropriate people of the injury. Put in place an injury reporting system. The moment an injury occurs, follow the correct procedures. If someone needs to go to the hospital, call an ambulance. Make sure you write down everything that occurred.

Providing a safe place for employees to work and a safe place for customers to dine is the responsibility you take on the moment you become a restaurant owner or a restaurant manager for someone else, and it is a responsibility you must not take lightly.

Well thought out and well-planned restaurant concepts have fewer accidents than poorly designed and underanalyzed competitors. The money you will save by doing things right the first time shows up in many ways—lower insurance costs, fewer workers compensation and liability law suits, and even better customer and employee satisfaction. That is the reward for reducing your risks.

The Least You Need to Know

➤ If you are in the restaurant business, you are in the risk business.

➤ You cannot totally eliminate risk, but you can reduce it.

➤ By creating a comprehensive policy and procedures manual and consistently enforcing the procedures, you can significantly reduce your restaurant's risk.

➤ Many types of insurance are necessary, and you will need to get reputable advice to know what you will need for your restaurant.

➤ The work environment, food and beverage service, poor employee behavior, and injuries are the areas to worry about.

Chapter 11

Basic Accounting: It's More Than Just Counting the Beans

In This Chapter

➤ The importance of cash control

➤ The accounting cycle and you

➤ Basic accounting lingo

➤ Important financial statements

➤ The joy of taxes

➤ Acceptable forms of payment

This is an ode to the bean counters, because they will rule your world. No, the beans in the kitchen don't necessarily need to be counted, but your money does and the folks who do this counting, accountants, are affectionately called "bean counters." Counting the beans is up to you (at least weigh them!), but accounting is not an option. Many restaurant owners treat it as such, however. Well, ex-owners. See, many restaurants don't keep a good eye on the bottom line and then they run into trouble and the owner wonders why.

The best way to prevent financial trouble and figure out how your restaurant is doing is to find out where the money comes from, where it goes, who gets it, and why. It's called accounting, and it's a way of keeping score. In our competitive society, people like to be challenged and like the concept of keeping score. Sharing your restaurant's key performance numbers with all of your team members is a good way to motivate them to increase sales and profits.

This chapter tells you how to keep score in the restaurant business. In it, you learn about the critical financial statistics that are important to the success of your business. You also learn about accounting tools, such as cash-control systems, in-unit accounting forms, the profit and loss statement, and more. You learn how to pinpoint critical numbers, such as sales, food cost, labor cost, cash overages and shortages, and profitability, and why you should share these numbers on a regular basis with all of your employees.

Cash-Control Systems

Control cash? Who wants to do such a thing? Cash is fun and should be spent! Right? Wrong. Controlling cash is traditionally the first step to improving and analyzing your bottom line and is critical to your success as a restaurant owner.

Restaurant owners constantly play a game called Watch the Cash. Money is king. If you have it, you try to keep it. The difficulty comes because you are not the only one who touches your money. It would be nice if every minute of every day you were the only one touching that hard-earned money. And it would be nice if you had a team that loves you so much that not a single one of them would ever think of stealing your hard-earned money. And it would be nice if a genie granted you three wishes, and your fairy godmother showed up with a fourth. It would be nice, but it's not reality.

So what can you do? Fret, accuse, lurk? No. You need to keep an eye on your money, a close eye. And the best way to do that is with a real system. If everyone knows that you keep track of every penny, you will win the game.

Tip Jar

Keep your eyes peeled, even when you are all welled-up with tears from the slicing and dicing of a 20-pound bag of onions. You need to know what is going on everywhere. You need numbers. Look for numbers, follow the numbers, and question the numbers.

Cash Overages and Shortages and Possible Theft

"Hey boss, I just counted out Jim's cash drawer from the dinner shift, and he's $7 over."

"Say what?" I ask.

"I thought you would be happy because he wasn't short."

"No," I say. "Absolutely not! In fact, I am very concerned."

A cash shortage is bad, but a cash overage is almost always worse. A cash shortage could simply be the result of the cashier giving a customer back too much change. A cash overage shows some strange activity. Here is the question: If Jim was $7 over in cash, where did the money come from? Is a customer being overcharged? You could lose a customer forever this way. What if something worse is happening? Is the person stealing thinking that leaving a dollar or two in the register is covering up any theft? If the record shows a trend of cash overages for a specific cashier, that is particularly worrisome.

Take a breath. Sit down. I have some bad news for you. It took me quite some time to realize this because I like to believe in the goodness of people. But the reality is that people steal. They would steal if they were put in the right circumstances at the wrong time. This is a difficult concept for me to teach, but it must be passed on. Let me illustrate.

I believe that every person has a personal threshold of principles that can be very high for some and, sadly, very low for others. However, situations and circumstances change continually. The truth is that anyone has the capability to steal under the right circumstances. For example, if someone threatened to harm your family unless you stole something, would you do it? You probably would determine your options and do the best you could to stay true to your current level of principles. But in time if no other options presented themselves, you would steal. I know I would. I would save my family. Most people would do the same, and others find other reasons.

Theft is very much that way. People justify. Truth is, you will never completely know the personal financial situations and needs of your employees, and their threshold before they begin stealing could be just around the corner.

Cash overages and shortages are warning signs of something bad. I have always used the following rule of thumb: Cashiers should be able to consistently hit between 0 and short 99 cents on any register count out. If they cannot, something is wrong.

Food for Thought

Theft tends to occur most often when it is easy. If you make it tough for workers to steal, they will decide in time to just go work someplace else where they can get into the cookie jar more easily.

Tip Jar

You can make bank deposits in a couple of different ways. You can hire an outside vendor, such as Brinks, to pick up the money. Another way is to do what is called a double-custody run. A double-custody run is where you have two people handle the deposit from the time it is counted at the restaurant to the time it is deposited at the bank. Two people count it, two people fill out the deposit slip form, and two people take the money to the bank and deposit it.

Bank Deposits

A priority to any restaurant owner or operator needs to be to get the money in the bank. I've seen it a thousand times: An owner expends incredible amounts of time, advertising resources, and energy to build sales and get the cash registers ringing and doesn't build a system to reduce theft or control deposit handling. Remember: Profits don't count until you put them in the bank!

Industry averages show that a typical restaurant loses between 2 to 4 percent of its sales volume to some form of theft or cash mishandling. That is a ton of cash. As a restaurant owner, you need to spend time investigating ways for your employees to steal. Think like a crook. Some of your employees will.

To combat theft, you need to establish systems. Remember that word? You're in business now, so the word *systems* is part of your new capitalist religion. Systems rule. You need to put systems in place to track every dollar from the moment the customer gives it to you to the moment it is deposited in the bank.

Even with great systems in place, you won't be able to stop all theft. Nor can you stop all cash-handling mistakes because sometimes people really do just make mistakes. But by keeping your eye on the ball, you will get the dollars to the bank more consistently. After all, your business richly deserves the money it earns. It's the American way.

Bank Reconciliation

Banks make mistakes. Following up bank deposits to ensure that all of your money is credited to your account is critical. This process is called a bank reconciliation.

The bank sends you a copy of all of your banking activities. Go through this paperwork line by line, and physically check off every deposit and every check that you wrote and make sure that the transactions you believe you have made match the transactions the bank believes you have made.

The Power of Restaurant-Based In-Unit Accounting

You don't need to be a certified public accountant (CPA) to own a restaurant. However, you need to have some basic accounting knowledge. Restaurant-based in-unit accounting resembles balancing your personal checkbook. This type of accounting involves these basic elements:

➤ An income log tracks sales, sales tax, and deposits. You write in the sales column the amount of sales you had for the day. You write in the sales tax column how much your sales tax was for the day. You write in the cash accountability column how much cash you should be depositing (your sales + your sales tax − any payouts = cash accountability). You write in the deposit column how much money you deposited in the bank. Chapter 24, "Restaurant Checklists, Forms, and Guidelines," has a copy of this log for you to use to set up your own in-house system. This log gives you the required data to follow-up on if any income issues arise. Keep in mind that knowing your results is half the battle to improving your results.

Food for Thought

Keeping track of invoices seems obvious, but I once spent the better part of a Super Bowl Sunday looking for a $312 freezer repair bill in the backseat of a 1972 Datsun pick-up. I learned this concept the hard way. Keep track of your invoices.

➤ An outgo log tracks invoices, payments, and debits. In your checkbook, you write down any money you spend. In business, you do it in this log. I also recommend having an invoice register (see the "Invoice Register" form in Chapter 24) attached to an envelope to provide quick and easy access to invoices and security with a clasp. Keeping existing invoices in an envelope is the ultimate checkbook log: It provides an easy method of tracking expenses without your having to slow down to fill in paperwork or find an empty space in your office to store invoices.

Recipes Revealed

An **in-unit profit and loss statement** is compiled every week and gives you a snapshot of how you are doing month-to-date. By matching your in-unit profit and loss statement with your professionally prepared income statement (which is completed once per month), you can get a pretty good feel for how accurate both tools are.

➤ A product inventory and usage sheet (see the accompanying figure) tracks the amount and the value of the products in the building: 7 pounds of bacon, 31 pounds of cheese, 3 bundles of napkins, and so on. It also has the cost of each item by the same unit measure (per pound, per bundle, and so on) and a place to calculate the value of each product in the restaurant.

➤ An *in-unit profit and loss statement* totals up everything. This statement summarizes by individual line items or categories.

With these basic forms, you can get an idea of how much the restaurant is making and how much it is spending. The biggest costs in the restaurant business are food and labor. Determining what percentage of revenues these big costs eat up is easy and important to do. To figure the percentage of revenue you spend on labor, for example, take your cost of labor (say $6,000) for the week and divide it by your sales for the week (say $27,000). Your labor percent would be

22.2 percent. You can do the same with food. Take your cost of food and beverage (say $8,000) and divide it by your sales (say $27,000). Your food and beverage cost would be 29.6 percent of your sales.

*Product Inventory and Usage Sheet

Date of Inventory 11/15/02   *Inventory Taken by: Mary Jo*

Name of Item	Unit of-Mea sure	Starting Inven-tory (+)	Purchases (+)	Available Inventory (=)	# of Units on Hand (–)	Item Usage (=)	Unit Cost $	Item Cost of Usage
Crackers	CS	.5	1	1.5	1.0	.5	$8.56	$4.28
Turkey	Lb	27.25	114.75	142.	33.5	108.5	$2.26	$245.10
R Beef	Lb	12.5	40.25	52.75	9.25	43.5	$2.86	$124.41
Juice, Grape	CS	2.5	4.0	6.5	1.5	5	$11.15	$55.75
Beans, Black	CS	3	6	9	2.25	6.75	$2.58	$17.42
Pickles, Kosher	CS	2.5	7	9.5	1.5	8	$19.44	$155.52
Raisins, Seedless	CS	.75	3	3.75	1.25	2.5	$24.61	$61.53
Pasta	CS	2.75	4	6.75	.75	6	$9.73	$58.38
Cup-Coffee	SL	10	20	30	13	17	$2.14	$36.38
Napkins	PK	14	12	26	8	18	$3.05	$54.90
Grand Total								$813.67

A sample product inventory and usage sheet.

The Books: Simplify Your Accounting

Your main job is to run a restaurant. Use your restaurant-based in-unit accounting for the data you need to make the restaurant work and leave the serious accounting for the bankers, lawyers, and CPAs. Even so, you have to keep the books for the restaurant, so you must learn a little accounting. This section describes the accounting cycle and defines basic accounting terminology.

Understanding the Accounting Cycle

An accounting cycle begins with the transaction and includes a group of systems that makes it easy for you to see the whole of your business on paper. This cycle has many working systems, but it basically consists of four main parts:

➤ **The transaction:** A customer says, "I'll have the Texas burger with a large order of fries and a vanilla shake." The cashier replies, "That'll be $5.99." This exchange is one transaction. Making a payment to your produce vendor is another transaction. A transaction occurs when you either receive or distribute payment of any kind.

➤ **The journal:** Each transaction is documented in a journal as it occurs. The same type of process is used to add deposits and deduct withdrawals from your personal checkbook log. The journal is a general file to temporarily hold transactions until they are classified by specific transaction type.

➤ **The ledger:** Journal entries are classified by type once a week and are then moved into individual accounts in the ledger. These accounts are labeled with such account names as Food, Labor, Supplies, and Paper and are usually determined by your accountant by using a standard format of restaurant accounts, which he or she will have.

➤ **The reports:** Reports are the ultimate scorecards for any entrepreneur. They include the income statement, the balance sheet, and the cash flow statement. These reports are generated by the data that was inputted from the transaction, the journal entry, and the ledger.

Wet Floor!

Don't compare yourself to other restaurants. Compare yourself to what numbers you are currently running and where you feel you can get some improvement. Also, contact your local, regional, and national restaurant associations or contact *Nations Restaurant News* to get industry averages, but only use them for a starting point.

I have witnessed plenty of restaurants that seemed to be running better numbers than their competition go out of business.

Deciphering Basic Accounting Terminology

Not only does accounting have crazy forms and numbers, but it also has its own language. Accountants love big words and enjoy using the hundreds of accounting terms. But you don't have to learn the language to communicate with your CPA. If you don't know what an accountant is talking about, ask. The only stupid question is the one you don't ask.

Read these key definitions to start learning the lingo:

➤ **assets** Anything that has some kind of value that can be converted into cash. Real estate, investments, and equipment all qualify.

➤ **current assets** An asset that can be converted into cash within one year. The same as the list above but usually saved for items that can clearly be converted to cash easily—certificate of deposits, stocks, bonds, mutual funds.

➤ **fixed assets** An asset that will take more than one year to convert to cash. This is usually more focused towards real estate and property.

➤ **accounts receivable** Money that you are owed. When you allow a customer to purchase your products today and pay for it at a later juncture, you are creating accounts receivable. The restaurant business is mostly driven by cash, checks, and credit cards, which are all considered cash. However, if you do catering, you may have house accounts or lines of credit or sometimes large groups will make reservations for a wedding party or a graduation bash, and you may agree to bill them at a later date. These are all considered accounts receivable.

Recipes Revealed

Straight-line depreciation is the simplest form of depreciation and the most common. It takes the value of the item being depreciated and divides it by the item's life expectancy (how long it is expected to last). A $3,000 item with a life expectancy of five years will be depreciated $600 a year for each of the five years.

➤ **accounts payable** Money that you owe to others. You purchase $75 worth of lettuce, tomatoes, and onions from Gatto's Produce Company to make your tacos and burritos at Taco Bob's, and this purchase becomes an accounts payable bill.

➤ **notes payable** A multimillion dollar loan to build your restaurant or a $750 loan from your brother to set up the business's legal structure both represent a notes payable.

➤ **inventory** The products, supplies, and ingredients you have on hand to make your delicious menu and serve your customers.

➤ **depreciation** The process of an asset gradually wearing out, becoming obsolete, or losing its value to the point of worthlessness. You can account for this depreciation in a variety of ways; your accountant can give you some insight as to which style of depreciation would be best for you to use. The most common is *straight-line depreciation* because it is the simplest method.

The Three Most Important Financial Statements

The more you learn about the financial side of your business, the better decisions you can make. Three key financial statements put the performance of any business in perspective:

➤ The income statement

➤ The balance sheet

➤ The cash flow statement

The dozens of other financial forms or reports are used more for line-item analysis and investigation than they are for determining the overall health of a business. These other reports include variance reports, labor reports, food cost reports, theoretical and ideal food cost analysis, aging lists, and so on. But ultimately, your restaurant's health can be determined from these three main reports. Keeping a close eye on these critical financial statements will become second nature to you as you grow comfortable as a business owner.

The Income Statement

Of the variety of wonderful reasons to start your own restaurant, the most popular reason by far is to make money. So how will you know if you're succeeding? The income statement is the easiest and most direct way to determine whether you are making or losing money.

An income statement (sometimes called a profit and loss statement or P&L for short) is usually completed on a monthly basis and shows the business owner four key bits of information:

➤ Sales volume during the reporting period

➤ Business expenses during the reporting period

➤ The difference between the sales and the expenses resulting in a profit (making money) or a loss (losing money) during the reporting period

➤ The performance of the business versus the projected budget

Chapter 24 has a blank income statement form for you to copy and use for your own restaurant.

Income Statement

For the Period of 8/1/02 to 8/31/02	$	Percent of Total Sales
Sales	97,324.15	100
Food	80,390	82.6
Beverage	16,934	17.4
Total Sales	**97,324**	**100**
Cost of Sales		
Food and Beverage Cost	26,959	27.7
Paper Cost	2,822	2.9
Total Cost of Sales	**29,781**	**30.6**
Gross Profit	**67,543**	**69.4**
Controllable Expenses		
Direct Payroll	18,784	19.3
Indirect Payroll, Taxes, Employee Benefits, etc.	7,299	7.5
Misc. Operating Expenses	3,601	3.7
Repairs/Maint.	1,071	1.1
Utilities	3,786	3.9
General Admin.	4,477	4.6
Advertising	4,574	4.7
Total Controllable Expenses	**43,592**	**44.8**
Profit Before Occupancy Expense	**23,951**	**24.6**
Rent	4,250	4.4
Taxes	3,000	3.1
Insurance	2,787	2.9
Interest	703	1.8
Depreciation	1,879	3.0
Net Profit	**+$11,332**	**11.6**

A sample income statement.

The Balance Sheet

What is your business like today? The balance sheet is a closely cropped snapshot of a given date and time and determines the financial health of a business on the day the statement was completed. For instance, on July 29, 1999 (my birthday, by the way—cash is a fine gift, thank you), the restaurant had a financial picture that looked one way. But on August 3, 1999, the restaurant could have looked totally different financially. Keep this in mind when looking over a balance sheet.

The balance sheet lists the value of all company assets, subtracts the liabilities (such as debts, taxes, notes payable, and so on), and generates, in essence, a net value or net worth for the company. Over the long-haul investors and others use these balance sheets to look for trends either up or down to determine the overall health of the business.

Sample Simple Balance Sheet (July 29th 1999)

Assets		Liabilities and Net Worth	
Current assets		Current liabilities	
Cash	15,200	Accounts payable	17,200
Food inventory	6,600	**Total current liabilities**	17,200
Beverage inventory	2,100		
Supplies inventory	800		
Total current assets	24,700		
Fixed Assets		Long-term liabilities	
Leasehold improvements	141,000	Bank loan	82,000
Furniture, chinaware, etc.	22,000	**Total long-term liabilities**	82,000
Preopening expenses	7,100		
Total fixed assets	170,100		
		Total liabilities	99,200
		Net worth	
		Owner's investment	70,000
		Retained earnings	0
Total assets	$194,800	**Total liabilities**	$99,200
		Total assets	194,800
		Net worth on date listed above	+95,600

The Cash Flow Statement

Do you have cash? Can you make it flow from those who owe you to those whom you owe? Cash flow is what makes the business world go around. Cash flow is what pays the beverage bill, the employee payroll, the electric bill, the rent, and every other expense you have. Yet cash flow and profit are two different things, and you can easily have one without the other.

The cash flow statement is a report that tracks the cash coming into the business (in-flow) and cash going out of the business (outflow). Most business owners look at this statement every day.

Simple Cash Flow Form

Income	Jan	Feb	March
Food sales	55,200	58,290	
Beverage sales	9,600	10,555	
Sales receivables	0	0	
Other income	0	0	
Total income	64,800	68,845	
Expenses			
Cost of food	14,352	17,580	
Cost of drinks	2,400	2,900	
Controllable expenses	3,900	4,595	
Payroll	17,650	19,800	
Employee benefits	2,950	3,300	
Direct operating expense	4,200	4,500	
Advertising and promotion	2,950	4,750	
Utilities	1,200	2,800	
Administrative and general	2,595	3,000	
Repairs and maintenance	725	600	
Occupancy costs			
Rent	3,250	3,250	
Property taxes	312	312	
Other Taxes	187	187	
Insurance	565	565	
Interest	1,094	1,094	
Other deductions	0	0	
Total cash disbursements	58,330	69,233	

	Jan	Feb	March
Cash flow			
Income	64,800	68,845	
– Total cash disbursements	58,330	69,233	
= Net from operations	6,470	–388	
Cash on hand			
Opening balance	22,657	1912	13,739
+ New loan (debt)	0	0	
+ New investment	0	0	
+ Sale of fixed assets	0	0	
+ Net from operations	6,470	–388	
= Total cash available	29,127	18,739	
– Debt reduction	5,000	0	
– New fixed assets	0	0	
– Dividends to stockholders	5,000	5,000	
– Stock redemption	0	0	
– Loans to officers	0	0	
= Total cash paid out	10,000	5,000	
Ending cash balance	19,127	13,739	

A sample cash flow statement.

Food for Thought

If I received my order of Maine lobster tails on Monday morning, and Mr. and Mrs. Hayes orders it and pays for it Monday night, and I don't have to pay the bill to Bruno's Seafood until the middle of the next month, I have created a positive cash flow. I have the $123 cash in hand from Mr. and Mrs. Hayes, but don't have to pay for my food invoices, payroll, or facility use for some time yet. That's cash flow. Positive cash flow is sweet, simple, and the most wonderful of experiences for any business.

Cash flow statements vary greatly in their complexity, but I have always preferred, much like everything I do, to keep them simple.

Wet Floor!

Some restaurant companies can act like pre-bubble dotcom companies. Before the bubble burst, many high-tech dotcom companies increased cash by adding new customers and getting more investment capital infusions. They had positive cash flow, but they were not making profit off of the customer's business. The expenses were outweighing their revenues. But as long as they kept growing revenues, their house of cards stood tall. The minute the top line revenues stopped increasing, it became time to pay all the bills and they didn't have the cash to do it. Restaurant chains make the same mistake by building restaurants quickly and forgetting about the bills that show up six months later.

Taxes Can Be Taxing: What You Need to Know

I once met a tax expert for the IRS at a restaurant. The moment I found out who he was I told him my name, Eckniv Rewerb, and my occupation: back-up singer for Bozo the Clown. After these formalities, we had a wonderful conversation, and I learned more about taxes in that two hours than nearly any conversation I have ever had.

The tax code for the United States takes up thousands of pages of text. The IRS doesn't even understand its own rules, regulations, forms, and guidelines. The best tax advice is to hire a reputable tax expert.

Like anything else, do your research. To find a reputable tax expert ask your lawyer, accountant, friends, and competitors who they use. There is no sure-fire thing to finding the right expert. Just ask around and, no matter who you choose, make sure they have dealt with restaurants before.

But even tax experts aren't always expert. Every time I meet someone who does taxes for a living, I hear the claim that they are *the* expert regarding taxes. But after further investigation, I always find out that this person pays many times more in taxes than he or she should based on the tax code. Tax experts may not be perfect, but their job is to know the tax code. Your job is to know restaurants.

So let's prepare you for what you are getting into and then advise you to go find your own tax expert or an accountant who can provide both accounting and tax expertise. You will, of course, be responsible for paying all kinds of taxes in the restaurant business including but not limited to: sales tax, income tax, property tax, liquor tax, and taxes on wages.

Forms of Payment

"Hey boss, Mr. and Mrs. Tiller at table 14 just ordered the chateaubriand, the red potatoes with chives, the house salad, and two bottles of champagne and want to pay us with Monopoly money and a contract from their time share in Maui. Should we take it?"

You can choose a variety of forms of payment when you open your restaurant, but keep in mind that more options are not always better. Instead, stay conservative and provide similar options to what your competition offers. Let the big companies do the trial-and-error stuff. The three mainstream forms of payment are cash, checks, and credit cards. (Timeshares, for me, just seem too risky.)

Food for Thought

In some parts of the country, the list of tax forms and tax responsibilities are so long and varied that if a baseball team decides to build a new stadium it may very well show up as some kind of new tax for the local restaurant owners.

Cash

Cash is always nice, as long as it is real. Unfortunately, you must be on the lookout for counterfeit bills. There are now markers that can help you distinguish the real stuff from the fakes. Other than this small hassle, cash is sweet and simple.

Checks

Fast-food establishments may find it unnecessary to accept checks, but casual-dining and fine-dining establishments may find it necessary to do so if they want a satisfied customer base. However, you should think twice before accepting checks. Checks can slow down your service inside your restaurant and can slow down your cash flow if it turns into a bounced check situation followed by a collection nightmare.

If you do decide to accept checks, use one of the many bad-check collection services and check verification services that are available. You do not want to have to call Mr. Thomas, who frequents your restaurant three times a month, to tell him he bounced a check for $27. He may be embarrassed, and then you may never see him as a customer again.

Credit Cards

Americans are using credit cards more than ever. Even though restaurants have to pay a 2 to 4 percent fee for every transaction, nearly all restaurants are willing to pay this price. Even fast-food places will be taking credit cards on a regular basis within the next five years. In fact, many already are.

Keep Your Losses to a Minimum

Regardless of whether you accept cash, checks, credit cards, or some combination of the three, none of these forms of payment guarantees that you will collect all of your cash. Any reputable CPA will tell you that all businesses have a certain amount of money that is written off as a loss due to nonpayment or fraudulent transactions. Depending on your concept and the part of the country you do business in, you should expect to keep this loss between .5 and 1 percent of your sales. Fight to keep it down. Then accept it and move on.

The Least You Need to Know

➤ Controlling cash is a must if you want to be successful.

➤ Keeping track of the numbers yourself is a necessary step to understanding the business.

➤ Hire a reputable accountant, and if you don't understand a tax or accounting term, ask him or her what it means.

➤ The income statement, balance sheet, and cash flow statement are the three financial statements that give a picture of the health of your restaurant.

➤ When deciding on how many forms of payment to accept, more is not necessarily better. Look at what your competition offers and what most of your customers want when making this decision.

Chapter 12

Purchasing: It's More Than Buying a Can of Corn

In This Chapter

➤ How to choose vendors

➤ What to negotiate

➤ Why you need a purchasing system

➤ How much to order

In order to sell things, you usually have to buy things first. To run a restaurant, you need lots of stuff, from tomatoes to sugar to lightbulbs. You probably aren't going to be growing your own tomatoes, and chances are good that your neighbor won't have a spare 2,000 cups of sugar for you to borrow for your expanded dessert menu. And driving to the hardware store every time you run out of lightbulbs is not the best way to stock your restaurant. You need to learn the fine art of purchasing, which is the procuring of goods and services.

Purchasing involves much more than simply buying stuff. Some ways of buying make more sense than other ways. Big restaurant chains have entire purchasing departments and spend a lot of time wheeling and dealing for the best prices. The sheer size of the chains usually ensures that they get the best prices. You are not going to be so lucky, but you can be just as smart.

This chapter is about the process of purchasing. In it, you learn how to choose your vendors, how many vendors you need, and what is negotiable. You also learn the value of building a purchasing system and the elements of such a system.

Food for Thought

One of the best vendors I ever had was Franz Bakery in Portland, Oregon. My account representative was Lyman Smith, who has sadly since passed away. Lyman always understood my needs and treated each of my employees with respect and love. Franz Bakery did not have the best prices, but they had the best service, the best products, and the best relationships. These qualities were well worth the extra price.

Wet Floor!

Some vendors will try to get your business by giving you free tickets to games and other events. Don't give in to temptation. It's better to get quality products and services at lower prices and then buy your own tickets to whatever you want.

Choosing the Vendors

Open up any yellow pages or any industry trade magazine, visit any industry Web site, or attend any of the hundreds of restaurant conferences or trade shows and you will see them: more product and service vendors than you could ever need. So how do you know which ones are any good?

The best way is to interview vendors as you would a prospective employee. Do reference checks. Dig deeper and get to know the company, the staff, and the way they operate. A vendor is more than just someone selling you something. Ideally, a vendor is a business partner.

A vendor should be willing to go the extra mile to help you succeed. After all, when your business succeeds, the vendor can sell more products to you. A good vendor understands that connection.

How do you decide which vendors to use? You want reputable vendors who can provide the products and services you need at the level of quality and service you require. In other words, don't just pick vendors based on price. Many restaurant owners and operators lose sight of quality and service issues when determining a list of vendors and allow price to be the determining factor.

The truth is that price is secondary to quality because no one will pay to eat in a restaurant that serves bad quality. Price should be one of the last factors you discuss with the vendor. Instead of worrying over price, find relationships that work.

In addition, try to use as few vendors as possible. The convenience of one-stop shopping is well worth a little extra money. Sure, you can buy meat cheaper by going to a butcher, and you can buy milk cheaper by going directly to the dairy. You also can buy produce cheaper by going directly to the orchard. But there are only so many hours in the day and spending that time placing, receiving, and accounting for 36 different orders isn't worth the 17¢ you may save on a gallon of milk.

Keeping the number of vendors you use to a minimum makes it easier to control all aspects of the purchasing process and to establish relationships. Traditionally restaurants go with one main distribution company that purchases literally hundreds of thousands of products from a seemingly inexhaustible list of suppliers and manufacturers. This strategy provides for one-stop shopping with only a few exceptions. These exceptions are usually quality upgrades on products or unique products or services (such as pest control or specialty dessert items) that the distributor doesn't have.

Negotiating the Particulars: Wheeling and Dealing

Securing your vendors involves a great deal of negotiation. Most of the time when the word *negotiate* is mentioned the first thing that comes to mind is price. But as I've stated, price is one of the last things to discuss. Your negotiations should include the following as well:

➤ Product guarantees

➤ Delivery schedule

➤ Payment terms

➤ Price

Product Guarantees

Standards of quality must be more than just words. Product guarantees are important. After determining product specifications, you must inform your vendors of your expectations of quality and then hold them to delivering at or above those standards. During negotiation your standards should not be negotiable. Instead, the discussion should be about what the vendor must do if the agreed-upon standards aren't met.

Common sense says that if you are delivered 60 dozen eggs and half of them are broken the vendor needs to replace them. But with some vendors, once you sign off on the invoice and the product is left in your care, it is no longer their problem. Other vendors care about how their own products are perceived and do not want restaurants serving up stale or bad products.

Tip Jar

Vendors are great sources for building your business reputation, credibility, references, and creditworthiness. When Sysco Foods or Pepsi Cola has extended you a line of credit, you can use the power of their name recognition and credibility to get credit from other vendors. As you conduct business and build new business vendor relationships, you can secure more funding options.

Recipes Revealed

When a product is **back-ordered,** the vendor or warehouse ran out of it. If backordering happens with one particular vendor too often, it shows that the vendor needs help, and you may want to drop that vendor. You don't want to lose sleep at night waiting for the distribution house to get its act together.

Another consideration is if products are continually *backordered*. In the negotiation, discuss what process will be used to provide you with an equal or better product (a substitution) at the same unit cost. Also discuss who will take care of getting the specified substitute for you and who has the responsibility for the cost. If the distributor made the mistake, the distributor should pay. But you must have this arrangement in writing.

Delivery Schedule

You are not the only restaurant that buys from your vendors. They are busy delivering products and services to many other restaurants. Therefore, you need to negotiate an effective and efficient delivery schedule.

Keep in mind that you cannot always get what you want. You need to be flexible because a vendor cannot possibly deliver to every restaurant at only the times they want. However, you must hold firm to these two things with regard to the delivery schedule:

1. No deliveries should be accepted during any peak revenue periods. If you have a huge breakfast business, arrange for delivery in the afternoon, for example.

2. Delivery should occur within a two-hour window. If the scheduled delivery time is 3:30 P.M., then it should arrive no earlier than 2:30 P.M. and no later than 4:30 P.M. This time window allows your deliverer ample time to fight traffic and so on. For your staff members, the two-hour window lets them know when to expect the delivery without having to wait all day for it to arrive.

Finally, try to get your delivery to arrive the day before your biggest sales volume day. This delivery schedule will ensure full inventory on the days you need it most and small inventory during the slower portions of the week when you are least likely to use the inventory and when you are most likely to be counting it as part of your regular tracking duties. Having less to count makes your inventories more accurate and less time-consuming.

Payment Terms

When you buy groceries at the grocery store, you pay for the groceries before they leave the store (except for the few grapes you ate out of the fruit bin). In the restaurant business, these transactions are conducted as a buy-now, pay-later arrangement with varying terms on the pay-later part. In other words, you get the products and services provided today, but you don't have to pay for them for a certain number of days.

The number of days you have to pay off your purchases is negotiable. Each vendor is different, but vendors usually want their money quicker than you want to pay them. Thirty-day terms are not unusual and should be considered a target to shoot for or exceed with each vendor.

Price

Determining price is about more than $1.35 per pound or $6.17 per unit. *Yield* and *margin markup* come into play as well.

Don't let a few cents lower in price tempt you to compromise your quality expectations. You may find that the cheaper product has a worse yield than the more expensive one and ends up costing you more than you realized.

Building Your Purchasing System

Every restaurant on the planet should have a well-defined purchasing system. It doesn't matter what size the restaurant is. A system is the only way.

Recipes Revealed

Yield is the amount of usable product a given item delivers. A 16-ounce cut of meat may produce only 13 ounces of usable product after the fat has been trimmed.

Margin markup is the markup above what the distributor paid for the item from the manufacturer. If the distributor paid the manufacturer $2.34 for a frozen chicken pot pie, you need to ask how much of a markup the distributor is going to add to this price.

This system is equivalent to your grocery-shopping list at home with some notable upgrades. This system spells out the four main pieces of your purchasing process:

➤ Par level

➤ Product specifications

➤ Personalized yellow pages

➤ Order guide

Without this purchasing system, you will experience inconsistency as well as lack of product, service, and vendor control. Ultimately the customer can feel all of these issues and can become dissatisfied.

Par Level

Par in the restaurant industry has a similar meaning to par on the golf course except that, unlike Tiger Woods, you don't want to come out under par. A par level for an item or ingredient is the amount you think you need to ensure that you don't run out before your next delivery. It is calculated based on how much you need per $1,000 of sales. For example, if you used 30 pounds of salt in a week and your weekly sales were $16,000, your par level for salt would be 1.9 (rounded to 2) pounds of salt per $1,000 of sales.

Adding 15 to 20 percent to your par level provides a safety cushion to ensure you will not run out of an item and also controls the expensive situation of having too much on your shelves. Using the salt example, you would take the 2 pounds of salt per $1,000 dollars of sales and multiply it by 20 percent. This number becomes 2.4 pounds of salt usage per $1,000 of sales.

Product Specifications

Product specifications are related to size, grades, cuts, yields, age, color, and so on. This area is where you and your chef determine in advance what is and isn't acceptable in the way of products and services. You need to determine the size of a tomato or the grade of the cut of meat or the color or freshness of the fresh fruit you want delivered.

The benefits of determining your product specifications in advance are easy to see. You won't be rushed to make a purchasing decision or to accept just any product that seems "good enough." Knowing exact product specifications is also beneficial in helping you narrow your choice of vendors based on which ones can hit your standards and guidelines.

Wet Floor!

Never pay any vendor of any kind in full before you receive your goods or services. Many owners have war stories about times when they paid for land-scaping, construction, and so on in full before the job started and never got the work completed or finished to a satisfactory level. Any reputable vendor should be more than satisfied with 50 percent (or less) up front and the rest due upon completion or with terms.

Personalized Yellow Pages

Finding vendors is as easy as thumbing through pages upon pages of possibilities. Once you find them, though, make your life easier by building your own personalized yellow pages or vendor directory. This directory makes it easy you and the rest of your staff to access your approved vendors. You want to stick to using approved vendors because dealing with the billing process of unapproved vendors takes time and effort and can be quite a hassle.

In your personalized yellow pages, list each and every vendor (utility providers, pest control, electricians, and more) you do business with. Provide contact names and information, ordering procedures, and any other pertinent data.

Order Guide

An order guide is akin to the venerable *TV Guide* that we all held so dear prior to beginning our restaurant businesses. This guide lists all the items that you have determined meet your standards and are necessary for you to operate your restaurant concept. It includes everything from food and beverage items to cleaning supplies, paper supplies, and more. If you need to buy it for your restaurant, it should be in the guide.

The order guide should also have the item order number, the case or container size, the cost per unit, the par level (see the "Par Level" section earlier in this chapter), and space to track your last eight orders. These eight orders will give you a good track record of what you ordered in the past, and traditionally you won't need to go to much above or below that in the near future. Make multiple copies of this guide and begin a new one every eight weeks. In this way, you can see your ordering trends for the previous eight-week time frame.

Determining How Much to Order

The modern world offers many ways to place orders, including telephones, e-mail messages, Web sites, and fax machines, but the essentials of determining how much to order and how to place the right order apply regardless of the ordering method. The process involves three steps:

➤ Determine your inventory level

➤ Determine your usage

➤ Calculate your order

Inventory on Hand

Doing inventory is critical, but many people make this process more difficult than it needs to be. Counting inventory is no different than counting your cash drawer and has many of the same ramifications. The products sitting on those shelves are just like money.

So how do you do inventory? First, pick a unit measure to consistently determine how much of a given product you have and the price of that product per the same unit measure. Some items, such as meat, may be weighed by the pound. Canned goods may be measured by the can; paper by the case; or frozen pie by the pie. It doesn't matter as long as you stay consistent.

Tip Jar

Keeping your inventory well organized makes it easier to count. To improve the accuracy of your inventory count, begin your inventory process at basically the same time on the same day every week. Also, count all products in the same order every week. The best way is to count shelves and storage areas from top to bottom and from left to right.

It is easiest to use the same unit measure for each item that vendors use to bill you. This way the invoice and inventory and order all match. Thus, you do not need to convert unit measures just to figure out accounting.

Once you have a unit to measure, count it. If you have 25 pounds of chicken in the building, you write down 25 pounds of chicken. Inventory is not like a golf score. In this game, there are no mulligans, and every stroke counts.

Tip Jar

Many restaurants fill out an order moments after completing their weekly inventory. This is the most effective, efficient, and accurate time to place your order because it is the time when you have the truest sense of what products you have on hand.

Tip Jar

Consider the number of days between when you place your order and when it arrives. The shorter the gap, the better off you are. In the meantime, you need to account for those days of product usage in your ordering. Go back to your par level number and your sales projections for those few days, figure out additional needs, and add it to your weekly total.

Determining Your Usage

Every restaurant inventory shows the following information in one form or another:

➤ **beginning inventory**   This number is your ending inventory from the last time you did inventory.

➤ **purchases**   A record of purchases during the week.

➤ **ending inventory**   How much product you had on your shelf at the time you did this inventory.

With these three numbers and the following equations, you can easily figure out your usage for any item:

Beginning inventory + Purchases = Amount available

Amount available – Ending inventory = Usage

Suppose you want to figure out your milk usage. You ended last week with 8 gallons of milk, so your beginning inventory for this week is 8 gallons of milk. In addition, you purchased 31 gallons of milk this week. After taking inventory, you find that your ending inventory is 5 gallons of milk. First, you figure out the amount of milk you had available by adding the beginning inventory (8 gallons) to the purchases (31 gallons), for a grand total of 39 gallons of milk. Then you subtract the ending inventory (5 gallons) from the amount available (39 gallons) to determine that your milk usage for this week was 34 gallons.

Calculating Your Order

When you have your inventory and usage numbers, making your order becomes simple. If you are projecting that you will do $25,000 in sales next week and your par level for a given item is 1.1 cases per $1,000 of sales, it becomes quite elementary how much you will need to have on hand:

$25 \times 1.1 = 27.5$ cases

If you have an ending inventory of 14 cases, you will need to order an additional 14 cases (seldom will vendors allow you to purchase half cases) to have enough on hand to get you through the week.

Receiving the Order

The order has just arrived at the back door—now what do you do? You have to do more than just put the product away. What more is there to it you ask? You have to do the following:

➤ Check in the order

➤ Date the product

➤ Properly store and shelve the order

Having the same person "put the truck away" every time when possible allows for more consistency and quicker receiving and shelving. Plus, you will always have someone who knows where every item is.

Checking in the Order

All orders should be checked when they come in. Not only are you checking to see if the number of items is correct, but you are also checking to ensure that the right item was delivered and that the quality is up to your standards. Check in items by writing a check mark next to each item on the order to ensure accuracy and a written record. Then sign the invoice or statement when the entire delivery meets with your approval.

Dating the Product

When the product is brought in the door, date it and shelve it in accordance with the *FIFO* rule. Following this rule helps ensure a proper rotation of your inventory and product quality for your customers.

Wet Floor!

Putting together an order at the last minute or trying to guess what you have on hand by sitting at your office desk are two ways to end up with an order that is significantly short of the products you need or significantly overstocked on products you don't. Pick an appropriate time when you can focus on getting the order right.

Recipes Revealed

The **FIFO** rule states that the product on the shelves should be used before you use the products that are newly coming in. FIFO stands for First In, First Out.

133

Most restaurants want to date only perishables. I prefer having my staff date each and every item for consistency and ease of training. I also use the month/day/year method of dating. That is, 3/4/01 is March 4, 2001. You can use your own method, but be consistent.

Shelving and Storing the Order

You must abide by a variety of storage standards, and these standards are covered in more detail in Chapter 17, "Operational Execution, Part 1: Quality," which discusses product quality.

From a purchasing as well as an organizational perspective, shelving and storage is critical. If you have no storage system, your inventory will become inaccurate, causing your order to become inaccurate.

The Least You Need to Know

➤ A vendor relationship should be a partnership.

➤ The more vendors you have, the harder they are to manage. Fewer vendors is better.

➤ Figure out what you are buying before you go to buy.

➤ Build a system to purchase things so that you don't end up short or way over on some items.

➤ Count inventory the same day and the same way every week.

Restaurant Marketing 101

"Eat Here!" blinking in neon atop a roadside diner is certainly marketing and so is Ronald McDonald. From a blinking neon sign to a clown to a rock n' roll jingle to a 2-for-1 coupon to passing out your business card, marketing is a big part of the formula for success in the restaurant business.

The successful competition really knows how to market itself. McDonald's spends more in marketing dollars than most restaurant chains receive in sales. All the big chains spend many, many millions of dollars in marketing per month. Can you compete with that? You can in your neighborhood. You just need to understand how to make marketing work for you so that you can be seen and heard amidst all these marketing Goliaths.

This chapter is about the critical function of marketing your restaurant. If nobody knows about your restaurant, chances are you won't have very many customers. In this chapter, you learn some basic tactics, five marketing rules for a start-up restaurant, the importance of a grand opening, and other tips.

A Tactical Approach

Spending money and time on marketing is easy as pie. Spending it wisely is more difficult. But, like a recipe, if you take it step by step, you can cook up a great marketing strategy. Resist the temptation to jump into something flashy for the sake of your own ego and take some time instead to figure the right way.

First, understand that there are really only three ways to increase sales:

➤ Increase the frequency of visits of your current customers

➤ Increase the check average of your current customers

➤ Find new customers and entice them to use the services of your restaurant

If you have Mr. and Mrs. Goldschmidt dining at your Italian eatery two times per month, and you find a way to have them frequent your restaurant three times per month, you have positively impacted sales. If Mr. and Mrs. Goldschmidt spend on average $14 for their meal every time they stop in, and you find a way to have them spend $15 on average, you have positively impacted the check average. If Mr. and Mrs. Sisty have never eaten at your restaurant and you find a way to get them to give your restaurant a try, you have positively impacted the trial of new customers. Restaurants who are great at sales building always have plans in place to affect all three areas of sales.

Tip Jar

Focus groups are a powerful form of research. A focus group involves gathering 15 to 20 people to conduct a group discussion led by a facilitator (who may very well be you) who introduces particular topics, assesses the conversation, and then analyzes these comments. Focus groups serve as a miniature spy operation that can give you a way to see your products and services through customers' eyes.

To create your marketing plan, you need information about your current customers and those you are trying to attract. Collecting market research takes a lot of time and effort, and you can't do it over a weekend. But you can do it. In Chapter 3, "Choosing Your Restaurant," you learned about the importance of research in making your concept work. You can use this same research to build a marketing plan. You want to find out information about where you operate, who frequents your restaurant, and what messages resonate. Once you have this knowledge, you will be more prepared to move on to the next step: defining what route you are going to take to try to increase sales.

Marketing Rules for a Start-Up Restaurant

You have completed your research, and you now understand what you are trying to impact. Now what? How do you build an effective and efficient strategy? After all, many other restaurants are spending much more than you can.

Don't lose faith. Five key rules can help your start-up restaurant compete immediately for sales, even without the big marketing budget.

Rule #1: Let Them Know You Exist

Be memorable. McDonald's and other restaurants aren't giving away even one sale without some advertisement to argue the customer away from you. A ton of competition is reaching the consumer with a message a minute. To stand out from the crowd, you need to be different, unique, strange, funny, noticeable, bright, crazy, and more if necessary. But mostly, be memorable.

This rule applies to the hospitality, quality, service, cleanliness, and overall experience you provide in your restaurant as well as the marketing and public relations you execute outside of your restaurant. Make customers know your restaurant exists and make them remember it.

Rule #2: Get Your Customers Talking About You

The best form of advertising for any restaurant is word of mouth. Whether you are serving a child or wiping up a spill, make a visit to your restaurant a treat. This rule is crucial. Make sure that customers leave your restaurant with nice things to say about their meal, your facility, your team, and their overall experience. If your restaurant is not a good place to eat, those few who do eat there will tell everyone they know. If it is a good place, they will also tell the truth, and that truth grows. There is supreme power in truth.

Rule #3: Keep Messages Short, Clear, and to the Point

The average consumer sees thousands of marketing messages and logos in a given day. Americans have become desensitized because of so many advertisements. You don't need complicated messages. You

Food for Thought

A Taco Time dropped thousands of Ping-Pong balls from a helicopter. One was full of cash. A delivery pizza start-up followed the delivery drivers of competitors and went to the door and offered the competitors' customer free soda, free pizza, and a coupon to use on their next order. An Italian restaurant had an outdoor dance with all comers dressed up looking like members of the 1950s Mafia. Such tactics are outrageous only if they don't work.

need messages that are short, clear, and to the point. Some examples that have probably left an indelible mark on you, as well as the rest of America: "Have It Your Way," "We Love To See You Smile," "Beef: It's What's For Dinner," and "Got Milk?" Short, simple, memorable.

Tip Jar

A handful of well-placed words is significantly more memorable than a 500-word dissertation on why someone should order your new lemon chicken dish.

Food for Thought

A Pizza Hut franchisee in Southern Wisconsin throws a "Zoo Crew" party once a year for three days in the summer to benefit a small, undeveloped zoo. Proceeds go to purchasing animals, maintaining and running the zoo, and helping kids learn about animals. While bands play, people buy trinkets embossed with the Zoo Crew logo. Best of all, many food and drink choices exist, with pizza and pasta from Pizza Hut leading the way.

Rule #4: Community Involvement: Own It or Forget It

If being a good community partner is important to you (and it should be), then own it or forget it. Pick some program, charity, institution, or group that you believe in and are committed to helping and then deliver. Leave your mark.

Don't be just a part of something that makes you one of the dozens of sponsors. You are better off being the main or only sponsor of something else. No one remembers the businesses that simply sponsor things, but they do remember the business and the leader who makes an impact on something important in the community.

Rule #5: Start Right

Marketing starts early, way before you open. Write down your marketing goals. Formulate a plan. Build action steps. Then execute the plan.

It is best to get professional help devising a marketing plan and building the appropriate action steps. Marketing is a very tricky game. Thus, it is worth every penny to find a firm or an individual who has played the game in the restaurant industry many times before.

Use Your Brain

The only bad ideas are the ones you don't have. You need ideas, lots of dreams, plans, and visions. Write down all of your ideas. You can analyze them later.

Start by thinking about creative and memorable ways to implement the following common marketing tools:

➤ Your company name and logo: Your name and logo should be recognizable, memorable, and somewhat descriptive. You want the customer to realize you are a restaurant, so it is best use words that clearly state the obvious: eatery, café, deli, pizza, taco, fish, steak, etc.

➤ Letterhead: This is one more chance to brand your restaurant, so make sure it looks professional and has your logo and address on it. Then use it for every letter you write.

➤ Restaurant signage: Make it visible from a long way off and make it easy to read. Remember, if cars are driving by, small letters are very difficult to read.

➤ Web site: You need to have a Web site. It does not need fancy bells and whistles, but it does need to give your potential consumers a way to look at your menu offerings and your potential applicants a way to apply for a job. Add in your logo and contact information and you have it. Anything else is frosting and that's good, too.

➤ Business cards: Make them professional and keep them current. Then, give the darn things out. They do you no good sitting in a box, and they can be a very good way to generate trial customers if you give one to virtually everyone you meet.

➤ Menu boards (dine-in, drive-thru): Make your menu boards easy to read, well lit, and featuring a few eye-catching graphics and pictures. Everyone who visits your restaurant will be looking directly at these tools of the trade.

➤ Menus (carryout, catering, delivery, special season or event, dine-in): Many of the same points I mentioned above apply here except being well lit. (That may be kind of difficult.) By the way, keep them new and untattered as well as clean.

➤ Chamber of commerce membership: If you want to make this a memorable tool for you, you are going to need to be more than an everyday member. Provide the meals for the meetings and the outings. Volunteer for some of the boards and projects and make a real lasting impact.

➤ Carryout and delivery container designs: These are great word-of-mouth tools for any restaurant. Think about it—someone is walking around the streets with your logo on a cup or bag. This is a great advertising opportunity. Make your logo big and noticeable.

➤ *Point of purchase* (P.O.P.) signage (pictures of food, drink, and so on): These tools are big in the restaurant industry. Point of purchase signage should be rotated every four to eight weeks and should be professionally done and

Recipes Revealed

Point of purchase signage comes in a variety of types of materials, from table tents, to counter cards, to window stickers, ceiling danglers, and wall posters.

put in places where the customer will see it. Pictures of great looking food will help sell the food.

➤ "Coming soon" countdown campaign (see "Have a Great Grand Opening" later in this chapter).

➤ Grand opening campaign (see "Have a Great Grand Opening" later in this chapter).

Spend three or four days considering all kinds of marketing concepts and ideas. You will come across dozens and possibly hundreds of good ones, but you can't do them all. Once you complete this marketing brain dump, take your entire list and begin to whittle out the ones you don't want to use.

Even if you have lots of good marketing ideas, keep in mind that you don't want to use them all. A few very well-executed and tightly woven together marketing ideas are much more powerful than a bunch of poorly executed and unrelated concepts and plans. Don't try to be everything to everybody.

Examples of this, both good and bad, are on display every day across the industry.

Restaurants great at executing a tightly woven marketing idea send one solid and distinct message. You see their television ad, and it is talking about their new lemon Dijon chicken. You get a direct mail piece or an insert falls out of the newspaper, and it talks about their lemon Dijon chicken. You hear a radio spot from them, and it talks about their lemon Dijon chicken. You walk into their restaurant craving their lemon Dijon chicken, and you see their lemon Dijon chicken plastered in their point of purchase material, and the employee asks you, "Would you like to try our new lemon Dijon chicken?"

On the other side of the equation, you see plenty of restaurants that are sending so many different messages that the consumer really doesn't hear any of them. You've seen the places. They talk lemon Dijon chicken on television. They do print pieces with a steak fajita. The radio spot talks about their garden salad. The point of purchase in the restaurant is selling gift certificates or worse yet "now hiring" signage, and the business section of the newspaper is talking about XYZ experiencing sales declines, and the company leadership can't explain why. Well, the reason is staring them right in the eye.

Don't worry at this juncture about any particular order or cost of implementation. Just create ideas and concepts of your own and borrow ideas from successful restaurants you have seen. Put these ideas in an idea file and update it often.

The Cost of Marketing

Ideas are great, dreams are wonderful, and reality is reality. Imagine, then dream. And then see the Super Bowl. In 2001, the average 30-second Super Bowl commercial cost $2.2 million. I'm only guessing, but I'm betting you aren't made of money. So a couple of spots on the Super Bowl may not be the most realistic marketing idea you will develop. But you will need to market your restaurant, and you will need to spend money.

How much will you need to spend on marketing? This question is important because all marketing plans begin with a marketing budget. The marketing budget is a percentage of your projected yearly sales, usually somewhere between 2 to 7 percent. In the beginning, though, count on needing significantly more.

Waiting to have the sales in hand to pay for the marketing, however, is a backward approach. Marketing leads to sales before sales lead to more marketing. If you don't market the restaurant, the customer may not even know it exists. In order to come up with a marketing plan and budget for your new restaurant, you are going to have to make some educated guesses.

When you are opening a new restaurant, estimating your yearly sales is very much a guess. You probably pulled your projected sales number out of the sky, and you could easily do significantly less or more in sales than you projected. But you have to guess something. So guess by using as much data as possible.

For example, if you expect your most popular menu item to be a hamburger, french fries, and a soda, which goes for $5.50, then use $5.50 as your projected check average. If you think you are going to average 800 customers per day, each of 800 customers buying $5.50 worth of food and drink would be $4,400 worth of sales per day. If you expect all seven days to be about equal from a traffic perspective, your guesstimate for sales would be $30,800 per week or $1,601,600 per year. Figure the percentage of this total you want to use for marketing. And then comes the fun part: deciding how to spend the money.

Have a Great Grand Opening

On the day when your dreams come true make sure that the customer believes eating in your restaurant is as much of a dream come true as you do. The opening of a restaurant involves more than picking a day and opening the doors. A restaurant opening is an event that you use to create a first impression.

You need to take a three-pronged approach in order to create a great first impression. Plan the following campaigns:

➤ A preopening countdown campaign

➤ A grand opening campaign

➤ A spread-the-word campaign

Tip Jar

Every restaurant has its very own formula for how much or how little the owner feels that he or she has to spend in a start-up marketing campaign. The best formula is one that allows you to make a big enough splash, so your potential customers know you are on the map without you having to break the bank.

Food for Thought

I once opened an Arby's Restaurant in Longview, Washington that did $70,000 in sales its first week. At the time, it set an Arby's franchise record for first-week sales. The restaurant management and I created the staggering success of that first week with the three-pronged attack of a preopening countdown campaign, a great grand opening, and a spread-the-word campaign.

Wet Floor!

An untrained team can be deadly to a grand opening campaign. So try a soft opening without the pomp and circumstance of a grand opening during the time you are trying to learn the operational ropes of a new restaurant. Many restaurants wait two to four weeks after officially opening to have the grand opening. That way the staff can gear up for the occasion.

A Preopening Countdown Campaign

Fliers should be everywhere around town long before your restaurant opens. Have a team begin putting out the message two months before the restaurant is ready: 60 Days to Open. Continue the preopening countdown messages by replacing the fliers as the opening gets closer: 59 Days Until Roast Beef, 58 Days to Curly Fries and Shakes, and so on. The signage and fliers are bright, noticeable, ever-changing, and, most of all, memorable.

The Grand Opening Campaign

A grand opening, regardless when you schedule it, is critical to the opening of a restaurant. But it is only worth the trouble if it is memorable. It's called a grand opening for a reason. Make it a grand experience.

A grand opening doesn't have to cost a lot. Build yourself a realistic budget, plan some fun and exciting things, and execute them. The following are some fun things I have seen to kick off a grand opening in style:

Horse and carriage rides	Circus performers
Clowns	Pie-eating contests
Face painters	Limousine service
Bobbing for apples	Parades
Dunk tanks	Chili cook-offs
Magicians	Live music

Keep it fun, make it festive, make it memorable, and make it tasty! Try some cross promotions with local businesses, where they give away free products or services during your grand opening. This strategy will create goodwill in the business community, and your customers will love it.

Spread-the-Word Campaign

Making sure that everyone knows you're going to open is quite simple and inexpensive: You just have to tell everyone somehow. Try the following ways:

➤ Have your employees tell all of their friends and family.

➤ Have someone dressed up in a costume out in front of the restaurant waving to passersby.

➤ Give the local radio stations lots of free food.

➤ Hand out fliers at nearby malls and traffic centers.

➤ Give away free meals.

Three Long-Term Marketing Questions

A one-time grand opening fun-for-all will not continue to bring business your way. You must build a marketing plan for the longer haul.

In order to plan, you must answer three questions:

➤ What are you selling?

➤ What is the core message?

➤ Who is the target?

Of course, your marketing plan must fit with your marketing campaigns, your budget, and your public relations objectives, but answering these three components clearly makes mapping out your marketing plan much easier.

What Are You Selling?

Some restaurants sell convenience. Other restaurants sell an experience. Some sell service while others sell a lifestyle. What you sell is best answered by asking, "What is it the customer is buying when they frequent my establishment? What is the benefit to the customer?" All marketing has to answer this critical question.

Figuring out what a fast-food restaurant is selling is easy. Customers want their meal quickly and conveniently. They are not expecting a five-course meal and exemplary hospitality and ambience. If you are in the fast-food business, you should be selling what the customer wants: Food that is prepared and served quickly. Other restaurant concepts become a bit more difficult to analyze. Asking customers why they frequent similar concepts can give you a pretty good feel for what you want to sell.

What Is the Core Message?

Knowing what you are selling is a step toward selling it. The core message must be clear and concise and must point out the two to three key benefits of eating at your restaurant.

143

If you're selling your high-quality, upscale menu, then your message becomes built around the food. Pictures of entrées and chefs push this message of fresh, tasty, and mouth-watering food prepared by professionals.

If speed of service is your benefit, maybe lightning-fast drive-thru service will be your core message, and your marketing message will revolve around how fast service fits busy lifestyles.

Who Is the Target?

Your target customers change. Don't find a target and forget about it. Your restaurant's market is constantly changing and, therefore, your target is changing as well.

People move, competition increases, tastes and styles change, and what was hot one day may be cold the next. In time, you will begin to constantly try to target where your core market is and where it is going to be.

Marketing Tips to Consider

Marketing is a multifaceted endeavor. Use this list of tips to create great marketing:

➤ **Packaging:** Put your logo on things the consumer carries out of your restaurant (cups, bags, and so on) and make it noticeable. In contrast, putting your restaurant logo on a paper napkin that is going to be used and immediately tossed in the trash is an expensive endeavor with not much reward.

➤ **Point of purchase (P.O.P.):** Make P.O.P. more effective by placing your message in a position that customers are most likely to see. Go stand in line and see what they see or drive through your drive-thru lane and then make adjustments.

➤ **Coupons:** Put an expiration date on a coupon to drive the customer to your restaurant by a given date. Make the coupon of interest to the consumer (make it of decent value) and make the date of expiration noticeable (don't use that small type that no one can read).

➤ **Discounts:** Do not discount food and beverage in the drive-thru, at the menu board, or on the menu. Think about it. The consumer is already in line to buy your products at full price. Why would you discount them now? The only reason to discount is to drive people into your restaurant.

Tip Jar

If the coupon comes in after the expiration date, you gladly take it. Refusing a coupon that is past an expiration date makes no sense. The customer using the expired coupon is probably a new one who may decide never to walk in your restaurant again if you don't accept the coupon.

➤ **Bounce backs:** Use a bounce back to drive customer frequency. A bounce back is a coupon that is given to a customer who is using your business establishment. Coupons taped to pizza boxes or handed out to customers when they pay are forms of bounce backs.

➤ **Cross promotion:** Find one or two businesses that will hand out coupons randomly for your business and do the same for them. Pick a business that is off of the normal traffic pattern of your restaurant. The idea is to get new customers that you wouldn't normally get.

➤ **Fluff campaign:** If you are going to decorate your restaurant for the holidays, do something special and put extra effort into it. It may cost you a bit more, but it will be memorable for the guests and employees. Spending $500 on a complete Christmas blowout that people talk about is better than spending $100 on a tree and a few decorations that no one will even notice. Do it up big, or don't do it. Save the $100.

➤ **Menu marketing:** Deciding the price range of your menu, bar, and wine list is critical. Initially, your prices will relate directly to the overhead and expenses you project for your business. If your rent is $13,000 a month and you only seat 80, you probably won't make it if your most expensive entrée is $6. Certainly, a close awareness of what other restaurants in your category and geographic area are charging and serving is essential to operating competitively as well. In time, you will learn that "what the traffic will bear" means how much of a price increase will chase away customers. The restaurant's concept and target market determine the parameters of menu prices. A quick-service Mexican restaurant may have a limited menu that offers food in the 99¢ to $3.89 range. The selling price of each item must be acceptable to the market and profitable to the restaurateur.

Wet Floor!

Don't do mass bounce backs to every customer that comes in. All that does is teach customers to frequent your business only when they have a coupon. This problem has caused the pizza business an immense amount of pain and suffering (buying a delivery pizza without a coupon is close to a sin). Use bounce backs sparingly and randomly to maximize their effect.

Food for Thought

Some restaurants build their menus with a wide range of prices to accommodate a wide range of customer meal occasions and spending habits. Remember that price ranges are major factors to menu selection.

Tip Jar

Over time, survey your prices:

➤ What is the competition charging for a similar item?

➤ What is the item's food cost?

➤ What is the cost of labor that goes into the item?

➤ What other costs must be covered?

➤ What profit level is expected?

➤ What is the consumer willing to pay?

➤ Is the price at a level where the consumer will frequent the restaurant on more than one occasion?

➤ **Suggestive selling:** You can raise your check average by simply asking your customers nice questions, such as "Would you like to try our wonderful new dessert?" or "Would you like an ice cold Coke to go with your meal?" So spend quality time training your crew how to suggestive sell. Keep in mind that if you try to suggestive sell 10 customers, only a couple of them will buy anything extra. Oftentimes employees give up suggestive selling as a result, thinking that it is not worth the effort. But those 2 out of 10 customers that spend more can drive tens of thousands of dollars in extra sales into your restaurant in a year.

The Performance Analysis

Knowing what works is important to any restaurant owner. You don't have the time or the money to throw at marketing concepts and campaigns that don't make a mark. So finding out what works is a key goal in your overall marketing approach.

Don't expect everything you do from a marketing perspective to be a home run. Hitting a bunch of singles and having a high batting average is more important. Steady growth is good.

Analyzing your marketing performance can be quite simple (unless you talk to marketing analysts—they make it more difficult than it needs to be). Ask yourself: Did you improve what you were trying to improve?

➤ **Frequency of visits from current customers:** If your regulars come in more often, you have a successful campaign.

➤ **Increased check average:** If your check average was $5.50 before the marketing campaign and $6.15 after the marketing campaign, you were successful.

➤ **New customer trial:** If you have customers coming to your restaurant who have not tried you before, you have a successful campaign.

Once you find a successful campaign, use it again and again.

The Least You Need to Know

➤ The three areas you can target with marketing are frequency of visits, check average, and new customers.

➤ In the beginning you will spend more on marketing to announce your arrival.

➤ Have a great grand opening by making it fun, festive, memorable, and tasty.

➤ Marketing doesn't stop. Three good long-term marketing questions to ask yourself are: What are we selling? What is the core message? Who is the target?

➤ Marketing must fit your restaurant's core message and theme.

Part 4

Open for Business: The Basics of Operating

What does it take to satisfy a customer? It takes execution of all parts of your concept, from the kitchen to the bus station to the bathrooms. What does it take to satisfy the customer? It takes a smile, a good meal, a fair price, and more.

Part 4 is about the hands-on restaurant stuff that every aspiring restaurateur should learn to love. It explains how to set up the back of the house and the front of the house. It also emphasizes the critical importance of hospitality and explains why quality, service, and cleanliness are not options.

Get It Right on the Back End: The Back of the House

As a customer sips a beverage and enjoys the ambience of your dining area, a very different world is buzzing behind the doors marked STAFF ONLY. The back of the house, otherwise known as the kitchen, is where the production happens.

The kitchen is the nerve center for any restaurant, regardless of its concept or service style. Before you set up your restaurant's kitchen, you need to ask yourself some important questions: Is your nerve center going to be built for speed and efficiency? Is your team going to have the equipment it needs to do the job right? Do you plan to purchase premade products that will allow you to operate without much equipment? What happens if your chef doesn't show up or decides to quit? Do you, as the owner, know how to work a mixing bowl and a measuring cup? You need to know the answers to all of these questions in advance of setting up your kitchen.

This chapter provides tips on how to make your restaurant's kitchen work for you. It covers equipment issues, wares (bowls, cookware, and so on), bar considerations, and checklists that help everything run smoothly.

Tip Jar

If you are not capable of holding your own in the kitchen, go with a higher percentage of convenience foods. Chefs of the world may disagree with me on this issue, but if you consider the alternative, prepackaged food makes sense. You can easily find very good prepackaged food items that can save even the best chef's time, money, effort, and kitchen space.

Food for Thought

Do you need it? Suppose you must spend $8,000 to purchase one piece of equipment necessary for one food item. If you could just as easily provide the same quality food item without this expensive piece of equipment and save the space in your kitchen and the money in labor, wouldn't a premade version of the food item be worth considering? Of course it would.

Equipment Needs

Formats for the back of the house vary from restaurant to restaurant. A fast-food restaurant, such as Taco Bell, has a completely different back of the house than a fine-dining establishment. Taco Bell restaurants, for example, have what is called a k-minus or kitchen-minus concept. They have done everything they reasonably could to design their restaurants and menus in a way that requires as little kitchen and storage space as possible. At Taco Bell, most items are prepared, sliced, diced, and precooked off site. In contrast, if you walk through the kitchen of the legendary Cajun restaurant Broussard's in New Orleans, you'll see the chefs and kitchen staff preparing the menu themselves with the necessary equipment.

This comparison of Taco Bell and Broussard's illustrates the fact that your equipment requirements depend upon two factors: your menu and your use of convenience or prepared products. The more extensive your menu is, the more equipment you will need. Conversely, the more convenience products you use, the less equipment you will need.

You need to analyze every food and beverage item in terms of what equipment you need to prepare it. Make a list showing the menu item and the equipment needed to prepare that item. The following list provides some examples of menu item equipment needs:

➤ **Homemade soup:** Refrigerator, production table, range

➤ **Fried chicken:** Refrigerator, production table, deep fryer

➤ **Pizza:** Refrigerator, production table, dough proofer, pizza oven

You get the idea. After you've gone through every item on your menu, you will have a complete list of equipment you need. Then you can whittle down your equipment list by reducing any duplication. You don't need a separate refrigerator for each item, so you may decide to go with a walk-in cooler instead for more space and ease of access.

Also, talk to product providers and distributors (they are product experts) and compare, compare, compare. Don't lower your quality standards; however, some products are so good that it is virtually impossible to know that the product wasn't made in-house.

Take a bite of one of the many pies, breads, and cookies on the market and try to guess if they were made in house or not. You will not be able to answer with confidence.

The Size of Your Equipment Does Matter

All pieces of equipment are not created equal. Nearly every piece of equipment you can think of comes in a variety of sizes, from single-serving size to industrial behemoths.

When buying your equipment, consider the following factors:

➤ How much money are you willing to spend?

➤ What is the size of the space you have reserved for this piece of equipment?

➤ How much food or beverage do you need this equipment to produce?

➤ Will the equipment do the job you need it to do, not only in terms of quantity but quality?

➤ Is the piece of equipment essential to your restaurant concept or can you prepare the same product using another process or piece of equipment?

➤ Is the equipment safe?

➤ Does the equipment look good and will it be easy to clean and keep sanitary?

➤ Does the equipment come with a warranty and can it be serviced locally, easily, and affordably?

➤ Is the equipment cost effective and can you get it up and running without a ton of expense for utility hookups?

Wet Floor!

I have heard operators say "It doesn't matter what my equipment looks like if the customer can't see it." I say baloney. What about your internal customers? The people who work for you deserve to see your restaurant and their work environment at its best as well. And, of course, don't forget that the health inspector will make periodic visits.

Tip Jar

Discuss all your equipment needs with two to three equipment vendors. They are experts in the equipment game and can help with determining your needs, measuring for space, determining where and how to reduce your equipment expenses, and setting up and starting up each piece. Use two to three vendors to compare multiple opinions.

Rent or Buy?

You can rent equipment, or you can buy it. I regularly do both for my clients. If they have the cash or strong credit, I buy. If they don't have the cash or they have weaker credit, I lease. Leasing is quick and easy, and nearly anyone can do it. Buying takes more of your money now or requires a loan, which makes it more difficult.

If you are not all that good at taking care of preventive maintenance on your toys, go with a lease. If you buy it, you are stuck with it and normal wear and tear can take a serious toll. If you lease it, the normal wear and tear will still take its toll, but you just lease another one.

Another alternative is to buy used equipment. Plenty of great used pieces of equipment are sold for pennies on the dollar. Where does this equipment come from? Most often from failed restaurants. You can look in any yellow pages to find used restaurant equipment vendors.

But when you're shopping for used equipment, keep in mind that a low price doesn't always make a bargain. You don't want to buy someone else's headache. Use the following considerations to determine whether going with used equipment is worth the trouble:

➤ Determine whether the piece is dirty or just plain old. If the equipment just needs a good bit of elbow grease, but is otherwise functional, great. If it is old, you don't need it, regardless of the price.

➤ Used nonmechanical equipment is more appealing than used mechanical equipment that has many working (or possibly nonworking) parts.

➤ Have the piece tested to ensure that it is mechanically sound before buying it. Have someone who knows equipment look at it. (In time, you will be able to analyze and fix your equipment on your own, which is just one of the skills you will pick up in the restaurant trade.) Go to another used equipment dealer or even dig in the local telephone book and find someone who specializes in equipment. Another option is to call one of your many restaurant buddies. Chances are one of them is an equipment expert.

➤ Is the manufacturer of the equipment still in business? If not, don't buy it.

➤ Price is in the eye of the beholder. I won't buy used equipment unless I am saving big dollars (50–90 percent off the price of buying the piece new).

Paper or Plastic? The Ware and Tear

The question of paper or plastic comes up all the time in the grocery store, but in the restaurant business, the question is even more complicated. It includes china, silver, crystal, stainless steel, wood, and so on. The great variety in restaurants is reflected in the equally great variety in ware, including silverware, dishware, cookware, flatware, stemware, and the like.

Some kinds of ware work better with certain kinds of food, concepts, and decors than with others. Can you imagine, for example, opening a Chinese restaurant without chopsticks? Or how about using paper cups and plastic forks in a fine-dining establishment?

To find what works for you, consider these six factors when buying any kind of ware:

➤ **Concept congruency:** Does the ware make sense for your concept design?

➤ **Size:** Does the size of the ware make sense for your portion sizes, production needs, and so on? You shouldn't serve a lunch menu (smaller portions) on a dinner plate big enough to serve the largest Texas steak. A frozen drink in a thimble-sized glass doesn't look right, especially if Seven-Eleven is right next door.

➤ **Durability:** How well will the ware hold up? And not just for you, but also for your customer? We have all had cheap, paper to-go cups nearly melt in our hands. You must consider dishwasher abuse, daily wear and tear (employees can be tough on ware), and chips and cracks (do you really want the tacky look that comes with chipped plates?).

➤ **User-friendliness:** Is the ware easy to clean? Easy to pick up? Easy to get a lid on? You don't want stuff that no one likes to use because of the hassle.

➤ **Cost:** Consider the cost of the initial purchase, the replacement cost, life span, and shipping costs.

➤ **Ease of reordering and replacing:** You don't want to buy any ware that takes months to replace, is the last in a product line (so if one breaks you can't replace it), or needs to be specially produced. Plenty of wonderful designs are available. Go with one of them.

Tip Jar

When buying any cookware or small wares, go with the best you can afford. It must put up with hot and cold temperatures and the banging and pounding that any chef or line cook is going to put it through. If you go cheap, you will be replacing it anyway. Also, if you hire a great chef, he or she most likely won't put up with cheap cookware.

Tip Jar

Ask your vendors to help you project your needs for each item. They are ware experts and will take great care of your ware order.

Look in any industry magazines or yellow pages, and you'll see plenty of advertisements for your ware needs. Call four or five ware vendors and compare.

As for ordering, your projected sales volume, restaurant size, concept, and the type of ware you need all play a role in how much you need to order. Be sure to order extra ware in case of breakage or loss. How much extra you need is dependent on how long it takes to reorder the item and how critical it is to your concept.

Eight Ways to Raise the Bar

The bar is a kitchen for your beverages, a production area with a caveat: It happens to be out in the open for customers to see. The bar comes with its own equipment and ware needs. The following list describes some ways to improve the performance of the bar. I call this list "Eight Ways to Raise the Bar":

➤ If you expect to do a big bar business, hire a bar manager. Much like a chef is to a kitchen, a bar manager is an expert on the bar and beverage business and pays for his or her own salary many times over if he or she is any good.

➤ Build the bar space for speed and efficiency. The fewer the steps needed for your employees the quicker Mr. Coppock can get his beverage, and the less hassle your employees have to go through to get it.

➤ Go with durable and dependable mixers, glass washers, ice makers, and so on. Any decent bar volume will test the life spans of your wares and equipment.

➤ Have a decent variety of beers, wines, and alcohols, but don't go overboard. The reality is that having 71 different brands of beer takes up a lot of space, requires a genius to order and inventory, and doesn't drive any more beer sales. You can't be everything to everybody, and most customers will gladly order something from the list you do have.

➤ Control the cash and the inventory. Have tight systems in place for pouring (automatic measuring nozzles), product inventory, theft reduction, and cash control.

➤ Hire and train bartender-quality hospitality experts. Behind the bar is where the whole hospitality concept began. An unfriendly bartender is as worthless as an accountant who can't add or a chef who can't cook.

➤ Allow people to drink, but don't allow them to get drunk. You are running a restaurant, and you need to protect yourself from allowing people to turn your restaurant into a saloon full of drunks. Don't be afraid to professionally and privately cut people off if they seem to be reaching their limit. Doing so reduces your liability and is just good business.

➤ Make your bar concept congruent with your restaurant concept. If your menu is Caribbean, you must have margaritas and other tropical drink selections, as well as beers and wines. If you serve hot dogs and hamburgers, you could probably get by without offering $125 bottles of California wine.

Check It Out

If you spend any quality time in the back of the house of any well-operated restaurant, you will notice many checklists. A restaurant must use checklists if it ever expects to be a well-oiled machine. There are just too many details to try to remember without them.

Each restaurant owner and operator traditionally devises his or her own set of checklists and does so in a way that can be easily updated and revised without much hassle or expense. These lists are usually created on a personal computer and then put under plastic or lamination for safekeeping and easy access. Many times these checklists are also put on a clipboard for mobility and follow-up purposes.

The following is a partial listing of checklists you may decide to use to help improve productivity, efficiency, and effectiveness:

➤ Opening: This is a checklist on what to do to open the restaurant properly and on time.

➤ Prep: This checklist is used to determine how much preparation of food needs to be done to be ready for the projected business volume.

➤ Maintenance: This pinpoints what needs to be cleaned, sanitized, fixed, and maintained to keep your facility up to par.

➤ Prerush: This is the checklist to ensure you are stocked and ready for the next peak revenue period.

➤ Postrush: This is used to get the restaurant back to the way it was before you got slammed with customers. Floors mopped, tables reset, registers cashed out, and more.

➤ Closing: This is the checklist that is critical to getting your restaurant prepared for business tomorrow. With this tool every night your restuarant should be looking as good as it did the moment you opened for business that day.

➤ Freezer pull: This form tells you how much product needs to be pulled out of the freezer and thawed for the projected sales volume tomorrow and the next day.

➤ Product quality: This is a checklist where you will track temperatures, freshness, and overall product quality.

➤ Hold time: This is used to keep track of how long products have been held prior to serving.

➤ Temperature: In some states this needs to be an extension of the product quality form and the health departments want a form that tracks temperatures of many food items done every hour. Check with your local health inspector to find out your specific requirements.

➤ Training: This form is used to keep track of the training levels of each of your employees.

➤ Zone duties: This checklist is used to give each employee their own zone responsibilities and duties they must complete prior to clocking out for their shift. A zone may be the dining area or the kitchen.

➤ Ten-minute tasks: These are tasks that the employee does during moments of free time in between serving customers to help keep them productive.

Most of these checklists are self-explanatory. For example, opening and closing checklists walk you through the opening and closing procedures for your restaurant. Chapter 24, "Restaurant Checklists, Forms, and Guidelines," provides both an opening and closing checklist for you to copy and use for your restaurant.

Other checklists, like the freezer pull checklist or hold time checklist, may not be quite so self-explanatory, but any restaurant operator becomes familiar with them in very short order. The freezer pull checklist helps you estimate how much product to thaw based on your future business needs. The hold time checklist helps you keep track of how long a given product can be held before it must be tossed out.

The Food Manual

If your restaurant offers a great lemon chicken and your chef quits, do you still offer a great lemon chicken? If you have a food manual, you do. A food manual is the kitchen staff's playbook (and you thought every item was thrown together without a recipe and made from memory).

You should have your food manual put together by a certified chef. If you don't have a certified chef, think about hiring or *outsourcing* one just for this purpose.

The food manual should have the following elements:

➤ The recipes for your dishes

➤ The specifications for your raw ingredients

➤ The cook times for every item

➤ The cook temperatures for every item

Recipes Revealed

Outsourcing is when you pay someone who is not an employee of your restaurant to do a project, such as build a food manual. Many times, the person you hire for the project has his or her own full-time business or a little part-time business on the side.

➤ The size of each portion

➤ The preparation procedures, including thawing, slicing and dicing, storage, and more

➤ The hold times and procedures

➤ The leftover and storage procedures

➤ The complete food safety procedures

➤ The cost analysis for each food item

➤ The suggested pricing for each item

➤ Menu options (if you have a revolving menu)

And you thought all a chef did was cook. Ha! A certified chef is a food doctor, a food lawyer, a food mover, a food shaker.

With an expertly designed food manual, a cooking novice should be able to follow the easy-to-read recipes and provide a great quality, safe-to-eat meal. Without it, you may want to go with a can of condensed soup.

Back of House Organization

Effective and efficient kitchens and bars all have one thing in common. They are well organized. When the heat is on during a Friday night dinner rush and you need to find the nutmeg, having a well-organized spice rack is imperative. The same can be said for your entire storage layout, including dry storage, cooler, freezer, and liquor.

Take the time and design your storage organization to provide for quick and easy access. Put light things on top, heavy things on bottom, more frequently used items close at hand, like items near each other, and so on.

In addition, most health departments don't allow for storage to be within 12 inches of the floor, and most fire departments don't allow for stuff to be stored within 12 inches of the ceiling. (And you thought your spouse's rules for how you handle your dirty socks were tough?) So check with your local authorities before setting up your storage areas.

The Least You Need to Know

➤ Your kitchen is the nerve center of your restaurant, so plan and organize it well.

➤ Homemade products are not always better than convenience products that are already made. It depends on your situation.

➤ If you buy used equipment, make sure you get a deep discount.

➤ When buying cookware and other equipment, consider its durability as well as price.

➤ A bar manager can be as important as a chef.

➤ A good restaurant uses lots of checklists.

Chapter 15

Upfront Effort: Setting Up for Service

In This Chapter

➤ How to allocate space

➤ What the concept of flow means to a restaurant

➤ Where best to store things

➤ How to pick tables and chairs

If the kitchen is the nerve center of your restaurant, the dining room is the heart and soul. Will the heart and soul of your business be fast, friendly, or forgettable?

Much like the back of the house, the front of the house needs to be a well-oiled machine, but the front of the house is a different kind of machine. The back is built for production like a car engine. The front is built for service and beauty like the chassis.

This chapter is about setting up the front of your restaurant where the customers meet the service. In it, you learn to be aware of traffic flows and how to make service more consistent, efficient, and effective.

The Dining Room

The design of your dining room is based on your concept. For example, a fine-dining restaurant is designed for comfort, relaxation, and a feeling of exceptional quality. In a

Food for Thought

Many fast-food restaurants have become far from fast and equally as many full-service establishments are far from anything that could be considered service.

fast-food restaurant, the dining area is much like the kitchen: It's designed to push through volume effectively and efficiently. Casual-dining restaurants are set up with both relaxation and speed in mind.

Matching the Space to the Concept

So how do you begin planning your dining room? Begin by thinking about your concept. The concept also determines the amount of space for dining. A guest in a fine-dining establishment is given far more space than one in a banquet dining or self-serve restaurant. The following table allocates square footage by type of dining experience per seated guest.

Type of Dining	Dining Room Area (In Square Feet)	Total Restaurant Area (In Square Feet)
Fine dining	16–20	28–36
Casual dining	14–18	24–32
Counter service	12–16	18–24
Banquet dining	10–14	18–24

These estimates of dining space required are based solely on your concept. There are, of course, other considerations, such as additional space needed for unique table arrangements, dining room waterfalls, salad bars, and the like.

Another determining factor of how you allot your space is the price you are paying per square foot of the property. In low-rent districts, you may be able to afford to give an extra foot or two of space to each patron. In a high-rent district, tight seating is part of the normal order of things.

Turning the Tables

Table turns are an important aspect to consider in planning your dining room and the space required for your concept. You do not want to push your customers to hurry up and eat their meal and go, but you can do some things to improve your table turns, thus allowing for more customers and reducing your need for dining room additions. And you can do these things without pressuring the customer to finish his vegetables!

➤ Ensure the kitchen is effective and efficient. If possible, use items that do not take long to prepare or use premade foods. Just don't sacrifice quality.

➤ Have enough employees on the schedule to provide prompt service.

➤ Take used dishes away as soon as the customer is through with them. This action makes the customer more comfortable and makes it easier to reset the table when the customer leaves.

➤ Reduce bottlenecks and teach teamwork to your staff. Don't make customers wait just because one waiter is running behind.

➤ Teach your staff how to read customer signals. For instance, when customers close the menu and lay it down, they are ready to have their order taken. Go take it.

Go with the Flow

Try this: Go to your favorite restaurant and ask to be seated next to the kitchen or close to the garbage cans or at least near a storage area. The look you receive will be priceless.

No one wants to sit near these areas, yet a restaurant cannot afford to let them be empty. I bet you have had the opportunity to be seated near the kitchen or bus station during a visit to a restaurant, probably on more than one occasion. And how did you feel about your seat? And yet now, from the ownership perspective you are acquiring, you realize that in order to do a decent enough business to survive, you must use all your space.

You must also go the extra mile to provide no bad seats. You must find ways to make wait stations and kitchens either quiet or more out of the way. You must ensure that storage areas are not obtrusive and that equipment is basically invisible and silent.

Creating a smooth flow in your restaurant is essential to creating a comfortable atmosphere. Restaurant flow usually means traffic flow, where the people, both employees and customers, funnel

Recipes Revealed

Table turns is the number given for how many times a given table is occupied per hour, thus determining the average stay. It is highly dependent upon your concept, your speed of service, and your service staff's ability to bus, clean, and reset a table. A fast-food establishment may average four turns per hour (meaning average stays of 15 minutes). A fine-dining establishment might average less than one turn per hour.

Recipes Revealed

Slide deployment is a maneuver of a well-trained staff in which staff slide from their main responsibilities to help with a bottleneck. This maneuver demonstrates the power of teamwork and training in helping a customer and a fellow employee in need.

in and out within their traffic patterns. If bottlenecks occur, they should be reduced with a redesign of your concept or eased with a simple *slide deployment* as they occur. But flow is more than just getting rid of bottlenecks.

Consider flow in the dining room from the broader perspective of concept flow. To your customer, flow is more of the feeling than the traffic. Traffic is a part of it. No one wants to have a waiter's behind hanging over your table every time the table next to you is served. But there is more to it. Is the table quiet, uninterrupted, visually appealing? That's flow to a customer. How does it feel?

Your design and layout often determine concept flow. But from an operations standpoint, you impact your flow in three ways:

➤ Front of the house organization and storage

➤ Dining room zones

➤ Equipment selection

Tip Jar

To reduce congestion and improve flow, try these tips:

➤ Divide large open spaces into smaller, intimate spaces. Use walls, plants, and so on.

➤ Provide adequate aisle space for wait staff to maneuver.

➤ Use a variety of table sizes and layouts, so you can accommodate a variety of group sizes without interrupting your concept flow for larger groups.

➤ Avoid bottlenecks near doorways or traffic areas, such as restrooms.

Organization and Storage

Where do you find the napkins when your dispenser runs low? If you're looking under the customer's feet, you may want to rethink your organization.

I have seen storage in ceilings, under booth seats and salad bars, in the middle of the dining room, along the wall, and even in bathrooms. The organizational and storage decisions you make play an important role in how customers feel about their dining experience. And how they feel plays an important role in whether they come back.

Certainly, some restaurants are not designed or built with storage and organization in mind. In these restaurants, finding an appropriate place to hide the necessary goodies is difficult and maybe even impossible. But at least give it a try. Think it through a bit versus just piling stuff in any old place. Here are some suggestions:

➤ Try to store as much out of customer contact areas as possible. If you need to, add a small storage shed to your kitchen or even on the roof of your kitchen. (Make sure to get the appropriate approval from health inspectors, zoning commissions, and building inspectors in your area prior to undertaking this endeavor.)

➤ Try to keep storage of items as close to the place where you will need them as possible without breaking the first rule.

➤ Talk to your product distributor about more frequent deliveries due to your limited space.

➤ Space is limited in all restaurants, so make purchasing decisions with space in mind. For instance, there is no reason to have four and a half cases of toilet paper in the building when the restaurant only goes through a case a week.

Zones of Service

How do waitresses determine which customers they will personally serve? Simple. They use a zone system, much like a zone defense in basketball or football.

The dining area is broken into zones, and each waitperson is responsible for his or her own zone. Just as a defensive back may cover a portion of the field in football, a waiter covers his own zone of the restaurant. This zone may consist of 3, 5, or 10 tables, depending on the projected volume of customers and your restaurant concept. More upscale service and a higher projected volume usually call for a smaller number of tables in a zone.

Most restaurants have the dining room broken out into many different sizes of zones based on the number of wait staff scheduled. Each possible zone setup is mapped out on a different chart that shows the dining room floor plan, with each of the tables numbered. If one waitress is working, the entire dining room is her responsibility. With two waitresses, the zones are split a different way, and so on.

In practice, zone coverage works like this: You look at the schedule. If eight wait people are scheduled for this dinner hour, you pull out the eight-person zone chart. Then serve, serve, serve! A good zone system provides better service, less employee traffic for the customer, and easier handling for the waitperson.

Wet Floor!

Be careful not to have more deliveries than is necessary. Many distributors, but not all, have minimum order requirements and delivery charges. You do not want to have added expense if it is not absolutely necessary.

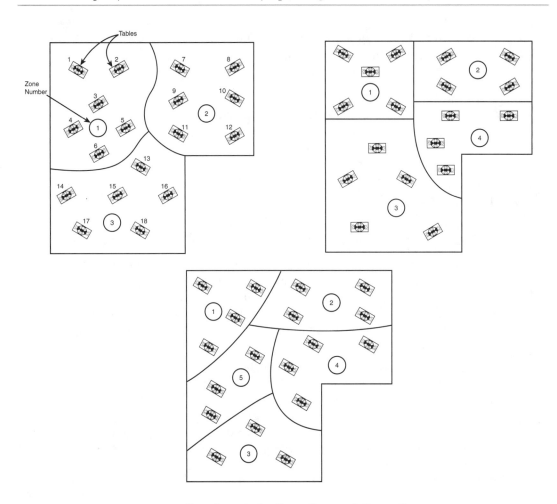

Zone layouts for three, four, and five waiters.

Front of the House Equipment

When you buy equipment for the front of your restaurant, you need to think a little differently than you do when you buy kitchen equipment. You consider many of the same issues you had to for the back of the house, but do it with an understanding that customers will see this piece of equipment. Whether it is a condiment stand, a salad bar, a beverage mixer, or a service cart, you must understand that each and every customer will see this piece of equipment up close and personal, thus, it must fit a few other criteria. Ask yourself the following:

➤ Does it look good and will it stay looking good?

➤ Does it fit in with the look and feel of your dining room concept and decor?

➤ Is it quiet? You don't want to disturb your guests' dining experience with some loud motor noise.

➤ Does the size of the equipment make sense for the size of your dining area and your portion sizes, production needs, and so on?

➤ How well will it hold up? A broken piece of dining room equipment needs to be replaced immediately, while many pieces of equipment in the back of the house can easily be replaced with an alternative method. If a slicer breaks down you could cut your vegetables by hand and the customer would not know. On the other hand, if your salad bar goes down the world will know it.

➤ Is it easy for your employees and customers to use? This is critical when it is being used right in front of your customers. You really don't want to have stuff that no one likes to use because of the hassle.

➤ Is it easy to reorder and replace? You don't want to buy anything that takes months to replace, especially if that leaves a gaping hole in your dining area.

Probably the most noticeable pieces of equipment in the dining room are the tables and chairs. Like everything else, your choice of tables and chairs is determined by your restaurant concept and decor. Upscale and fine-dining establishments go with rich-looking tables and chairs and spend big dollars to do it. Fast-food restaurants go with less expensive stuff that is more or less built for speed and ease of handling and durability.

When choosing your tables and chairs, keep in mind the concept congruency. Putting plastic tables and chairs in a restaurant that boasts a French chef and high-end entrées just isn't right.

Everything you get should last and look good for a long time. Go with sturdy stuff that sits well on your floors (not wobbly) and doesn't stain easily or break under the pressure of your special-recipe pound cake. It also should be easy to clean and repair. Stay away from potential vinyl tears, cracked glass, and so on.

Tip Jar

When buying tables, chairs, cups, glasses, flatware, salad crocks, and so on, consider that if the item chips easily, it will look tacky. Durability is important in aesthetics as well as functionality. If it chips easily, forget it—no matter how great it looks new.

When buying your dining room accessories (forks, knives, linens, and such), stick with pieces that are easy to reorder and easy to clean. (See Chapter 14, "Get It Right on the Back End: The Back of the House," for more tips on buying accessories, also known as ware.)

Your Service System Guide

Having a service system guide ensures that your staff understands each guideline for the front of the house. It provides a similar step-by-step approach to service as your food manual and checklists serve for the use of your kitchen (see Chapter 14).

This manual should cover the entire process of customer service from the moment a customer walks in the front door to the moment the customer leaves and nearly every possible scenario while the customer is in your restaurant.

This manual should include the following:

Food for Thought

The front of the house uses checklists just like the back of the house. Go to the Restaurant Operations Institute Web site at www.roiontheweb. com and pick up the complete CD-ROM of virtually every restaurant form you could ever need. This CD allows you to download over 50 different forms and adjust them with a simple click of the mouse to suit your particular needs.

➤ The wait staff zone layouts based on every possible scheduling scenario.

➤ The specifications, processes, hold times, and guidelines for all products that your service staff must prepare. Many restaurants have their service staff prepare food as well as serve. They might prepare the salad bar or make individual salads, make coffee or tea, slice lemons into wedges, or prepare desserts.

➤ Service equipment guides for coffee machines, ice cream dispensers, and any other equipment that the service staff uses as well as procedures for operating this equipment.

➤ Hosting, bussing, and register procedures.

➤ Customer complaint procedures.

➤ Complete service procedures and guidelines.

➤ Suggestive selling and upselling procedures.

➤ Dining area music guidelines.

➤ Dining area lighting, temperature, and ambience guidelines.

➤ Table setting layout.

Other Stations

Other stations need to be set up in the front of the house to ensure a smooth operation. They may include the host station, the bus station, wait stations, drive-thru stations, and register areas.

The key to each of these areas is to keep them as small and unobtrusive as possible while still making them efficient and effective places to conduct the necessary tasks. You do not want to waste large chunks of your dining room with wait stations and bus stations. Make these stations as unnoticeable to the customer as possible, and keep them away from places where they could cause a bottleneck, such as doors or bathrooms.

Multiple smaller stations are preferable to gigantic catchall stations. Remember that these stations need to be set up for speed and efficiency regardless of your concept. When you design these stations, use organizational tools, such as plastic containers and dispensers, to increase the stations' user-friendliness. If work at your restaurant is easier to do, employee morale, overall employee performance, and ultimately your profits will improve.

The Least You Need to Know

➤ The design of your dining room must fit with your concept.

➤ Understanding traffic flow and concept flow will help you design a more enjoyable and efficient eating space.

➤ Hide your storage and your employee stations as best as possible while making them efficient and effective.

➤ Write and use a service system guide to ensure your customers are treated well from the time they arrive until they leave.

➤ Durability and looks are important factors to consider when you purchase front of the house equipment. Remember, customers will see this equipment.

Chapter 16

Dinner at Your House: Treating Customers Like Guests

In This Chapter

➤ Understanding the basics of hospitality

➤ Creating a hospitality team

➤ Building a hospitality culture

➤ Improving hospitality in your restaurant

➤ Tracking performance

➤ Handling complaints

If people are going to pay you to cook them some food, don't you think you should at least be nice to them? No matter what your concept is, you are inviting people over to eat, and you should show them some hospitality. Yet many restaurants disregard hospitality, and that disregard spells disaster for their business.

But what exactly is hospitality? Hospitality is simply having a friendly, respectful, polite, warm, and welcome approach to dealing with other people. Customers have made it clear that outstanding hospitality is always appreciated, rewarded, and remembered. If you operate with a high level of hospitality as one of your core values, retaining and growing your sales and customer base will never be an issue.

In this chapter, you learn what hospitality is and how to make outstanding hospitality happen in your restaurant. The many insider tricks of the operator's trade and simple ideas and concepts in this chapter will help you and your team turn into hospitality legends.

Wet Floor!

One happy customer may talk to others about you, but an unhappy customer will almost certainly tell 7 to 10 other people about his or her poor experience. So the relationship between your staff and customers is crucial. The main job description for any of your employees should be to connect with and serve the customer.

Food for Thought

It costs six times more to attract a new customer than to keep a current one. So treat your customers like royalty.

Are You a People Person?

Hospitality is many different things to many different people. It is devoting the time to take someone's jacket or pull out someone's chair. It is asking Mrs. Jones how her child did at soccer camp and wishing Mr. Smith best of luck on his fishing trip. It is caring. It is knowing the names of your customers and ordering an extra dollop of ice cream for Billy because you know he loves it. Hospitality is enjoying people just because. Hospitality is enjoying life and the place you work and having a genuine desire to share. In short, hospitality is about relationships.

The business world has a great concept called relationship marketing, which is the idea that employees build a personal and lasting relationship with customers. Relationship marketing has very little to do with any actual marketing and more to do with building a relationship with your customer. In time, those customers become a great marketing tool for you and your business through the use of word of mouth advertising. (You'll also be able to count on the relationship.) In the restaurant business, relationship marketing works. Customers who enjoy the atmosphere of your restaurant will keep coming back and will bring their friends and family with them.

You can personalize the concept of relationship marketing within your restaurant by building concepts and training materials that are more unique to you and your team. For example, my teams use a concept called "connecting with thy customer." This catchphrase is easier for staffs to understand and helps my teams focus on what their role is. "Connect with thy customer" has become one of my team's restaurant commandments and cultural distinctions and has made a long-lasting positive impact on sales.

Do You Pass the Ho-Hum Test?

"Ho-hum" is how the customer mentally defines restaurants if they are just another one in the crowd.

When the customer leaves your restaurant are they smiling? If they aren't smiling they weren't impressed.

When the customer talks about their dining experience with you, was it wonderful? Or was it good? Good isn't good enough.

Delivering outstanding hospitality is how you can avoid being just another one in the crowd of "ho-hum" restaurants.

Rate your restaurant versus your competition in the following form. Use a scale from one to five, with one being poor, three being average, and five being great.

The Ho-Hum Test

Competitor's name: _____ Date: _____

Category	My Score	Competitor's Score
Politeness	_____	_____
Smiles	_____	_____
Eye contact	_____	_____
Greeting	_____	_____
Listening	_____	_____
Thanking	_____	_____
Bidding farewell	_____	_____
Positive attitude	_____	_____
Customer focus/connection	_____	_____
Hospitality consistency	_____	_____
Total hospitality score:	_____	_____

Comments: _____

_____

With 10 questions, a score of less than 25 is poor. A score of 30 is average. A score of 40 or more is good. A score above 45 is excellent. Of course, your score versus your competitor's score has more value as a test. Are you significantly better in the area of hospitality? If not, you don't pass the ho-hum test.

The Seven Basic Characteristics of Hospitality

Hospitality has seven very basic characteristics. Spend time teaching these characteristics to your team and you will have a team that will reward customers with better hospitality, resulting in better customer comments, better employee morale toward customers, and better sales. What's in it for the employees? How about better compensation and better tips? That should get their attention!

What are these seven characteristics?

➤ Be polite

➤ Smile

➤ Manage eye contact

➤ Greet

➤ Listen

➤ Thank

➤ Bid farewell

Be Polite

The basic rules of etiquette, and magic words such as "Please," "Thank you," "Excuse me," "Pardon me," "Bless you," and "May I help you?" have gotten lost in much of society. But if you want to have a successful restaurant, you should make sure your staff follows these rules and uses these magic words. Yes, you may have to teach politeness classes for your staff. I do.

Smile

"That's what you pay me for, sir."

This line was one of the greatest that I have ever heard from an employee. I was eating in a restaurant in Orlando, Florida, at Disney World when I saw a young lady with a truly outstanding smile. I said to her, "Young lady, you have one of the greatest smiles I have ever seen."

She simply replied, "That's what you pay me for, sir." She wowed me with that answer. You see, she clearly understood two very powerful things. First, she understood that I, the customer, was paying her salary. Second, she made it clear that the smile was nonnegotiable—it was a must. Wow!

This kind of attitude is infectious and makes work more enjoyable. "Hire the smile" is common advice, and I concur. However, I believe you can train the smile as well. To get your staff smiling, you have to smile and truly enjoy people and then work with your employees.

Indifference toward the customer is the ultimate silent killer. It will take the life out of your team and destroy the commitment to your hospitality vision. To battle the effects of indifference, you must show the customer you care. To borrow a concept from a very bright young lady: "Smile—that's what they pay you for."

Manage Eye Contact

Eye contact is more than looking at someone; it is eye management. Eye contact is a sign of confidence, interest, and even people orientation. Working with your employees to manage their eye contact helps them build better relationships among themselves and with their customers. An important part of managing eye contact is knowing what not to do; stress the following rules to your staff:

➤ Don't roll your eyes. This action shows frustration and/or indifference.

➤ Don't stare at the customer (even a very attractive one). Staring is disrespectful.

➤ Don't look past the customer. Doing so shows lack of interest.

Greet

Greeting people can be as simple as "Hi, welcome to _____," or "Hey, great to see you. Welcome." Which would you prefer? Corporate America has made the greeting so generic that many times it is no longer personal, sincere, or of interest to the guest. The key to a greeting is to acknowledge the guest's presence and show a sincere and hearty welcome. Greet from the heart and teach your staff to do the same.

One of the best companies I have seen at this is Waffle House. Anyone who frequents a Waffle House for breakfast recognizes the cheery Waffle House "Good morning!"

Listen

Consumers rarely think that employees listen. Work with your employees to get them to be able to take mental notes of what the customer wants. Many restaurants are emphasizing such listening skills by having the wait staff memorize orders instead of writing them down. You have to decide on the accuracy levels of this method, but order memorization is a good skill to learn. Being able to hear and respond to a customer's request for more ice water is important.

Tip Jar

Videotape is a great way to show your employees how great they look when they smile and how bad they look when they don't. Even try saying, "Hey, whatever you do, don't smile" to your employees. They won't be able to stop themselves from grinning. If you get a few going, the next thing you know you'll have miles of smiles.

Thank

Thanking the guest is much like the greeting. Your message of thanks can't be insincere, impersonal, or canned. Ask the customer if everything was to his or her liking and thank the customer for his or her patronage. The tacky signs posted across America that say "Thank You For Your Business" mean nothing to the customer and are a waste of money. Skip the sign and invest something of much more value: real words from the heart. Thank you!

Bid Farewell

Bidding farewell is your last point of personal contact with the customer and is critical to the customer's view of the overall dining experience. Bidding farewell is saying "Have a great day," "See you next time," and "Drive carefully." Bidding farewell is so simple and says so much about the true feelings of the staff. You already have the customer's money, your work is virtually done, and now you come to good-bye. Will you seal the deal for the next visit? Of course you will.

Wet Floor!

U.S. News & World Report claims that 68 percent of customers quit going to certain restaurants because of the indifference of employees. Indifference shows up many ways, including body language, lack of eye contact, and even facial expressions. Eye rolling, poor posture, and frowning also indicate indifference. Indifference also rears its ugly head with sarcasm and negative comments made toward the customer, especially during a customer complaint or immediately thereafter.

The Four Critical Components to Better Hospitality

After you have implemented and executed the hospitality basics, you need to have four critical components to improve hospitality:

➤ A cultural commitment to excellent hospitality: Your culture must be committed to hospitality. This is not cheap or easy and your commitment level will show when the heat is on.

➤ A team that is driven and focused on hospitality: You are only as good as your worst hospitality employees. If every employee is not committed, you will suffer some pain and so will your customers.

➤ Hospitality leadership: Are you going to be the visual, vocal leader who is the perfect example of hospitality?

➤ Consistency and constant improvement: Stay true to your hospitality vision and continue to add aspects to it that will make you constantly improve for your customers.

These components work in any restaurant, regardless of concept, size, volume, or venue. The absence of any one of these critical components can have an adverse effect on the performance of your restaurant.

Committing to a Culture of Hospitality

As you create your restaurant team, consider your restaurant's culture. The culture of your restaurant must be grounded in hospitality.

Show me a restaurant company where the office staff carries more clout than the operators and I'll show you a company that has lost touch and doesn't care. A restaurant must be run from a restaurant for many reasons, especially hospitality. Great hospitality happens in the restaurants and with the customers, not through any office setting. Culturally, the people who serve and connect with the customers must lead the show so they don't lose touch.

Committing the restaurant's culture to hospitality takes time and energy, but it is well worth it. If you know what the hospitality concepts in your restaurant will look like, you can implement them. For instance, what training tools will you use? What will your catchphrases become, and who will be involved in the concept execution? This culture building doesn't happen overnight, but with the right focus you can be proud to call your restaurant a home of hospitality.

Building a Hospitality Team

The best way to build your hospitality team is to instill an attitude of caring in your employees. The first step in this process is to treat employees and your customers well. But you must also spend some time teaching your team so that every member is in tune with your hospitality goals and objectives and is passionate about delivering on them. Hospitality starts with you and resonates through the staff to the guest.

Tip Jar

Phone etiquette is a component to hospitality that is often overlooked. Place a mirror by your phones and have your employees look into the mirror as they talk to customers on the phone. This technique will help them sound friendlier, fluctuate their voice inflection, and even be more personable to your phone guests.

Food for Thought

Positive mental attitude (PMA) rallies can be very effective, quick meetings that, if executed properly, can significantly improve your hospitality culture. The purpose of these rallies is to instill a higher level of morale. They should be two to three minutes in length and should be held at the beginning of every peak revenue period. They are a great time to bring up new ideas and concepts, but getting two-way communication is paramount.

177

So how do you build a hospitality team? You hire hospitable people, train them in your way, and keep your standards sky-high.

Hiring hospitality gurus is not difficult. It starts with changing the types of questions you ask during an interview. Stop asking "Tell me about a time" questions and begin asking "Let me give you a scenario and you tell me how you would handle it" questions. Listen for answers that are friendly and customer oriented.

Also, watch how applicants interact with your staff. Observe their comfort level around people they do not know. In short order, you will be hiring for hospitality.

Being a Hospitality Leader

Hospitality starts simply. Look in the mirror. Who is that person? Are you friendly, outgoing, personable, and approachable? Do you like your neighbors? Do they like you? The reality is that hospitality starts with you, the leader. Just as an athletic team is built in the mold of the coach, a restaurant hospitality team is built in the mold of the manager.

Teach all new hires the importance of a positive mental attitude. Talk to them about your restaurant's hospitality culture and your expectations and let them know that you are there for them if they are having a bad day and just need to talk. And then be there if it happens. By being hospitable to your employees, you show them a great example of relationship marketing, and they pass it on to the customer.

Improving Hospitality

If all you do is the seven basic characteristics of hospitality (smile, greet, thank, and so on), you will be further ahead than most of your competition. But then what? You must create a hospitality distinction. You must attack your competition by really separating yourself from the crowd.

Suppose *The New York Times* restaurant critic stopped by your restaurant. Would the critic get surly and rude service? I should hope not. Get your team members to treat every customer like the local food critic by demonstrating that they care what the customer thinks of them.

Wet Floor!

If an employee is not reaching your hospitality expectations during training, spend the necessary time to train and retrain this employee. If after providing further hospitality training assistance the employee is still lacking a hospitality focus, chances are very good that he or she never will hit or exceed your standards. Now is the time to make the tough decision to fire that person. Do not procrastinate.

Food for Thought

All managers lead by example. If a manager is friendly, outgoing, and hospitable, the team will follow that lead. And if a manager berates an employee for not smiling, he shouldn't be surprised when his staff has trouble getting on the hospitality bandwagon.

Don't be afraid of being unique in your quest to improve hospitality. Try designing a short set of classes for your staff to help improve hospitality in your restaurant. These classes should be 15 to 30 minutes in length and designed to cover the seven basic characteristics of hospitality as well as increasing awareness, connecting with the customer, reading customer body language, improving small talk, and more. These classes are also a great time to talk about your team's hospitality performance and other best practices.

Hospitality Scorecards

After committing your culture, your team, and yourself to hospitality, how do go beyond classes to improve even more? You do what any other business does. You measure and adjust.

Keeping score on hospitality seems difficult because it is such a subjective area. The main thing to keep in mind is that the customer's perspective is what's most important. That's why keeping score on hospitality begins and ends with customer feedback. Such feedback is a powerful tool that will help improve your overall hospitality performance.

The best ways to get this feedback are comment cards, secret shoppers, focus groups (see Chapter 13, "Restaurant Marketing 101," for information on focus groups), and customer interviews. Being able to see your hospitality performance from the eyes of your customers gives you the necessary information to put the proper pieces in place going forward.

In addition to customer feedback, an award, such as the often-used *ABCD award,* is helpful in boosting your team's commitment to hospitality. Rewarding employees for providing good hospitality is much more effective than reprimanding the employees for not smiling and not being friendly (which makes them feel even less like smiling and more unfriendly).

Recipes Revealed

The **ABCD award** is an award some restaurants give to employees who go above and beyond the call of duty (ABCD). Traditionally this award is a plaque that comes with either free tickets to a ballgame or a concert and is given in front of the staff to reinforce the message that those who provide high levels of hospitality will be rewarded on a continual basis.

Comment Cards

Comment cards should be oriented around hospitality issues. These cards should ask simple questions and provide simple multiple-choice answers. Don't overwhelm customers with a huge number of questions and be sure to leave plenty of room for them to voice their comments. Chapter 24, "Restaurant Checklists, Forms, and Guidelines," has a sample comment card for you to use in your own restaurant. Make sure you track your comment cards on a monthly analysis form to watch for trends.

Secret Shoppers

The best use for secret shoppers is to find out how your staff handles a complaint. Tell the secret shopper to make up a fictional complaint and have the shopper describe exactly how your staff handles the situation. Tell the shopper to watch for eye rolling, body language, and so on.

Plenty of secret shopper survey companies out there will do a very detailed secret shop on your restaurant for a fee of $25 to $100 plus the price of the meal. However, I recommend using friends, family, and neighbors. It's cheaper, you can style it to your liking more easily, and they'll all love you for the free meal.

Customer Interviews

My favorite way to get input is to simply ask for it. Every chance you get, whether you are in your restaurant dining room, at the club, in an elevator, at a church function, or anything in between, ask people what they think about your business.

Don't make it a systemized approach and don't spend too much of their time. Just communicate as if you are talking to long-lost friends. Ask people these questions: Have you eaten at XYZ restaurant? Do you like it? What don't you like? What would you change? Don't tell them you are the owner. Just ask for their opinions. People love to feel their opinion matters, and you'll love to find out what they think.

At the end of the conversation, feel free to thank them for their thoughts and give them a free meal card to visit. A good customer interview turns into a great relationship marketing opportunity and a win for all concerned.

Do-or-Die Hospitality Points of Contact

Hospitality is an all-day, every day commitment, and dropping the ball even one time is a serious offense to the customer. With that said, however, the most critical do-or-die point of contact is the customer complaint.

Handling complaints is the most sensitive point of any restaurant-customer relationship. The customer is vulnerable, and the employee, at times, can and does take the complaint personally. It is a potentially explosive situation. This moment is when all the hard work and staff training you have done on hospitality pays off.

Great hospitality-focused organizations really separate themselves from the also-rans in this arena. Any time you have a complaint, the employee who is involved needs to remember this key phrase: It is not a personal attack. Also, instruct your staff to remember to remain calm and focus on the customer and fixing the problem.

Most customers do not waste their time to complain. Instead, they just don't come back. You should look at complaints as the customers showing you that they care enough about you and your business to take their valuable time to give you a free education.

One Priceless Question to Save Your Business

What can I do to make it right?

This question is the most effective way to ask customers to give you the opportunity to keep their business forever. Regardless of how well your restaurant runs, customers will complain from time to time. You will nearly always stop these customers right in their tracks if you ask them, "What can I do to make it right?" With this question, you are asking them from the heart for their wants and their needs. Then you must deliver.

Remember, you can take care of any complaint effectively and efficiently by using the following steps:

1. Relax.
2. Listen.
3. Apologize.
4. Ask "What can I do to make it right?"
5. Fix the problem.

The Least You Need to Know

➤ Hospitality is critical to the success of any restaurant, regardless of its segment, location, or concept.

➤ Hospitality starts with the boss and resonates through the staff, not the other way around.

➤ Hospitality is never driven by a program, but rather by a mentality and a cultural distinction.

➤ Customers tell you the facts about your restaurant's performance by word of mouth and by the use of their feet.

➤ Handling customer complaints well is critical to your overall hospitality performance and culture.

Operational Execution, Part 1: Quality

To a person dining in a restaurant, the concept of quality is simple: Either the food is good or it's not. The reaction of the consumer is the ultimate measure of your quality. Their reaction is pure, almost childish; the food is yummy, delicious, scrumptious, fantastic, and succulent, or it is not.

When restaurant operators talk about quality, they tend to be thinking on a much broader scale than taste. For them, quality is the ultimate restaurant science because human lives are at stake. The safety of food and beverages takes precedence by law. After all, people are going to put your meals inside their bodies.

Quality also includes such marketable and profitable measures as texture, eye appeal, hold times, and product yield. Taste, of course, is also important. But quality is even more than that. From the moment the food or beverage is produced, grown, packaged, delivered, stored, cooked, and served, some very detailed guidelines need to be considered to guarantee quality.

Quality begins with a commitment, and this chapter is about that commitment. In this chapter, you learn to deliver a product that is satisfying to your guests and safe to serve. You also learn why the health department is your friend, how to borrow a page from NASA, and how to know how long you can keep your food before it goes bad.

Quality Doesn't Just Happen

You and your staff are creating someone's meal. That is a huge responsibility. Providing someone a meal is establishing a personal relationship with that customer. Your food is what they are putting in their body for taste and for life.

The food you are serving must be safe; there is no margin for error in this area. But quality is more than food that is safe. Quality is hot food served hot, cold food served cold, fresh products that are fresh, and frozen products that are frozen. Quality is the same item on your menu served the same way every time a customer orders it.

Quality cannot be an occasional occurrence. It happens every time, and it happens only one way: through systems. Achieving quality in any restaurant is about managing the details, so you must have a system for every aspect of dealing with food and beverage.

Developing these systems is the key to quality. Much research has already been done to help you achieve quality, and many experts are available to educate you along the way.

Food for Thought

Most restaurant people are system machines because they've learned to ensure quality products from the beginning of their restaurant career.

The Health Department

Some rules in the restaurant business can seem silly. But the rules of the local health department are not at all silly. The rules of the local health department can save the lives of your customers and, secondarily, the life of your restaurant.

Sure, the health inspector may nitpick, but the health inspector also will help you install systems to make your (and his) job easier. The health inspector wants to help you.

Again, although some restaurant rules don't make sense, the ones governing your health absolutely do. You will most likely eat in restaurants other than your own on occasion. Don't you want the health inspector to go over those restaurants with a fine-tooth comb? Of course you do. Yet some restaurants fight the law, and the law wins. And that's good for you and me.

HAACP: A Proactive Approach

HAACP is the Hazard Analysis Critical Control Points system that was developed to ensure the safety of food for United States astronauts. From NASA to your restaurant, this system is now coming into play in mainstream America. The reason is that these guidelines make good sense.

Yes, these concepts were tested at altitudes you will never reach, unless an angry customer kicks you into orbit for making him sick. But they make perfect sense at your altitude, too (and altitude does make a difference).

The HAACP system focuses on three key elements to food safety: food microbiology, quality control, and risk assessment. This system is not as focused on inspection as it is on safety for safety's sake.

The HAACP system consists of six steps:

➤ Identify hazards and assess the potential risk. You know, like what can happen when your employees don't wash their hands.

➤ Look at the four most critical control points: personal hygiene, cross contamination, cooking, and cooling.

➤ Establish and implement step-by-step procedures to ensure quality controls and safety controls on every item you produce.

➤ Monitor the critical control points. In the case of our hand washing example, this is where they make sure you have the necessary signage, tools, dispensers, and training materials.

➤ Take appropriate action when a critical control point is violated, such as revising your procedures to meet new and improved standards.

➤ Continually confirm that the system is working. Follow-up is always critical to continued compliance.

The HAACP system gives you systems to work with. And as you know, the restaurant business is all about systems. Establishing food safety systems may seem overwhelming, but once you have established your initial systems and procedures for every product you serve, the process becomes just minor maintenance going forward.

Tip Jar

NASA developed the HAACP system, and you should use it. It may be one small step for man, but HAACP is a giant leap forward for restaurant-kind.

Understanding and Dealing with Food Contamination

Food can become contaminated in many ways, but three ways make up the majority of the cases:

➤ **Foreign substance contamination:** This contamination occurs when hair, dirt, plastic, gum, bandages, and so on get into food.

➤ **Chemical contamination:** This contamination occurs when substances such as those found in cleaning supplies or pesticides get into or onto food.

➤ **Cross contamination:** This contamination occurs when safe and contaminated foods come in contact with each other. This contact may occur when the same piece of equipment is used to prepare two different products without being cleaned and sanitized in between uses or when two different products are handled without hands being washed in between, or when a host of other situations occur.

Avoiding these three types of contamination is imperative to staying in business. Start avoiding contamination by trying these steps:

➤ Have an organized and well laid-out kitchen and preparation area to provide the necessary room for product handling.

➤ Insist that staff wear either hairnets or hats when they are working in the kitchen area.

➤ Have kitchen staff members wash their hands many, many times throughout the day and in between the handling of different products.

➤ Wash all food items thoroughly prior to preparing them.

➤ Keep all cleaning supplies and chemicals away from food items.

➤ Keep your restaurant clean. (See Chapter 19, "Clean Is Your Only Choice," for details.)

➤ Keep cooked and uncooked products away from each other.

➤ Do not store anything above food preparation areas.

➤ Wash every piece of equipment or small wares after every use and between uses of different products.

➤ When in doubt, toss it out. If you think something has contaminated the food for one reason or another, play it safe. Throw the food away.

FIFO: First In, First Out

Quality is essential in the restaurant business, and FIFO is a key ingredient to ensuring quality. FIFO (first in, first out) is the proper way to store and use food products. The first product that came in is the first one you should use.

Following this strategy is important to maintain freshness. You do not want to have the same case of lettuce on the bottom of the stack for weeks. If you do, guess what? It rots.

Just as was discussed in Chapter 12, "Purchasing: It's More Than Buying a Can of Corn," your system needs to be set up so all products are dated on the container when they come in. Even in the holding bin, you want the first chicken breast to go into the holding bin to be the first one to go out. You have to track hold time, so you will know which one it is.

Hold Times

A *hold time* is the amount of time after a product is prepared that you can hold the item before the product quality deteriorates below serving standards. Certainly, you don't want to sell any item that deteriorates at all, but all food items deteriorate. And certainly, you can decide to never use items that are held after they are prepared. But if you plan to prepare every item to order, your speed of service will suffer.

Food for Thought

Nearly all restaurants from fine-dining establishments to fast-food joints hold some food. They have to if they expect to serve their customers in a reasonable amount of time. Some restaurants hold more food than others. Fast-food restaurants focus on their speed of service, so guessing volume and preparing food (hamburgers, french fries, and so on) ahead of time is very common in these places. Fine-dining restaurants may hold desserts, soups, or salad ingredients, but prepare the rest of the meal to order.

Your restaurant will probably hold some food. And every item that you hold has a different hold time that is dependent on the product, the preparation, the manner of holding, and even your restaurant's elevation above sea level. To determine hold time lengths for each product you serve, you must do some experimenting. Prepare the product exactly as you would for the customer. Then hold the product as your certified chef, health department, and even product manufacturer have determined is appropriate. They all will give you printed materials that will advise you on their recommendations and many times they will not advise you the same way. Here is where your better judgement needs to come in. Watch it, taste it, measure its temperature, pick at it, and prod it. If it's not a great product, why would you want to serve it?

When you start to see the product deteriorate to a point such that you are no longer happy serving it (well before it becomes a food safety issue) because of taste, texture, or visual appeal, mark down the time it took to get to that point. Take that time (assume it's 21 minutes) and reduce it by 33 percent (which would be 7 minutes) to provide a safety net. The maximum hold time for that product would then be 14 minutes. Make sure you keep a record of all hold times in the kitchen's food manual (see Chapter 14, "Get It Right on the Back End: The Back of the House," for more information on food manuals).

Tip Jar

I always round off hold times to the closest five-minute increment. Rounding makes the hold times easier for the staff to remember. I also never round up; I always round down. I don't want to lose my 33 percent safety net.

Bar Safety and Quality

The bar is part of your restaurant. Therefore, you must concern yourself with beverage safety and product quality in your bar as well as your restaurant. Following are 10 things you can do to ensure your bar has high-quality standards and is serving safe products:

➤ Wash all glassware in hot water (not lukewarm) with soap and sanitizer. Thoroughly rinse the glassware and allow it to air dry.

➤ Store clean glassware upside down to ensure nothing falls into the glass.

➤ Store all bar utensils in such a way that they are picked up by the handle.

➤ Keep all bar lines (the tube from the beer keg to the tap) clean. Clean them more often than what your local regulation calls for.

➤ Keep all cold beverages cold. This issue is a pet peeve of mine. I can't tell you the hundreds of times I have been served a warm or not quite cold enough beer. To prevent this travesty in your restaurant, make sure that beer is pulled from the storage area into the cooler early enough so that it has time to get cold before it is served. Also make sure the cooler temperatures are cold enough. If I come to your restaurant, I will want a cold beer.

➤ If you serve wine, learn the right way to store wine and then do it right. Wine connoisseurs will know if you did. So become a connoisseur yourself or find one to run your wine cellar.

➤ Toss all chipped or cracked glassware immediately.

➤ Keep your bar area clean and organized. Remember, the bar is a production area much like the kitchen.

➤ Make sure bar staff wash and sanitize their hands just as frequently as kitchen staff.

➤ Use different bar towels to wipe the bar and wipe down equipment. Use different color bar towels to differentiate what is a bar towel (for the bar table surface) and what is a cleaning towel for the rest of the bar.

Shelf Life

Every food or beverage item you use in your restaurant has a shelf life. Shelf life is a bit different from hold time, but it has many of the same attributes. *Shelf life* is the length of time a product can sit on a shelf prior to being prepared for consumption before it becomes outdated. The shelf life of some products, such as produce, is quite short; other products, such as canned goods or frozen items, have a very long shelf life.

In many cases, manufacturers determine shelf life guidelines for you. They know the proper storage procedures for their products and how long they stay usable. For example, some beverage companies use freshness dating, such as the "Use Before" dating that appears on milk and other products. In other cases, your local health department spells out the required guidelines in your geographic area for that particular item.

Even so, you should always keep an eye on shelf life for yourself, as well. Although you don't have the time to wait for six months to see whether that frozen dessert will hold up, you really shouldn't have to. With proper ordering procedures and par levels (see Chapter 12) and with your deliveries arriving on a reasonable schedule, you should not have to worry about too many shelf-life issues with frozen or canned products.

However, certain items you need to monitor at all times. These items are quickly perishable:

➤ Fruits and vegetables

➤ Dairy products

➤ Breads and bakery items

➤ Fresh meats and seafood

Often, restaurant operators schedule these items to be delivered multiple times during a week (and in some cases daily) to ensure freshness.

Wet Floor!

A food can have more than one shelf life depending on how it is stored. For example, the shelf life of a frozen food is much shorter once the food is thawed.

Product Consistency

How would you feel if one time you ordered a Big Mac and it had two all-beef patties, special sauce, lettuce, cheese, pickles, onions, and a sesame seed bun, but then the next time you ordered a Big Mac it had one chicken patty, sweet and sour sauce, a tomato, and no sesame seeds on your bun? Would you be confused? Would you think, "Is this a Big Mac or a Medium Ralph? What is going on? When I ordered a Big Mac, I expected a Big Mac."

Food for Thought

McDonald's excels in consistency. Everyone knows that a McDonald's menu item in Iowa is the same as the same menu item in a New York McDonald's. That is a cool thing. Customers reward McDonald's for its consistency by going often and in droves.

Wet Floor!

A dish needs to taste the same way it did the last time the customer tried it. Your customer relies on you to consistently hit that flavor. If you decide to change a recipe for an item after it has been on the menu, you need to indicate on your menu that the item has a new flavor.

In every restaurant environment, customers want to know what they are getting, and they expect to get it. If the menu says that the chicken is topped with mushrooms, then, by gum, mushrooms had better be on the chicken when it arrives at the table. The meal needs to look something like the picture on the menu. And if you have multiple restaurants, the items with the same name need to be produced the same way.

You can improve product consistency by using two types of controls:

➤ **Ingredient control:** Every menu item has its own recipe of ingredients with no room for discussion. If you are preparing a chili with green peppers, then yellow or red peppers are not options. Consistency is about even more than just what ingredients to use. It also involves how much of each ingredient is in the recipe. Don't use the terms *dash* or *pinch* in your recipes or the seasoning becomes too subjective. Use exact measurements.

➤ **Portion control:** Every menu item has its own portion guideline. The hamburger combination comes with 6 ounces of french fries and a 22-ounce soda. The lemon chicken dish comes with an 8-ounce chicken breast, a #12 scoop of vegetables, and a side dish of rice. The customer doesn't care about these exact measurements (and does not need to be told them), but because of them, your staff will be able to deliver the same-sized product every time and your customers will appreciate the consistency.

Other factors in product consistency include how the food is cooked (which affects taste) and how the food is presented visually. All of this information (ingredients, portions, visual presentation, and so on) should be clearly spelled out in the food manual you have prepared for the kitchen (see Chapter 14).

Temperature and Time

Many good chefs and cooks get so familiar with their product line over time that they do most of their cooking by sight and by feel, a style known as visual cooking. When the kitchen is pounding out many dozens of meals in a given half-hour time frame, you are going to need people who can do this.

That said, you must write down cooking temperature and time guidelines for each item on the menu. For example, you might write, "Cook for 17 minutes at 400 degrees. Let cool for 7 minutes and serve." These guidelines help prevent the inconsistency that comes with visual cooking and resolve overcooking and undercooking issues. Also, such information is a valuable resource for any staff members who are either new or not familiar with a particular menu item.

Visual Consistency and Appeal

What does the food look like when you serve it? Your products and menu items should be presented in a way that is visually appealing and consistent. Each item or menu selection should have its very own presentation or *plate setup*.

Give your filet mignon and herb-roasted potatoes to the wait staff and the customer in the same way every time. Regular customers with a favorite menu item especially appreciate this consistency.

I have been around food all of my life, and I know what looks good. Though I am no food stylist (one who is paid to make your plate presentation look wonderful), I know that presentation can make a difference. Most of all, consistency is the key.

Wet Floor!

Most foods cook much quicker at higher elevations and drier climates. You must test every item in regards to temperature and time in the restaurant location to ensure consistency. Don't be afraid to be flexible. You may need to adjust your oven temperature up or down 15 degrees to get the result you want.

Recipes Revealed

A **plate setup** is the design of how a product is served.

The Least You Need to Know

➤ Food safety has no margin for error.

➤ Quality is simply taste to the customer, but it is many things, including appearance, safety, and portion size, to the owner of the restaurant.

➤ Developing strict systems is the only way to ensure quality.

➤ Remember that the food that was delivered first should be the first food you use.

➤ Be consistent in food preparation; make all your cheeseburgers look and taste the same.

Chapter 18

Operational Execution, Part 2: Service That Sells

In This Chapter

➤ The difference between service and hospitality

➤ Ten steps to improve speed of service

➤ The importance of accuracy

➤ Service evaluation

➤ The shift quarterback

"Look under the bed."

So said the handwritten note on the bed of my hotel room. I was curious, so I got down on my hands and knees and looked under the bed. There was a piece of paper and another note. It said, "Yes, I clean under here, too! Have a great stay with us." The note was signed "Cathy."

Wow! Now that's service, not to mention ownership of a duty. Service-oriented employees like Cathy own (in their hearts) the responsibility to serve people the best they possibly can.

This chapter describes the service concepts necessary to ensure your restaurant has what it takes to give service above and beyond the call of duty. It covers the difference between the feel of hospitality and the specific tasks of service, explains why speed and accuracy are essential, and details the importance of every encounter with the customer. Finally, this chapter explains why restaurants need a quarterback for each shift.

Service and Hospitality Are Different

Although service is part of hospitality, service and hospitality are two different concepts. As Chapter 16, "Dinner at Your House: Treating Customers Like Guests," explains, hospitality is about building a relationship with the customer and providing a friendly environment. It's more of an attitude that your employees have regardless of whether they are at work.

Service is also an attitude, but it is more of a well-scripted, planned, organized, and systemized encounter. Service is about execution, speed, accuracy, and serving the customer's wants and needs.

Sure, having a hospitality-oriented team is an aspect of service. But a service-oriented team can provide more than just a smile. Service is being able to provide fast and fresh as well as friendly. A service-oriented team with all cylinders hitting is a great machine to watch.

Concept Execution Takes Dedication

Restaurateur Jeff Hayes has been responsible for districts and regions of fast-food franchises, as well as casual-dining restaurants in a corporate environment. He has been in charge of many restaurant concepts, yet his teams have always delivered excellent service.

Tip Jar

Design systems and a service machine, so to speak. Training, zone duties, hiring, and follow-up are all a part of the service machine. And checklists are a key part of the service machine. I have never experienced a well-running restaurant that doesn't use them. In all aspects of the restaurant, including service, use checklists.

After spending years watching Jeff and his teams, I have seen what separates his teams and restaurants from the crowd. Jeff's teams have increasingly higher standards for operational performance. They challenge themselves constantly to improve.

When Jeff Hayes runs a restaurant, he continually comes back to the basics of customer service that got him where he is, and he keeps trying to improve them for his specific concept. And Jeff Hayes always succeeds.

Jeff hires people based on their ability to deliver for the customer. He spends countless hours training and teaching his staff how to improve operations for the customer. Those who cannot provide outstanding service for the customer are no longer on the team. His service success comes down to this one rule: Do it for the customer.

Speed of Service: Move It or Lose It

When most people talk service, they immediately think about speed of service (SOS). America is definitely moving quicker than it was just yesterday. (Sadly, most restaurants are not.) For hunger or schedule reasons or most likely both, people are in a hurry to have their meals.

Regardless of the restaurant's concept, customers want their food as quickly as possible. Sure, in fine-dining places, the customer wants to enjoy the dining experience, but even then, the staff has no reason to do anything but hustle. Seven-course meals take a while to serve, so get it rolling!

To improve speed of service in any restaurant, use these 10 tips:

➤ Teach your staff to hustle at all times. When customers see a team hustling to make things happen, they assume you have a fast speed of service regardless of the actual number of minutes it takes to get their food.

➤ Have well-organized storage and work areas. Speed is difficult to achieve when you can't find the items you need or have to jump over a bunch of boxes just to get to the mop sink.

➤ Periodically use a stopwatch to time your staff completing different tasks. Tasks that are timed tend to be completed more quickly.

➤ Use convenience foods that are already prepared when possible. If you can deliver the same quality product with premade foods and improve speed of service, why wouldn't you give it a go?

➤ Be prepared for the shift and have everything stocked and ready to go (see "The Art of Shift Management" later in this chapter).

➤ Put the aces in their places. Have your best employees working when the peak period is happening. It is much easier to be fast when the task or position is second nature.

➤ Teach the concept that three customers is a line. (Two customers seem to be patient because there is no line. Three customers feel like they are in a line, and the line needs to be moving.) Just because it is not a peak period doesn't mean you should not hustle. Those customers don't like waiting any more than anyone else.

➤ If you have a drive-thru, understand the importance of speed to those customers. Drive-thru customers are telling you, "I am in such a hurry that I am not even willing to get out of my car to get food."

➤ Watch for bottlenecks inside your restaurant. Teach slide deployment (see Chapter 15, "Upfront Effort: Setting Up for Service") and the power of teamwork to ensure any slower spots in your service system go away.

Food for Thought

An understaffed restaurant usually cannot deliver good service. Sadly, most restaurant owners and operators don't realize this fact. The reality is that the more employees you have during your peak period times, the more time the employees have to relax and enjoy the finer points of service. They will have time to interact instead of just react, which in the end will generate more repeat sales. Although this theory can work to a point of diminishing returns, restaurants seldom reach that point.

Food for Thought

Complaints about accuracy in the industry are rampant, and reminding the waiter about your missing side dish seems to get a cursory apology from the waiter at best. Customers never complain about the waiter writing down their orders on a piece of paper.

➤ Be staffed at or above the projected staffing need for the restaurant shift. Employees who are furious because of understaffing are not likely to be fast.

Accuracy Is Right

The wrong food fast (no matter how fast) is just wrong! Your staff may be incredibly friendly, the decor may be wonderful, the food may be excellent, and the price may be right, but if you don't give the customer the right order, none of that will ever matter.

Most mistakes tend to be what I call a brain freeze, although such mistakes have nothing to do with eating ice cream too fast (though the resulting headache can be just as bad). These mistakes are more like, "You put ketchup on my hamburger, and I ordered it without ketchup." Or "You forgot my iced tea." Oops.

To add to the problem, many upscale restaurants are taking the order from the customer without writing it down. This kind of service is quite impressive until something is screwed up.

Accuracy is very important to the customer's perception of quality; it's a big part of the "Is it yummy?" question. So here are five tips to improve accuracy:

➤ Write down the order. If you decide to go without order pads, at least teach your staff to repeat the order back to the customer to ensure accuracy. And be flexible enough to allow your staff to write down particularly difficult orders.

➤ Teach your wait staff to visually verify every item at the *pass station* prior to accepting it for the customer. The wait staff must have high standards for their customers and should be checking for accuracy as well as product quality.

➤ Your employees should repeat the order when they are delivering it to the customer. This repetition allows them one more opportunity to catch their mistakes if they made any and, of course, correct them.

➤ Have a menu that improves accuracy. Huge menus encourage inaccuracy. Smaller menus are easier to execute. If you begin to have accuracy issues, analyze your menu. It may need to be weeded back.

➤ Be staffed at or above the projected need for the restaurant shift. Overworked employees are not usually known for their accuracy.

The Register Relationship

Running the cash register is much more than collecting the check and counting back change. In many restaurants, the register is either the first *customer contact point* (as in fast-food places) or the last customer contact point. Therefore, the cash register is more about a relationship.

Having a cashier who is great with the seven basic characteristics of hospitality listed in Chapter 16 is critical. After all, your restaurant will never get a second chance to make a first impression (or a last impression, for that matter).

Analyzing Service Performance

Customers make up their own minds about your service performance. Thus, if you can figure out what is going on in their heads about your service performance, you can improve your overall performance.

But how do you do that? You can push comment cards in front of customers, and sometimes that is fine. But it can also become quickly irritating for some customers. A better way is to look at the customer's actions. You can also try being a customer yourself to gain a new perspective on your restaurant's service. When you figure out what improvements you need to make, remember to go slowly and be consistent, so you don't make the customer uncomfortable.

Recipes Revealed

The **pass station** is the area where the food gets passed from the back of the house to the front of the house. Often it includes a hot hold on one shelf and a cold hold on another shelf. This station provides a place to set food once the kitchen staff has prepared it and a place for the dining room staff to pick it up.

Recipes Revealed

Customer contact point is the point where the customer and the employee come in contact with each other from a service perspective.

197

Read the Customer

Reading the customer has become a lost art form. In the old days, restaurant employees were taught to read body language, facial expressions, and customer movement. This old restaurant art form is not that difficult to master and can give you an insight into your overall service performance. When you read customers, note the following:

➤ If the majority of the people in the dining room have jackets on while they are dining, they are cold. Turn up the heat.

➤ A closed menu means the customer is ready to order.

➤ If the customers are fanning themselves, the dining area is too warm.

➤ Customers who are slurping through their straws need more beverage.

➤ If customers don't eat much of their meals, they probably didn't like them.

Wet Floor!

You can't judge your employees' service performance by the amount of tips they take in. In modern America, people tip regardless of the service.

Food for Thought

Service is an extended commercial that is a window into your entire business. How impressive are you?

These behaviors are easy to read. You will learn others as you open your eyes and try to get an insight into your customers and hopefully fix any issues before they arise.

The simplest read is this: Happy customers smile and interact with the staff. Unhappy customers do not. (Note: this read also applies to the staff.)

View Service from a Customer's Perspective

Often people only see things from their own perspective. With most things, perception is reality, and this statement especially holds true with customer service. The customers' perception of your service is reality. What you think customers should think doesn't matter. They think for themselves.

To understand how a customer experiences service, try seeing things from your customer's perspective. Don't be afraid to enjoy a meal in your own dining room or have a meal delivered by your staff to your home. Have your staff treat you like any other customer with no shortcuts and no special bells and whistles.

Seeing your products and services from a customer's view will help you understand your customers better. Watch your team and see how they execute on the entire package of service from start to finish. Take notes and teach your team members skills to improve their overall service performance.

Make Service Consistent

Every customer scores your overall service performance, but most don't bother to write down the score on a comment card. Subconsciously, customers rate your place of business in their minds on a plus, minus, or neutral basis. When they leave your restaurant, you either wowed them (which is clearly a plus), ticked them off (which is clearly a minus), or made no lasting impact whatsoever (which is a neutral).

Most restaurant owners understand that consistent minuses will kill a business and a consistent diet of pluses will help build it. What many owners fail to understand is the impact that inconsistent performance has on a customer's evaluation of service. Customers do not like to be surprised and prefer consistent mediocrity over inconsistency of any kind.

Inconsistency makes customers feel uneasy. They never know what to expect. They prefer the steps of constant improvement to the herky-jerky swings of service inconsistency. Your customers would rather see small incremental steps toward improved service instead of Super Bowl service during one visit and poor service the next.

The Art of Shift Management

Shift management is somewhat of a lost art in the restaurant business; few restaurants are any good at it. Yet if you become great at running shifts and can find one or two other people who can become great at running shifts, most of your operational headaches will be gone. The art of shift management can and should be taught if you expect your team to run as a unit.

Shift management is best described as having one quarterback who understands the restaurant concept and how to execute it. Shift management has four key components:

➤ Preparing for the shift

➤ Having a restaurant quarterback

➤ Scoring and analyzing the shift

➤ Following up and finishing off

Tip Jar

A key in the restaurant business is reducing customer defects. This term describes customers who once used your business and then stopped. The reason for this change is usually inconsistent service performance or employee indifference. As a result, the customers defect to another place of business.

Food for Thought

A football coach prepares by watching film of past games, deciding on his starting players, going through his pregame checklist, and building a game plan. A restaurant operator is not much different, except for maybe the film.

Food for Thought

The quarterback and the team should not have anything to worry about during the game (peak period) other than playing the game (operating the restaurant and serving customers) to the best of their abilities. Fans (customers) have paid to see a well-executed game plan (restaurant concept), and the players (staff) need to work hard and stay focused to win (satisfy the customer).

Preparing for the Shift

Being prepared for the shift means being staffed, stocked, organized, and geared up to handle the projected volume of business. Thus, food preparation is completed per the food manual, the dining room and kitchen staffs are in place and ready to go, the napkin dispensers are filled, and so on.

Being prepared means being ready for the peak volume of business an hour before you expect it to hit. If your restaurant begins getting busy at 11:30 A.M., you should review your shift checklist at 10:30 A.M. to ensure you are ready.

Having a Restaurant Quarterback

Similar to the way a quarterback runs the offense in a football game, a person in the restaurant runs the shift. He or she is responsible for everything that happens in the restaurant during that time. This restaurant quarterback determines where the other players are positioned and what routes they run (zone duties, tasks, and so on) and is responsible for each player doing his or her job to the restaurant's standards.

In the NFL, a coach works behind the scenes, and the quarterback leads the show on the field. At game time, the quarterback acts like an extension of the coach. Likewise, the person who is running the shift in the restaurant needs to be an extension of you, the coach. Sometimes the restaurant quarterback is you or the general manager. I for one always prefer to be the quarterback when I am in my restaurants because it allows me another opportunity to train my staff on how to become better at quarterbacking.

A great quarterback is critical to your chances of winning, as is building a quarterback system that fits your individual restaurant. Such a system is paramount to your restaurant's bringing home the championship. A great restaurant quarterback follows these seven commandments:

➤ **The quarterback must never leave the pocket during peak periods.** In other words, keep your butt on the floor during peak revenue periods. Run the restaurant!

➤ **The quarterback must not let linemen wander during the game.** Keep an eye on your team and direct activity.

➤ **Only the quarterback calls plays during the game.** The only thing that should be moving faster than your feet is your mouth. Verbally lead your team to enhance performance.

➤ **Positions should be decided before the game.** Cross-training is great, but when you are in the Super Bowl, have your stars play their best positions.

➤ **The quarterback should lead the team into and out of positions.** PMA rallies (see Chapter 16) are like huddles.

➤ **The quarterback should change the play if things aren't running smoothly.** When the heat is on, great quarterbacks show their greatness. Don't be afraid to make the needed calls on the fly.

➤ **Second-string quarterbacks may be called upon, but not until they know the playbook.** I want my best player leading the show, and my backups can learn the job when time and situations permit.

Scoring and Analyzing the Shift

Knowing whether you have won a football game is easy. The score is right there for all to see. Restaurant scoring is not quite so simple.

Great NFL quarterbacks have extremely high standards. It seems to be a common thread among them. Great restaurant quarterbacks have the same common thread. So create your own high standards, and then score the shift.

Wet Floor!

If any one-on-one discussions need to happen, do them in private. Reprimands have no place in front of everyone.

Score the shift the same way the customer does, with a plus, minus, or neutral rating. Then spend 10 minutes or so making notes about improvement, employees who need more training, or performance that was wonderful. Think of this time as your news conference without the media to figure out what went right and wrong with the shift and what you need to do going forward. Make your notes after every shift and keep them in a log for tracking and training purposes.

Following Up and Finishing Off

When the shift is over, thank the employees who did a great job and give corrective feedback to employees when necessary. Consider having a postshift (three-minute, stand-up) meeting with your team to give a few broad comments and hand out a game ball or two for a job well done.

Then begin to clean up the restaurant and get it back to where it was before the shift started. All shifts should begin and end with the restaurant looking clean, organized, stocked, and ready for the next shift's business.

The Least You Need to Know

➤ Service is more than just a smile. It is execution, speed, accuracy, and fulfillment of the customer's wants and needs.

➤ If your employees hustle in front of customers, you will be perceived as having fast service.

➤ Read customer body language to figure out what the customer wants. For example, a customer who is closing the menu is ready to order.

➤ Customers judge your restaurant as plus, minus, or neutral, and neutral means they think nothing of you.

➤ One person needs to be in charge of each shift to make service run smoothly.

Chapter 19

Clean Is Your Only Choice

In This Chapter

➤ Why having a clean restaurant is your only choice

➤ Which areas need the most attention

➤ Why you should have at least one clean freak on staff

➤ How maintenance affects cleanliness

➤ Why you need to be diligent

In golf, you do not just drive to a course, take your clubs out of the trunk, and begin swinging on the first tee without first paying some form of greens fees. If you did, even the nicest of course managers would become disgruntled with you. You must pay your greens fees if you want to play the game. Cleanliness in a restaurant is like greens fees on a golf course. It is the price to play. You must clean your restaurant and work to keep it that way if you expect anyone to come back for a second or third round.

This chapter is about keeping your restaurant clean. It covers the many important areas to keep clean, from the look of your menu to your high-traffic areas to your bathrooms. It also teaches the value of a clean-as-you-go philosophy and explains how to impart a cleaning mentality to your team. So pay your greens fees. Only then do you have the opportunity to play this course and win sales. And if you play well, the restaurant game is a lot of fun.

How Important Is Cleanliness?

Many market research companies have done surveys and found, virtually without exception, that the cleanliness of a restaurant is one of the top criteria customers use to choose where to eat. Now, paying your greens fees on the golf course or in the restaurant business does not guarantee you will score well (build sales growth), but at the very least it does give you the opportunity to play.

Obviously, your kitchen needs to be clean, and a great chef or restaurateur wouldn't have it any other way. But customers don't see the kitchen, and they analyze restaurant cleanliness based on what they do see, mostly in *high-impression areas*. They also make a lot of assumptions. They assume that if what they see looks bad, what they can't see probably looks worse.

To a customer, a restaurant can never be too clean. The only thing a customer notices is not clean enough. That's right, you are either acceptable or unacceptable. If you don't know how important cleanliness is, ask your customers. I dare you. They will probably look at you like you have lost your mind. Your restaurant is a place people come to eat, so cleanliness is very important.

Keep in mind that having a wonderfully clean restaurant does not drive sales growth, although it doesn't hurt. But having a restaurant that is not acceptable drives away sales.

Recipes Revealed

A **high-impression area** is a place that customers frequently see. In these areas, a high number (maybe all) of your customers will get their impression about your restaurant's cleanliness.

Food for Thought

Your restaurant exterior is your first calling card to any potential customer.

Lot, Landscaping, and Exterior Image

Restaurants lose sales all the time before a customer ever comes into the parking lot. If hungry drivers are turned off by your unmowed lawn, the jungle of weeds, the chipped paint, the broken lot lights, the burnt-out signage, and the garbage dump that is called a parking lot, they will never pull in at all. If you can't get them to pull in and get out of their cars, they will never get a chance to try your wonderful menu.

Door Glass and Entrance Area

Okay, so you got the customers out of their cars, but now they are walking through your front door. Is your door glass clean?

The door should also be free from cracks, scratches, and BB gun holes. Also, it shouldn't have any taped-up fliers, memos, help wanted signs, or any other generally tacky pieces of garb. Also watch the entrance area for mud being carried in from outside and dirty carpets or throw rugs. Carpets or throw rugs are fine, but keep them clean.

Finally, watch for cigarette butts and gum being disposed in this area. A scheduled cleaning as well as an eyes-open approach is best.

Floors

A dirty floor tends to get noticed by everyone except your staff. I am not saying this to slam the employees by any means. Your employees are familiar with the restaurant so they tend to look up and out. In contrast, customers, who are not so familiar with your restaurant, tend to look straight down toward their feet. When they do look down, you want them to be looking at your perfectly clean floors. By the way, don't forget to clean your floorboards, too.

Tables and Chairs

We have all been seated at a table that was either not clean or was getting the cursory wipedown while we were sitting there. Yuk!

Keep the tables and chairs clean. You should use one sponge or towel to wipe off the tabletops and a totally different-looking one for the seats of chairs. Using different towels seems more sanitary to the customer.

Menu Boards and Menus

All eyes are riveted on your menu, or at least you hope they are. Dirty menus and dirty menu boards do not increase the customer's appetite. All menus and menu boards should be wiped down before every shift to ensure they are clean at all times. By the way, an old and tattered menu or an unlit or burnt-out menu board, no matter how clean, seems dirty and should be replaced or fixed.

You spend a ton of money to get customers to look at your menu. Make sure that they do not need to wipe off ketchup stains or deal with sticky soda spills just to place an order.

Wet Floor!

If you put up a bulletin board or allow posting of any signage, you may cause a bottleneck in your entranceway. Keep this area free flowing. This area is an entrance or an exit, and that's all.

Tip Jar

Don't forget to check the undersides of the tables and chairs for gum left behind. For some reason, people think these are great places to dispose of gum. I think they learned it in school. You must clean up after them because the next customer will not think that the strawberry gum stuck to the underside of the table is a great free dessert.

Restrooms

Restrooms are critical to any restaurant's overall cleanliness picture. Customers can be brutal to any restaurant that has unacceptable restrooms, and I don't blame them. Your restaurant's restroom is not a gas station toilet along the interstate, nor is it your great-great-grandfather's outhouse. Restrooms should be checked dozens of times throughout the day.

Don't waste the time or the effort on the little signs on the back of the door with the neat little checklist that records the last time the restroom was checked by an employee. Most of the time checklist isn't updated, and no one particularly cares when the restroom was checked. Customers just want to count on the restroom meeting these expectations:

➤ Clean

➤ Well lit

➤ Free from graffiti and debris

➤ Free from odor

➤ Stocked

Remember that your customers put the restroom through this test every time they visit.

Tip Jar

Remind your staff members not to touch the top 2 inches of any glass and use the penny tip to help them keep fingerprints away from the drinking area. The penny tip is to ask them to imagine a penny on their serving tray. Tell them to pick up all glasses as if they were placing their pinky on the penny to hold it so it can't move. The pinky on the tray keeps fingerprints away from the drinking area of the glasses.

Eating and Drinking Utensils

Every restaurant has someone return a truly dirty knife or fork once in a while. You can't completely avoid that situation unless you have a fast-food restaurant with individually wrapped utensils. However, water spots or mishandling of utensils are bigger issues than the occasional dirty knife because they make the customer think the utensils are dirty. And in the restaurant business, customer perception is reality.

Teach your employees to look carefully at all eating utensils when they are preparing to either wrap them or place them in the clean utensil storage bin. Also, teach your staff to store utensils properly (face down or handle up) and to not touch the working end after the utensils are washed.

Employee Health, Sanitation, and Image

Dirty, ill, and unkempt employees work in dirty, ill, and unkempt restaurants. Clean uniforms, clean-cut appearance, and clean hands send the message that the employees have pride in themselves, as well as their restaurant. Such an appearance also gives customers the confidence in your restaurant that you dearly want them to have.

Get your employees to wash their hands many, many times throughout every shift. Teach them to keep their hands away from their hair, nose, and eyes and tell them that each violation of this rule results in another thorough hand washing. Finally, be sure to follow your local health department's guidelines for all cleanliness and sanitation procedures.

Find a Clean Freak

Every restaurant needs to have clean freaks, folks who just can't stand it if the place is dirty or disorganized. Yes, it's nice if the clean freak is you, but not all restaurant owners or operators are clean freaks. If you aren't one, hire a clean freak to make sure the place is clean and organized. I have even suggested to clients on many occasions to hire a cleanliness manager. The owner or operator just wasn't strong in this area, so we hired someone who was.

Ultimately, the goal is for the restaurant to get and stay cleaner. So analyze yourself. If you are a clean freak, fine. If not, hire one because it is difficult to create one.

Sure, you would like to think that the parents of all your employees taught them how to clean and organize their own rooms and toys when they were about three. But here they are at 16, 36, or 106, and these basic skills are often lacking. You can help, of course, with tight checklists, systems, and follow-up, but it can be a constant uphill climb. Nevertheless, finding a clean freak or two and letting them follow-up on everyone else should be the help you need in pursuing this climb.

Clean as You Go

If you see something dirty, clean it. This rule is referred to as clean as you go (CAYG), and it is a key to improving restaurant cleanliness. If you don't let messes pile up, messes won't pile up. When employees and the owner follow this philosophy, the restaurant is much cleaner. The rule is simple. If you see any kind of mess (whether you made it or not), clean it up.

Messes do get left from time to time. But cleaning as you go helps take care of any such overflow mess. This rule means that you clean up after yourself and any others who forgot to clean up after themselves as you go about your other duties.

Tip Jar

Sick employees should stay home.

Spring Cleaning

I remember when Grandma did her yearly spring cleaning. She would take every-thing off the shelves, paint the walls, varnish the floors, plant flowers, and basically tear the place totally apart and put it back together. I remember it vividly. On those days, her philosophy was simple. If you were sitting around, she would put you to work. Spring cleaning was not a day or two. It was more like half the month of May.

I use this concept in my restaurants. (Grandma played a big part in my success.) Every year my team and I attack the new summer business by taking the restaurant apart and then putting it back together. To share a wonderful quote from Grandma, "If God didn't in-tend for you to do spring cleaning, what did he in-vent elbow grease for?"

Tip Jar

End all business days by putting the restaurant back in the same or better shape than it was in when you opened. Start every day with a clean and well-organized restaurant. This strategy prevents the place from declin-ing over time.

The Little Things Make a Big Difference

When I was a young man just coming up through the ranks in the business, I always heard the saying, "If you've got time to lean, you've got time to clean." No matter how modern the restaurant business gets with equipment and newfangled menus and con-cepts, the old-school ways of running the business still apply.

The little tasks make the difference between okay and great. So keep your team busy with 10-minute tasks (usually cleaning or maintenance tasks). Assign each employee two or three of these tasks per shift and train them to complete these tasks when their core re-sponsibility of serving customers is caught up or if they have a minute or two with no customer traffic.

Wet Floor!

Use checklists for cleanliness. If you don't use them and follow-up on them daily, you will not have a clean restaurant.

Keep in mind that your restaurant is unlikely to have so many customers that your employees will be busy from the moment they walk in the door until the mo-ment they clock out and go home. The restaurant business just doesn't work that way. Your restaurant will have slow times, even dead times. Count on these times and give employees a few 10-minute tasks to keep them productive (remember, they are still getting paid) and help keep your restaurant clean and organized.

Managing Maintenance Impacts Cleanliness

If something is broken and still around, the customer perceives it as ugly and dirty. And customer perception is reality in the restaurant business.

The customer usually lumps upkeep and cleanliness into the same pile. Normally, if a restaurant is broken down with all kinds of maintenance issues, it is also dirty. I have seen lots of restaurants in my career, and I can't point out more than two or three exceptions to this rule. Broken really does seem to equal dirty.

Thus maintenance plays a significant role in the overall perception your customers have about the cleanliness of your restaurant. Broken-down equipment, heating and cooling systems problems, cracked glass and mirrors, overgrown or long-gone landscaping, wobbly tables and chairs, and dripping faucets all send a poor message to your customer about the upkeep of your establishment.

Pest Control and Maintenance

Pest control is a monthly (and even sometimes weekly) maintenance task for all restaurants. Even if your restaurant doesn't have pests (as far as you know), you can't afford to risk getting them. You are running a business that deals with a lot of food storage and food preparation, and one missed spraying of your favorite ant killer can turn ugly quickly.

For a very reasonable cost you can contract a pest control company to take care of this responsibility for you, and in fact, in some states having a professional company come do this is a legal requirement. Check with your local health departments to see what is required.

Even if it is legal to do it yourself, be a do-it-yourselfer with other things and let the professionals take care of the pests.

Never Give Up, Never Ever Give Up

Is your BMW scratched? If you owned one, would you allow it to be scratched? No? Most likely you would. Think about it. People stop noticing little nicks and scratches on their new cars quite quickly, even if the new car is a beautiful, sporty BMW that they have been dreaming about forever.

When people first buy the new car, they swear in the mirror that they will keep it spotless, but then time goes on. In short order, they stop washing and waxing it on the weekends. Then, they stop noticing blemishes. After all, the car is there day after day.

This story also holds true for new restaurants. Restaurant owners always start out with the best intentions. To begin with, they are very focused on keeping the place spotless and making sure all fixtures and equipment are in good working order and well maintained.

Tip Jar

Buy some basic tools and learn how to fix as much of your own equipment and facilities as possible. In time you will pick up some valuable skills, and based on the hourly rates of most service vendors, you'll be glad you did.

But time moves forward as it always does, and life happens. Things break, and messes occur. Such things happen every day, every week, and each year. The owner's focus shifts. Then, before long, the restaurant becomes a mess.

Winners stay away from complacency. They know to look at the business from the perspective of a new customer. They also realize that daily, weekly, and monthly preventive maintenance schedules and calendars are crucial.

We all know how important first impressions are. A first-impression approach to cleanliness is the only way to keep the highest standards. If you think about the first impression of a potential customer for life, your restaurant will always look brand new.

The Least You Need to Know

➤ If your restaurant is not clean, you will not stay in business. Cleanliness is nonnegotiable to the customer.

➤ Customers notice when your restaurant is not clean enough.

➤ Focus on a few key areas when you clean, including the exterior, bathrooms, tables, chairs, menus, utensils, and employees.

➤ Teach your employees to clean as they go.

➤ Don't leave broken equipment around for customers to see. Fix it or get rid of it.

➤ Check often for pests.

Part 5

Now What?
Growing and Optimizing

Your restaurant business is your dream come true, but this is no dream: You are really in business. As such, you may want to follow this quaint bit of philosophy that all entrepreneurs discover (either the hard way or the easy way): Profit is good.

This final part is about creating growth in your people, your sales, and ultimately, your profits. In this part, you learn the things to consider when you are thinking of opening a second restaurant or even a chain. Finally, this part provides examples of the forms that you need to run your restaurant.

Chapter 20

Retaining the People You Have

In This Chapter

➤ Why retention starts with you

➤ How to build loyalty

➤ Why the first 21 days are especially important

➤ How to train and develop your team

➤ How to give feedback

➤ Why your decision-making ability is a key to retention

The restaurant business is full of horror stories: "We can't find people." Or "No one wants to work anymore." Or "The people these days are so lazy." And "They just don't like being asked to work hard." Some owners say, "The restaurant business is too tough on them." And others offer, "The hours are too long." Yada, yada, yada.

Can't keep employees? Let me be direct. The solution to this problem is easy to find. Just look in the mirror.

This chapter is about how to avoid the greatest plague upon the restaurant business: employee turnover. In it, you learn how to build employee loyalty, why the first three weeks of employment are critical, why your people always need to keep learning, and how to build the self-esteem of your staff.

Do These People Like You?

Let me spend 10 minutes with each member of your team, and I will accurately predict your restaurant's future. If they care, I'll know. And if they think you care, I'll really know. No, I am not Nostradamus. I am a restaurant guy, and I know what I am looking for in the eyes and hearts of employees of the restaurants that I expect to succeed.

So what would I find out in that short 10 minutes? I would find out, from your employees, whether you understand the concept of getting things accomplished through other people. This concept is the most valuable asset any restaurant owner or operator can have. It is leadership, but it is also followership, friendship, and riding on the same ship (teamwork).

That's right, you will not succeed alone. Yet you alone can make success happen by motivating others to work with you and for you. You need people on your side who are not just paid employees but humans who care about you and your business.

Where Turnover Originates

If you don't fix your problems with employee turnover, the problem will turn nasty. It will affect every aspect of your restaurant from sales, to operations, to customer loyalty, and finally to profitability.

Think about loyalty. The question to ask is: How loyal are your employees? Businesspeople often talk of customer loyalty. Employee loyalty, though, is rarely discussed. Yet employee loyalty separates those owners who survive from those people who were restaurant owners.

Loyal employees speak well of your restaurant. They invite friends and family to dine, and they become veteran employees who have been doing their jobs at a very high level of performance for a long time. They love their jobs.

So how do you get employees to love their jobs? First, you must love your job. Then the key to getting employees to love their jobs is to never stop training new employees, even when they become old employees. Certainly, training new employees can be time consuming, as well as expensive, yet it is a good way to set a foundation. Also, if you build employee loyalty in the employees you have, thus increasing their tenure, you need fewer new employees.

Food for Thought

Customers love employees who love their jobs.

Beyond training, you can increase employee loyalty in five main ways:

➤ **Pay employees well.** Pay them at or above what the market will bear (see Chapter 9, "Whoever Gets the Best People Wins: It's a

People Game"). In addition, quarterly wage reviews are essential. You must continue to improve their compensation level.

➤ **Invest in employees.** Investing in employees may include providing them quality benefits, career opportunities and growth, training and development, bonus opportunities, and especially your personal time.

➤ **Care for and love employees.** Get to know who they are as people. Spend quality time talking with them, and not just about work. Build a relationship. If they like cats and dogs, you should know that. Also, you should know the names and activities of every one of their kids. But don't do it because you should. Do it because you care.

➤ **Learn why employees earn.** Why do they need the money? If you clearly understand that, you will more clearly understand what motivates them to come to work.

➤ **Put people on pedestals.** Make them feel good about themselves. If you make people feel low, they will act lowly. If you make them feel like they belong and are special, they will do special things.

Wet Floor!

Be sincere. Some employees can see right through you if you are only pretending to care, especially if you say one thing and do something else.

When the Boss Gets Fired

"You're fired!" As the owner or boss, when is the next time you expect to hear that? Probably never, right? You're the boss; you can't be fired, right? Wrong!

The last time one of your employees quit on you (not when they moved 500 miles away to another city, but got ticked off and left or found a job for 15 cents more per hour across the block), you were fired. It may have sounded like "I quit" or "I'm out of here," but it smelled of being fired. The boss being fired, that is. You were fired and maybe you deserved it. At least consider the possibility.

If you are a bad boss (and you are a boss, so deal with it), employees will get sick of you. For a while, maybe a month or so, you may fool them into thinking you are on their side. But if you are not, they will figure it out. They always figure it out. Some employees will see through you and will fire you as their boss by quitting their jobs.

Tip Jar

If you want to find out why people are leaving your company, ask them. Conduct exit interviews with every employee who leaves your company voluntarily. Those who leave will freely tell you the issues of your restaurant because they already quit. Learn from these ex-employees and move on.

As long as you are still in business, you can learn from your mistakes. An "I quit" means something has gone wrong. So learn what you can do better and grow from the experience.

The First Twenty-One Days Are Critical

A critical time for any employee is the first 21 days. Most people feel uncomfortable the first few days of any new job. They are not trained yet. They don't know their co-workers. They don't know where the bathrooms are. The workplace is not yet their home.

I have done surveys for many restaurant chains with high turnover, and the results were overwhelming. In those chains, approximately 80 percent (8 out of 10) of the employees who quit the job in the first year did so in the first 21 days. So, in these chains, if management could find a way to get the employees past the first 21 days, they would significantly reduce the odds of losing the employees in the first year.

Orientation as an Introduction

The orientation should be scheduled as the first activity of the first day of employment. It is critical to getting off to a great start.

Orientation is an employee's first real impression of you. Employees pick up some preliminary thoughts about you and your restaurant in their interviews, but they were nervous. They wanted the job and weren't spending too much time evaluating you and what you do. During orientation, they will get to know you. That's the point of orientation.

The orientation is like the first date (interviews are more like blind dates) and should be very personalized (preferably one on one) to the employee. If you show a video, sit with the employee while he or she watches it. Even if you have seen the same video 217 times, watch it again. Orientation is not about you. It's about being there for the new employee.

You should have an orientation checklist that lists each step of the orientation from opening hellos to closing good-byes. Your orientation process should include the following:

➤ A bit about you personally

➤ A brief history of the company

➤ A tour of the restaurant

➤ Introductions of the new employee to your current staff

Tip Jar

Orientation should be scheduled at a time when the restaurant will not be too busy with customers and in an out-of-the-way place where you won't be interrupted too often.

➤ An explanation of benefits, rules, regulations, and expectations

➤ Scheduling and payroll guidelines and processes

➤ Filling out the required forms in the employee personnel file

A good orientation should be one to two hours in length and should provide a wonderful opportunity for the employee to ask questions and for both you and the new employee to get to know each other better.

Training for Jobs Well Done

Training in the restaurant business is essential to ensure that employees know how to deliver your products and services per your hospitality, quality, service, and cleanliness standards and guidelines. Training is also imperative to ensure that cash is handled properly, accounting and marketing are done to your standards, and virtually every other one of the hundreds of tasks are effectively completed. If you intend to build a *learning organiza-tion,* training is an important component for the overall feel of the organization.

Training is about tasks. It occurs when one person instructs another on the steps to completing a given task. The training process itself usually involves a series of steps as well:

1. The trainer shows the trainee how to do the task.

2. The trainer tells the trainee how to do the task.

3. The trainer gives the trainee a chance to practice the task.

4. The trainer follows up with the employee to ensure compliance.

5. The trainer gives the trainee some feedback on how to improve performance on the task.

6. The trainee practices some more.

7. The trainer follows up again and provides more feedback on possibly how to improve.

Tip Jar

Contact Restaurant Operations Institute at www.r oiontheweb.com or call 205-323-5559 and request an orientation CD from The Train-n-Retain CD Series. This CD will train the employee on a variety of critical responsibilities, test them to ensure they were listening and that they retained the information, and store the information for future use if and when necessary. This product is guaranteed to train your employees and reduce your liability as a business owner.

Recipes Revealed

A **learning organization** is one where learning, growing, teaching, mentoring, and continued improvement and education are valued.

8. Practice and follow-up continue until the trainee is an expert at the task and is dosed with an ample but reasonable supply of rewards and recognition for a job well done.

For some busy owners, such a series of steps is a pipe dream. But in theory, something similar to this series of steps is the objective of training. It is tactical and systematic and is repeated frequently. Such training is not a pipe dream in great restaurants; it is mandatory.

Some Different Types of Training

Peak performance begins with superior training, and a good mix of the following three types of training provide an ample opportunity for the employees to enhance their skills:

➤ **Individualized training:** This one-on-one training sometimes takes place while the trainee and trainer are sitting down in the dining room; other times it involves watching a training video. Most times, however, this training happens on the floor while both the trainee and trainer are working.

➤ **Group training:** This training is more of the sit-down variety, but it may also happen in a quick rally-type format. It is great for team building, increasing morale, and doing a lot of training in the shortest amount of time. This type of training happens a lot just prior to opening a restaurant or even in the mornings and nights when you are not open for business.

➤ **Cross-training:** This is the concept of training your employees on more than one or two given positions or tasks. For example, you might teach a hostess how to run the register. Cross-training is critical for you and the employee. It gives you more scheduling options when you are building a schedule. It also provides better slide deployment of staff for improved customer service. From an employee's perspective, it keeps the job more fun and interesting. People love to learn new things.

The Role of Development

Everybody wants to improve his or her life. Development allows you to help your employees do just that.

Development is giving back to your team. It is about developing better soft skills, such as communication, leadership, people skills, and listening. It is classes and seminars that are often outside the realm of the job. It is about building your learning organization culture and providing a value-added payment to your employees beyond their paycheck.

Development is not mandatory. But it will show your employees that you care about improving their lives, and they will love you for it.

Simplified Leadership

If you expect your people to follow your lead, you must lead. Sure, everybody talks about leadership. Many books have been written on the subject, but it isn't complicated. When you are a leader, you ...

➤ Get people around you to do what they are asked to do.

➤ Do what you commit to do.

There you have it. If you can be great at these two things, you will be a leader.

How do you do these two things effectively?

➤ Improve how you give both corrective and positive feedback in order to get people to do what you want.

➤ Improve your decision-making, so you can do what you commit to.

Giving Corrective Feedback

Corrective feedback is giving the employee tips to help improve performance. These tips are given (hopefully) many dozens of times throughout the day. This corrective feedback is critical to achieving a lower turnover. Sounds weird, doesn't it? But it's true.

Your employees want to clearly understand what they need to do to improve. They want to know well before you get angry for their poor performance. They certainly don't want a customer or another employee to become hostile. Good employees want to learn and want to know what they are doing wrong.

Giving corrective feedback is easy to do. Sadly, managers often avoid giving it, causing frustration for the boss and the employees. Keep in mind that you do not need to give corrective feedback in private. (*Reprimands*, on the other hand, should be handled in private.) Corrective feedback is really

Food for Thought

Development is something you do for your people to enrich their lives just because.

Recipes Revealed

A **reprimand** is a serious disciplinary discussion regarding a particular performance issue. Reprimands are usually done behind closed doors (or away from others, such as while out on a parking lot walk with the employee).

an extension of training and can and frequently should be done right out in the open.

Making Decisions That Stick

Your decisions must be well thought-out and clear, not impulsive or wishy-washy. Employees do not like bosses who can't make a decision. Employees also do not like bosses who can't stick to the decisions they make.

To improve your decision-making, try these tips:

➤ Get ideas and input from your staff before you make a big decision. This tactic not only allows the team to say their piece, but it also provides good idea generation and gives you confidence in the decision you choose.

➤ Use your brain to think and your heart to tell you what feels right. Combining the two always makes for better decisions.

➤ Write down the pros and the cons of a decision on a sheet of paper. It's easier to determine which way to go when you can see it in writing.

➤ Try to make fewer decisions, but be better with the ones you do make. Five good decisions are better than 50 poor ones.

➤ If you make a decision, stick with it until it is absolutely clear that it is the wrong decision. Only then should you change your mind. You must give your decisions a chance at being right. Changing your mind every other day is tough on everyone involved.

Wet Floor!

Two of the bigger complaints from employees on employee surveys I conduct for client companies are the following:

➤ The management never tells us what is going on. They just expect us to read their minds.

➤ The management does not ask for our opinions and could care less about what we have to say.

Both of these points are communication issues: not speaking and not listening. With a concerted effort, both can easily be fixed.

When Discipline Is Necessary

Reprimands or disciplinary discussions are brought on by poor performance or the lack of improvement in a certain area after repeated corrective feedback. Employees get to the point where performance on a given item or task is insufficient or below standard for three reasons:

➤ **Lack of training:** If an employee (for one reason or another) hasn't been trained to properly do the job, it is your responsibility to pick up the training ball and ensure the employee knows how to do the task properly.

➤ **Lack of talent:** After training, the employee still doesn't have the ability to do the job. He or she may never be able to do it. This business just isn't for everybody.

➤ **Lack of desire:** The employee just doesn't care enough to either learn the job or do the job. In my restaurants, these employees lose their jobs.

Talk to the employee to find out which one of the three reasons applies to him or her. Once you have determined that, it becomes quite easy to build a plan of action on how you are going to help the employee get the appropriate training, improve upon his or her performance, or find a new job.

Positive Feedback

Positive feedback comes in many forms, such as pay increases, bonuses, paid days off, simple thank-yous, pats on the back, a nice card to express gratitude, and so on. Everyone wants to believe that they are great at giving positive feedback, but it just isn't so. Most people stink at it. We all have our moments when we get too busy, and we forget. It happens to the best of us.

You must recognize great performance. Teach yourself to say something positive about the performance of individuals on your staff many times throughout the day. Don't be afraid to tell your employees "Great job!" or "That looks nice." Pile on the sincere praise. Remember, recognizing great performance increases the chance that it will be repeated.

Your employees work hard, and the great ones deserve to be recognized. If you don't do it, a successful restaurant owner will.

Wet Floor!

If you don't shoot the turkeys (fire bad employees), you will have increased turnover. Good employees don't want to work with the turkeys, and they know who these turkeys are, just like you do. Keep your bad employees on the payroll, and you will forever need to find more people.

Tip Jar

Contests are a great way for you to remember to reward superstar performance. I suggest you make contests easy to track and short. A daily contest on suggestive selling and a weekly contest on comment card performance are two great ways to improve customer satisfaction and sales as well as keep the employees motivated. They will also help you remember to reward great performance.

The Least You Need to Know

➤ If you love your job, you will be easier to work for than if you are miserable.

➤ Pay people fairly. Everyone notices money.

➤ If people quit, find out why. You may learn a lot about your restaurant and yourself if you listen to ex-employees.

➤ Spend the time to train people properly, and then be sure they always get corrective feedback when necessary and positive feedback when possible. Lots of positive feedback is good.

➤ If you make a decision, stick with it unless you are sure the decision was wrong. Employees hate working for someone who is always changing his or her mind.

Chapter 21

Sales

The Art and Science of Sales Building

<hr>

In This Chapter

➤ Understanding the competitive nature of the business

➤ Motivating employees to focus on sales

➤ Recognizing the importance of hospitality, quality, service, and cleanliness

➤ Using various techniques to increase sales

➤ Raising menu prices

<hr>

You are selling many things in your restaurant, from service to quality to your decor, but at the end of the meal, it turns out, you are selling food and drinks. The more you sell, the more money you can pay your staff, and the more money you can keep. Selling is good.

Increasing sales is almost a prerequisite to building profits. (You can build profits by cutting costs, too, but you can't save much on costs unless you are already terribly inefficient.) And how do you increase sales? In Chapter 13, "Restaurant Marketing 101," you learned that there are only three ways to increase sales:

➤ Increase the frequency of visits of your current customers

➤ Increase the check average of your current customers

➤ Find and entice new customers to use the services of your restaurant

This chapter covers some specifics on how to do these three things. Although you can build sales in only three ways, the different strategies, concepts, and plans on how to make one of these ways happen are numerous. In this chapter, you learn how to focus on sales, what you can do to build sales, and when to consider price increases. If you spend quality time with this chapter, you soon will be spending more quality time with your banker making deposits.

Competition Lives

An old story tells the tale of two joggers in the woods who come across some bear tracks. One jogger comments on the tracks and then picks up the pace. The other jogger says if the bear comes after them, they will never outrun it. The other jogger goes a little faster and yells back, "I don't have to outrun the bear. I only have to outrun you."

This story makes the point that we are all in competition, and the restaurant business is no exception. Only so much food fits in each person's stomach at a time. And although some customers will just happen to walk through your door, others will consider you and all the competition before making a decision.

Yet some restaurants pretend the competition doesn't exist. The three most common reasons for restaurants not competing for sales are ...

Food for Thought

You are in business, so you are competing. You are competing for customers, sales, market share, employees, and advertising space.

➤ Not understanding the fact that they are competing for sales in the first place. If you are in business of any kind, especially the restaurant business, you are competing. Let the bear eat the restaurant owner across the street.

➤ Not knowing with whom they are competing. Your competition is on every corner. Target these restaurants and play hardball.

➤ Not knowing how to play the game. With every day that passes, you should learn more inside tips of the trade, and your restaurant skills should improve. Ask for advice and seek out mentors.

Manage It Up, Not Down

You build sales by having a viable restaurant concept, excellent people, extraordinary operational execution, and a systematic approach to following your tactical and strategic plans. Add in some fun and exciting marketing concepts, and you will build sales even more. And sales are good.

Think how much easier everything becomes with sales growth. Yet most restaurant owners and managers talk about controlling costs 10 times more than they talk about building sales. In some cases, owners almost never talk of sales growth.

Hitting some theoretical food cost or labor cost becomes a higher priority to some restaurant managers than building sales. This situation is called managing the business down (by controlling costs) versus building the business up (by driving sales). Managing down makes no sense in the restaurant business.

Sure, controlling costs is very important (and is discussed in detail in Chapter 22, "A Restaurant Named Profit: Hitting the Numbers"), but not at the expense of growing sales. That is too high of a price to pay.

The Crucial Roles of Hospitality, Quality, Service, and Cleanliness

If you are executing poorly on hospitality, quality, service, and cleanliness (HQSC), you may as well forget about building sales. HQSC have been, are, and will continue to be the lifeblood of the business. All restaurants must achieve a decent level of HQSC regardless of category, segment, sales volume, or company size.

HQSC will not go in and out like many fads. They will not be replaced by technology. They can't be bought with huge marketing budgets. They cannot be forgotten about, and they will not just go away. They are here to stay.

A high level of HQSC is what differentiates between a good operator and a bad one. The level of HQSC is the determining factor in customer satisfaction and customer angst, and it is the critical component for a repeat and loyal customer. If you and your team learn how to deliver HQSC at a high level, you can count on having customers.

To Build Sales, Focus on Sales

More sales make nearly all your restaurant ills go away. Yet many owner/operators do not spend the necessary time discussing how to build sales. Do the following six things to help put more focus on sales:

➤ Talk about sales at every employee meeting.

➤ Deliver operational excellence. Great HQSC will result in happy customers that return to your restaurant.

➤ Keep track of sales in every way possible: hourly, daily, weekly, monthly, quarterly, and

Food for Thought

Focusing on the basics of any business is the only way to succeed. The recent collapse of all the dotcom darlings is proof that ignoring the basics of business will kill you. HQSC are the basics of the restaurant business.

yearly. Also, track the check average and customer counts. People tend to improve upon things they keep track of (and keep score of).

➤ Stay hungry for sales. You can never have enough sales.

➤ Reward your employees for positively affecting sales with contests, contests, and more contests. And don't base a contest on something that doesn't affect sales.

➤ Have the employees help set sales goals and then keep them informed at all times about your sales and how you are doing versus your goals. There is no benefit to keeping these numbers a secret.

Do these things to help your team focus and you will get more sales. And sales are good.

Ideas for Increasing Sales

Each idea for increasing sales clearly falls into one or more of the following three ways of improving sales that were mentioned earlier in the chapter:

➤ Generating new trial

➤ Increasing frequency

➤ Increasing check average

Recipes Revealed

An **LTO** is a limited time offer. This new product or menu item is intended to drive new customer trial or higher customer frequency. It also gives you an opportunity to bring in a new item. Depending upon the customer traffic for that item, you may decide to make it a permanent item or a seasonal item (like a pumpkin pie only during the fall) or delete it all together.

The following sections describe a handful of ideas of the hundreds available to get you started increasing sales. You will be able to come up with many others on your own.

Generating New Trial

Generating new trial is about gaining new customers and then providing such wonderful HQSC for them that you retain them for future visits. The following list gives you eight ways to increase new customer trial:

➤ Try deep discounts, such as buying one dinner and getting a second one half off or free, to draw in new customers. The object of these discounts is to entice customers who you aren't currently coming to your restaurant.

➤ Offer *LTO* products to catch the eye of a potential customer who hasn't used you before.

➤ Supply free food for a local event (soccer matches, T-ball games, and so on) to introduce new customers to your menu.

➤ Celebrate something. Grand reopenings, mini-celebrations, radio remotes, and so on bring in new trial customers.

➤ Contact bus tour drivers and tell them you will give them a week's worth of free meals for every time they stop in with a load of people.

➤ Use mass media, such as television, radio, billboards, and newspaper inserts, to attract new customers.

➤ Work to break the habits of those potential customers who don't know your restaurant. Try direct mailing people who are clearly frequenting someplace more convenient based on where they live. Draw them out of that habit and into making your place a new habit.

➤ Provide top-notch HQSC at a fair price. This alone will get you new customers through word-of-mouth advertising.

Increasing Frequency

Increasing customer frequency is about getting your current customers to dine in your establishment more often. The best way to increase customer frequency is to give the customer outstanding HQSC at a fair price.

Customer frequency is based on whether the customer is impressed with your restaurant. If customers are impressed, you will probably see them again. If they are not impressed, you can forget about them.

Sure, an LTO will draw them in more often, as will an expanded menu with enough variety to make each meal occasion something different. But ultimately customer frequency comes down to operations. If you are good, customers will be back. If you are great, they'll be back and maybe bring new trial customers with them.

Tip Jar

Focus your sales growth strategy by day-parts. Every day-part (breakfast, lunch, dinner, even snack time) needs to have its very own strategy and a team that is passionate about building sales. Keep track of which team is improving which day-part the most. If the lunch day-part team is up 14 percent in sales versus last year, and the breakfast day-part is down 8 percent versus last year, you need to analyze and then come up with a strategy to fix it.

Increasing Check Average

Increasing the check average is about getting your average cost per customer visit to increase without having the customer feeling overcharged or taken advantage of. The idea is to increase the amount of money per visit without having the customer lower their number of visits.

The following list gives you five ways to increase your check average:

➤ Have a quality dessert menu with three or four selections. People love sweets.

➤ Teach your staff the concept of suggestive selling. The key to this kind of selling is to just ask. (See "Suggestive Selling Campaigns" later in this chapter.)

➤ Put add-on items in a visually appealing and high-traffic area. Place desserts, specialty coffees, wines, and so on in prominent places in the restaurant to drive the customer impulse to buy it.

➤ Put higher priced menu items in more prominent places on your menu or menu board. High visibility tends to draw more sales.

➤ Do not discount items inside the restaurant or in the drive-thru. The customer is already in line and willing to pay full price, so discounting now would be flushing away income. Use discounting to draw in new customers, not to reduce the prices for customers you already have.

Suggestive Selling Campaigns

Yes, suggestive selling does work and will increase sales. Keep these important points in mind when you encourage your staff to use suggestive selling:

➤ Teach your staff that not everyone is going to say "Yes." In fact, 80 to 90 percent of the people will say, "No thank you," which is perfectly fine.

➤ Don't waste the customer's time suggestive selling three or four different things during a given meal visit. Customers can handle only one attempt before getting annoyed.

➤ In fast-food restaurants, forget about suggestive selling when there is a long line and pound out speed.

➤ Don't suggest the same thing every time to every customer. Teach your employees to continue to serve the customer by suggesting things that the customer may need to complete his meal. Suggestive selling (if done properly) is another aspect of service and hospitality. It is not about getting the extra dollar of sales, it is about making the customer have even a more filling and well-rounded meal.

Tip Jar

Hire great salespeople who are outgoing and personable. These people make great salespeople for your restaurant as well as your menu.

Price Increase Decisions

Chapter 3, " Choosing Your Restaurant," gives some quality tips on how to determine the pricing of your menu. But once your restaurant is a going concern, you must consider some other aspects of menu pricing as well.

Every restaurant must raise prices from time to time. Inflation, which drives up the costs of products, services, utilities, and taxes, and increased wages and the expense of employee benefits mean that you have to raise prices to make the same amount of profit. Even when rising costs aren't an issue, a price increase can be a good business decision.

The question then becomes when should you raise prices and how much should you raise them by? The best time to raise prices is when economic changes that affect prices become news. If the Federal Reserve announces an increase in interest rates, the produce growers announce some big crop loss, the papers announce a minimum wage increase, and fishermen are reporting a shortage of red snapper, you should consider raising prices. Don't wait until you absolutely have to raise prices—react with the news.

Increasing prices at the same time as your competitors is prudent as well. After all, you are not doing all those pricing surveys (discussed in Chapter 3) for your health, are you? No, you are doing them to see what the competition is charging and what the market will bear.

If you notice, when the price of gas goes up 3¢ at one gas station, every gas station for blocks around raises its prices 3¢ as well. Restaurants more or less follow this same pattern. If five fast-food restaurants are located in a given area and three of them raise prices on french fries, the other two restaurants should at least seriously consider following suit. The market in that given area bears a bit more, and if you can justify a small price increase, now is the time to do it.

Tip Jar

Customers are more understanding of price raises during times when the restaurant business is being negatively affected by economic changes. Adding 10¢ to their favorite chicken sandwich isn't be a big deal to them when they know that the poultry supply has declined. They will be mad at the big news event, not you.

Wet Floor!

Be careful not to blindly follow suit with other restaurants' pricing changes. Pricing changes are serious business and must be thoroughly analyzed from all angles before any change is made. You do not want to overprice your products and services to where the customer decides to find someplace else to go or not to go out to eat at all.

How much should your price increase be? I have always found it easiest to take menu price increases in smaller (hopefully less noticeable) increments. I suggest you limit the size of your price increases between 2 and 5 percent.

You make as few price increases throughout the year as possible. Price increases can be a stressful change for both the customer and the employee, so keep the number of changes to a minimum.

Think about the following considerations when you are deciding new prices for your menu items:

➤ **Go with 9.** Price items at $2.99 instead of $3.00 or 89¢ instead of 90¢. Prices ending in 9 seem so much cheaper to the customer.

➤ **Think carefully before breaking certain pricing barriers.** Every 50¢ is a serious barrier to consider. Moving from 49¢ to 50¢ and 99¢ to $1 are big deals in the customers' minds. Avoid breaking these barriers if at all possible. If I have a hamburger that sells for $3.49, I am very cautious to move its price above that $3.50 barrier unless I really must.

➤ **Get the few cents.** If you have something priced at $2.91, you might as well move it to $2.99 because the customer won't care. You have not passed the 50¢ or $1 barrier, and they tend not to respond at all to this kind of an increase. The same is true of the $5.85 and the $5.89 price points. You may as well go with the $5.89 price and get the few cents extra.

Food for Thought

Menu bundling provides convenience and value for the customer and operational ease of execution for the restaurant. The value meal at your favorite fast-food place is an example of menu bundling as is a meal that includes salad and a side dish at a casual-dining restaurant. Customers like to order the whole meal package with one easy-to-understand price point. The restaurant operator should like this as well.

Restaurant Sales Growth: What Does It Say?

Many restaurants do not experience sales growth and continue to stay in business with flat sales (approximately the same amount of sales from one year to the next). Others even stay in business, at least for a while, with slowly declining sales (this situation turns into a slow death).

But sales growth is important even if you have good sales. In the end, any restaurant that continues to increase sales from one year to the next can be quite proud of that accomplishment. The customer base is telling you that they love what you do and how you do it. Being wanted by the customers is a great feeling, and continued sales growth is the ultimate compliment. What does sales growth say? It says: Good job!

The Least You Need to Know

➤ You are competing, so get in the game.

➤ Building sales has even more rewards than controlling costs.

➤ Focusing on hospitality, quality, service, and cleanliness (HQSC) will bring in sales through word-of-mouth advertising.

➤ If you must raise prices, do it when economic news seems to indicate that higher prices are a necessity.

➤ Sales growth means you are doing a good job.

Chapter 22

A Restaurant Named Profit: Hit the Numbers

In This Chapter

➤ Increasing profit with sales

➤ Cutting costs without cutting sales

➤ Keeping an eye on food and labor costs

➤ Saving money with checklists

➤ Considering additional expenses

Profit happens when your income (sales) exceeds your outgo (expenses). The more your income exceeds your outgo, the more profitable your restaurant will be. Profit is cash you keep, unless you invest it. Profit is how you get rich. Profit is good.

Obviously, if you can increase your sales and decrease your expenses, you will positively impact your profitability. But doing that is not as simple as it sounds because sales and expenses are interrelated. In this chapter, you learn why cutting costs at all costs could end up costing you customers. You also learn why the two key areas to watch are food and labor costs and why knowing the difference between being frugal and being cheap is so important.

Beware the Dumb Decision

Sometimes, a penny saved is a dollar lost. I know this first hand as a customer (well, former customer) of a major hotel chain. I used to stay at this particular hotel for meetings on all my visits to Chicago, and I spent a good $400 a night there because I liked the dining facility and meeting rooms. To me, it was worth the exorbitant price. For a while, I had received, in exchange, exorbitant service.

Then one night in 2001, I arrived from out of town and realized that I forgot to bring my toothbrush and toothpaste. So I called the desk and asked for my complimentary toothbrush and toothpaste, like you do. "I am sorry, sir," said the hotel operator, "but we stopped that service a few months ago because too many people were taking advantage of it. It was costing us too much money."

The front desk person insisted that the hotel must charge me $2 for the toothbrush and toothpaste. This charge came after I already paid the hotel $400 for the night and after I had already spent $400 a night many times in this same hotel. Yet the hotel needed my $2. Needed it, couldn't live without it. But now they do without me as a customer. When I go to Chicago, I always stay somewhere else.

Do the math: The hotel charged me $1.15 for the toothbrush and 85¢ for the toothpaste, but lost me as a customer. I was a customer who paid more than $400 per night for a room and stayed on average three to five days per month. And I consistently spent money in their overpriced restaurant.

Interestingly enough, this company has figured out a way to charge for virtually everything. Nothing is complimentary any longer. In a recent newspaper interview, the management called it "trimming the fat." The fat that got trimmed was the concept of having, keeping, and satisfying customers.

Wet Floor!

Pushing employees to reduce food costs or become more productive to reduce labor costs is a fine goal that can backfire if overdone. Sometimes, after constantly hearing these goals, employees decide it becomes more important to satisfy the need for profit than it is to provide great service. Soon, the place has fewer customers—resulting in better food costs and labor costs but fewer profits.

Controlling costs is important, but when it becomes more important than serving customers and increasing sales, you are starting down a very slippery-lope.

The Sales Coin Has Two Sides

Treating customers well is an essential part of restaurant sales, and garnering sales is the only way to succeed. However, you need to be able to treat people well and garner sales without negatively impacting profits in order to be successful.

Anyone can quickly realize increased sales. Begin selling your extra-large pizza with unlimited toppings for $2 and you will sell thousands of them. And though your sales will be at record high levels, you will be dead broke in no time flat. The pizza, you see, costs you significantly more to produce than what you are charging for it.

In the restaurant business, you must operate the front of the house (in the customer view) as if you have invited a friend over for dinner and you simply want to serve them to the best of your ability without any concern for profitability. This kind of atmosphere builds sales. Behind the scenes, you are controlling expenses and making decisions like Ma Bell (without cutting off any phone service). This strategy reduces expenses.

The trick is to not let your cost-cutting measures affect the customer. Anyone can pinch pennies and reduce expenses. And if you do, you will look profitable for a short amount of time. But when customers realize that you are charging them for a glass of water or adding 15¢ onto their bills for each pat of butter (both of which I have seen), they will think they are being cheated and may never come back.

Balancing a need to cut expenses with a need to increase sales is the only way to profitability. Customers come to your restaurant mainly for your hospitality, quality, service, and cleanliness (HQSC). In the end, cutting costs alone will not increase profits because you need to build an honest customer base to get sales. And you build sales honestly with HQSC. It is the only way. When you are done looking at all the numbers, you will see that profits always begin with sales.

The Consistent Path to Profit

Making a profit is the most basic objective of any restaurant, yet so many restaurant owners seem unable to figure out what it takes to make profitability consistently happen. That's right, you must *make* profitability happen if you expect to consistently achieve it.

Food for Thought

Building a profitable business of any kind (especially a restaurant) takes an unwavering commitment to building sales and controlling costs. Building sales is like having a great offense; controlling costs is like having a great defense. Having one of these elements is quite easy, but you need to be good at both if you expect to be profitable.

Tip Jar

Everyone who decides to start a restaurant dreams of the money he or she is going to make. And many people do make money at restaurants. But if you think you won't have to work at making money, you are doing more than dreaming. You are hallucinating. Building a profitable restaurant takes a lot of hard work, commitment, and dedication.

If you consistently build sales and consistently control expenses, you will become consistently profitable. Always giving customers great HQSC at a fair price plus never wasting money on things that don't improve the customer experience equals consistent profit. And profit is good.

Controlling the Big Two Costs

In the restaurant business, food and labor costs are called the Big Two because they account for more than half of a restaurant's expenses. Somewhere between 50 and 65 percent of restaurant sales go to paying for these two costs of doing business. If you control these two expenses, your restaurant has a chance to be profitable. If you do not, you can forget about it.

Recipes Revealed

A **menu mix** is the number of units and the percentage of sales volume each menu item represents in a given week. This percentage is calculated by determining the number of each menu item sold in a typical week, such as 868 cheeseburgers, 1,411 hamburgers, and 1,911 medium colas. Then multiply that number by the menu price and divide that number by the total sales. If you sold 868 cheeseburgers at $3.99 each, then cheeseburgers would account for $3,463.32 in sales. If you did $15,000 in sales in the week, then cheeseburgers would account for 23.1 percent of your menu mix ($3,463.32 divided by $15,000 equals 23.1 percent).

Controlling Food Cost

Food cost percentage is an important number. Figuring out this number and ways to alter it is slightly complex, but it is essential knowledge to have if you want to run a restaurant successfully.

What Food Cost Percentage Should I Run?

Each restaurant runs a slightly different food cost percentage. Most restaurants shoot for a food cost percentage between 25 and 32 percent depending on the menu, the service style, and the menu prices. Some concepts run much lower, and some run much higher, but this range is a typical.

If you are selling a meal for $8.95 and you know the ingredients necessary to produce this meal cost $2.41, you can easily figure out your food cost percentage. Pull out your calculator, divide $2.41 by $8.95, hit the percentage key, and you find that this meal costs out at 26.9 percent. (This calculation is referred to as costing out a menu item.) In essence, it's that item's individual food cost percentage.

So what should your overall food cost percentage run? It depends on what you sell. Take the time to cost out every item on your menu. Yes, even a simple 22-ounce glass of iced tea. It's good to know which things have a low food cost percentage (like iced tea) and which things do not (like many entrée items). Every item will have a very different food cost percentage.

Each restaurant also has a different overall food cost percentage every week. No, I'm not kidding. Your weekly *menu mix* will determine what your food cost percentage targets for that week should be.

If you know what the item costs to produce (by costing it out) and you know how many of them you produce in a typical week (by the menu mix), you can clearly determine the impact that menu item will play in your overall *theoretical food cost* picture.

Take your theoretical food cost and add in what is commonly called a *waste factor*. Traditionally, a .5 percent to a 1.5 percent waste factor is added. If you calculate your theoretical food cost to be 27.7 percent, your goal is to run an overall food cost between 28.2 and 29.2 percent.

The gap between the two different waste factor sums (28.2 percent and 29.2 percent in this example) is called your targeted cost of food (TCOF), a number which also includes beverage costs. In this scenario, if you run below 28.2 percent, your staff may be underportioning your menu (not putting the amount of ingredients in the meal that the food manual calls for). If you run above 29.2 percent, the staff may be overportioning, or there may be excessive waste, excessive spoilage, or theft.

How Do I Know What Food Cost Percentage I Am Running?

To figure out you food cost percentages for the week, you need to start with your restaurant's amount of food usage, which Chapter 12, "Purchasing: It's More Than Buying a Can of Corn," explained how to calculate. The following equations provide a quickie refresher on how to calculate this number. Note that you have to convert food amounts to their corresponding dollar amounts.

> Beginning inventory dollars + Purchase dollars for the week = Available food dollars

> Available food dollars – Current inventory dollars = Amount of food dollars used for the week

Recipes Revealed

A **theoretical food cost** is the total food cost you should run based on your menu mix and the food cost for each item. It does not take into account waste, theft, or spoilage and is an ideal number that gives you an overall food cost dollar amount and percentage you should have achieved.

Recipes Revealed

A **waste factor** is added to give the operator room to account for a small amount of necessary waste. This factor takes into account that some products will exceed hold time and need to be thrown away and a small amount of spoilage and mistakes will occur. No one is perfect.

Pull out your calculator. Enter amount of food used for the week (in dollars) divided by sales for the week, and then hit your percentage key. There you have your percentage for the actual cost of food (ACOF) for the week.

Let's plug in some numbers to help clear up any questions about calculating your food cost percentage. Suppose your food inventory was worth $3,415 and you ordered an additional $7,575 worth of food. To determine the dollar amount of available food on hand for the week, you would add the two amounts to get $10,990. After the week is over, you have $2,876 in food left, which means the restaurant used $8,114 worth of food. The sales for the week totaled $28,432, which means your actual cost of food (food usage divided by sales) was 28.538 percent (rounded off to 28.5 percent).

Food for Thought

In this age of high-tech sales volumes, menu mixes, food costing out, and theoretical and actual food costs can all be calculated with the simple push of a button. Such calculations can and do continue to be done by hand, but if you can, I recommend you purchase a point of sale (POS) system. There are many choices on the market with many different bells and whistles. A quality POS system is more than your cash register. Sure, it does that, but it also stores important information about your sales trends, menu and inventory usage, and much, much more. This tool gives you instant access to all the data you need to help find problems and devise quick solutions. A top of the line POS system can cost many thousands of dollars but will clearly save you 2 to 4 percent in food cost, reduce your theft concerns, and increase your sales opportunities. And this estimate may be a bit conservative.

So what do you do with the ACOF after you calculate it? You compare it with the TCOF to see how you're doing. If your targeted cost of food (TCOF) was 28.2 to 29.2 percent and your actual cost of food (ACOF) was 28.5 percent, you would celebrate because you hit your target. Great work!

But the ACOF is not always that simple. Many operations miss hitting their target on a continual basis. When you miss the target, you need to put systems in place (or commit to using the systems you already have) to fix the problem. Remember the ordering systems outlined in Chapter 12? How about the food manual and kitchen checklists covered in Chapter 14, "Get It Right on the Back End: The Back of the

House," or the food systems in Chapter 17, "Operational Execution, Part 1: Quality"? Go back and reread those chapters or just get back into the basic systems.

These percentages and systems may be boring, but they are absolutely effective. In the restaurant business, successful operations are full of checklists and systems.

How Else Can I Improve My Food Cost?

Running good food cost numbers is all about purchasing effectively (see Chapter 12), implementing systems, and training staff to use those systems (see all of this book). There is no other silver bullet, so to speak. But you can do plenty of things to improve your food cost. As you spend more time in the restaurant industry, you will begin to come up with many ideas on your own in this area, but here are a few tips to get you started:

➤ Randomly weigh products after they have been produced to check whether the item matches the serving weight it's supposed to have (according to the food manual). By randomly checking a product's weight (after the kitchen has made it, but before the wait staff has served it), you will know if your staff is overportioning or underportioning.

➤ Keep all high-cost items in storage areas that are high visibility and even high security. I have seen restaurant owners put certain items (alcohol, meats and cheeses, seafood) in locked storage areas. This kind of system is fine as long as it does not hurt the flow of your employees when they are trying to produce menu items.

➤ Track waste very closely. Use a waste chart and have your employees write down every food item they throw away. All restaurants have a certain amount of waste, which is normal. But if you track it, you control three things: excessive waste, not enough waste (remember, you must always think about product quality), and theft.

➤ Periodically dig in your trash once in a while. Make sure some of your staff members see you because a lot of internal theft happens by throwing things like 15-pound whole hams into the trash bin and then pulling them out of the outside Dumpster after the restaurant closes. If staff members know that you know about that possibility, they will probably reconsider stealing the food.

➤ Do daily or midweek inventory and food cost calculations. This calculating takes some extra time and effort, but if you are having food cost problems, it may be worth it. Do it the same way as the weekly calculations except you only use sales numbers, inventory numbers, and purchase amounts for the days you are calculating.

Hitting Labor Cost

To run a restaurant effectively and efficiently, you need to have the right number of people working at the right time. This mix is determined by one of the most important tasks that any restaurant operator has to do: create the schedule.

In Chapter 9, "Whoever Gets the Best People Wins: It's a People Game," you developed an effective and efficient schedule by using your ideal staffing needs. You also learned the concepts of stair-stepping, determining positions, paying folks fairly, and many more critical components about the whole people and scheduling game. But what about hitting labor cost? What is that all about?

A schedule is designed so you can operate the restaurant per the concepts, objectives, and standards. Labor cost objectives are about keeping people productive and controlling costs. All restaurant operators walk this fine line between concept execution and hitting labor cost objectives. The successful ones figure out this balance; the nonsuccessful ones usually don't.

Determine What You Need for Your Concept

Operational execution is what drives customer satisfaction. Customer satisfaction is what drives sales, and sales are the most important factor to improving profits. With that said, you first need to make the concept run right. Then, and only then, can you try to find ways to improve your restaurant's labor costs.

Most of the time I see restaurants start out by determining what their labor cost percentage needs to be (typically 15 to 25 percent of sales, not counting taxes and benefits) rather than what the concept execution calls for in the way of labor hours. That's right, many owners tend to staff their restaurants based on what they want to pay, not on what the service they claim to offer requires.

This comment may seem obvious, but I'll say it anyway: You have to make money before you can save money. Yet many restaurant owners try to save money before they make it.

Tip Jar

Think about making money before you think about saving it.

If your restaurant is running like you want it to with great HQSC (the customers will love you for it) and your employees are staying busy and your labor cost percentage runs at 24 percent, that cost percentage becomes your starting point for trying to find ways to improve labor costs. The two key points are that you have great HQSC and busy employees. These points cover your high standards and your need for staying profitable. When these two points are covered, you have come up with a labor cost starting point.

Work from Your Starting Point

The place is running well, and your employees are staying busy. Now is the time to drive productivity and efficiency and make the place print money, so to speak. Controlling labor cost from your starting point is one more major way to increase your profits.

Analyze every shift for places to improve systems. Enhance employee training and productivity, and think about where technology can help with systems improvements. Even look at outsourcing certain tasks to reduce the cost of in-house employees working on projects that are not related to service (such as landscaping). However, don't make any moves that will lower your HQSC standards.

There are technology options for virtually everything. The big boys in the industry are always pushing for more technology-driven systems, and that is good for all of us. The big company pays the tab, and the rest of us still get to purchase the items that help us run our businesses.

Some things worth looking at are POS Systems (as I mentioned earlier in "How Do I Know What Food Cost Percentage I Am Running?" in this chapter), "smart" soda dispensers that pour the exact amount of liquid with a simple push of a button, condiment dispensers that do the same thing, speed of service tracking devices, "smart" holding ovens to ensure consistent temperatures and digital temperature tracking and much, much more. Of course, technology can help with your training and retaining of employees immensely through the use of prepackaged books, tapes, and CDs.

If your labor cost starting point was 24 percent and you make some improvements to allow you to reduce your labor cost to 23 percent, you have made a good solid mark on your bottom line without affecting the customers. Nice work!

Beyond the Big Two: Control Other Spending

Plenty of other things cost a restaurant operator a significant amount of money, but they become important only after you have controlled food and labor costs. The key to controlling these expenses is to be frugal rather than cheap. Frugal is getting

Tip Jar

Some of the other big ongoing expenses in the restaurant business are utility costs, repair and maintenance expenses, and paper supplies. Use these tips to help control these costs:

➤ Use an equipment turn-on and turn-off schedule (provided by most utility companies) to ensure that you are controlling utility expenses.

➤ Lease equipment instead of buying it to reduce repair and maintenance expense. Also, learn to fix your own stuff.

➤ Put napkins, towels, bags, plastic forks, and other utensils in dispensers. This action reduces waste dramatically.

the quality of products or services you need at the most competitive price available (see Chapter 12). Being cheap is lowering your standards from a product quality perspective to pay a few cents less for the item. All effective and efficient restaurants must be frugal and avoid being cheap.

You will need to buy everything from paper supplies to cleaning supplies and from office supplies to forks. Whenever you buy something, buy it with this goal in mind: Buy it for the best price you can get. Remember to be frugal rather than cheap and then get back to the business of running your restaurant because the couple at table 5 needs an iced tea refill and a slice of your cherry cobbler.

Making your restaurant profitable takes extreme focus (often on that couple at table 5). But the focus you need to succeed always begins with HQSC. Treat people well. Then you can focus on the following:

➤ Build sales

➤ Control food and labor costs

➤ Worry about the cost of other items

Remember that profit always starts with sales. And did I mention that profit is good?

The Least You Need to Know

➤ Sometimes a penny saved is a dollar lost. Be careful not to cut service while cutting expenses.

➤ Sales are necessary, but don't give things away. You need profit.

➤ The only way to build sales is to deliver a good product with HQSC.

➤ Food and labor are your major costs, but always think HQSC first. Then measure, measure, and measure some more.

➤ If all your employees are busy, you have the right number working.

➤ Be frugal, not cheap. First find what you want, and then pay the lowest price possible.

Chapter 23

Double Your Pleasure

In This Chapter

➤ Why you should be thankful for choices

➤ What you should consider before expanding your restaurant

➤ How a start-up evolves into a chain

➤ What kind of energy and commitment you need

➤ Which way to go: market penetration or market saturation

You travel through the restaurant forest, and after finding success, you discover this amazing place where the path diverges. Down one path is staying put with your one restaurant. Down the other is the path of growth. No matter which path you take, you know you have the focus that will lead to success. Of course, your success with one restaurant has led you to imagine the increased burden of another restaurant. You know about the hard work and planning that is necessary to succeed. But thinking about growth sure is fun.

You know how to do it once. Can you do it twice? The path diverges: contentment on one side, expansion on the other. If you are content, that is one perfectly fine vision. And yet the path less taken beckons. Do you dream the big dream?

Life and the restaurant business are full of choices. This chapter is about the choices of the successful restaurant operator. In it, I help you decide your path and then, if you choose, prepare for opening your next restaurant. I also explain the different ways that you can expand your restaurant business. In short order, you can be opening another new restaurant and maybe even a few more. Remember, every restaurant concept you see, including every one of the big players, had to start as one restaurant. Now it may be your turn.

Crossroads

Should you be content with one restaurant? Should you expand? Or should you get out? Those are your options, and if you are successful, you may find yourself at a crossroads. So what do you want to do with your restaurant business?

Even staying with one restaurant doesn't necessarily mean your business will stay exactly the same. This business changes daily, and the key is to respond to these changes in such a way that you can continue to stay ahead of the competition without losing sight of your core concept.

Expansion

You never know if the formula that worked so well the first time around can be duplicated a second time. When you consider expanding your restaurant company, you need to ask yourself these questions:

➤ Should you? This is a much more important question than it seems. When I ask successful restaurateurs this question, I usually get, "Well, why wouldn't I?" I think you need to go back to checking inside yourself for what your motivation is behind this decision. Once you have answered that, you can begin to determine if this is something you should or shouldn't do.

Food for Thought

If you have been doing well at this restaurant game, you get to make the choice of what to do with the business. Take great comfort in that. If the business were failing, the choice would be made for you.

➤ Would you like to? This is a solid question to ask yourself to help you answer the "Should you?" question. It's a great dream, but are you truly excited about doing it again and building your restaurant dream even bigger, or is it more of an ego thing for you? Remember early on in this book we told you it was imperative that you knew what it was that made you passionate about this dream. Now it's time to reassess those thoughts.

➤ Can you? Sure you can—or can you? Think this one through, too. It's going to take more money, more effort, more people, and more focus. You need to have your ducks in a row like never before.

➤ Where? Where to expand is also a critical question to answer. Do you stay close to home or do you drop one of your restaurants in your favorite vacation spot half a country away? When you make this decision, make it based on what is right for the business opportunity.

➤ How? There are quite a few ways to build restaurant companies, but I must tell you, I have never been one to believe that building one successful restaurant was a trend or a track record. I advise people to keep things simple and basic for a while yet. Build your second restaurant, then your third, before you get too wild and crazy about acquisitions, unique points of distribution, and franchising. Then, maybe we can look at our more broad-based options.

Or what about getting out of the business altogether? The concept is up and running, and maybe taking a nice check and sitting on the beach contemplating life for a few months is more up your alley. Plenty of people will pay a pretty penny for a successful restaurant concept that has shown a winning formula.

You need to decide what you want. And once you do, make it happen.

Thinking It Through

Expanding a restaurant company takes an extreme amount of skill, hard work, and patience. The patience requirement may throw you a bit if you're hoping to open another restaurant right away, but going too fast can be a big mistake. Sure, plenty of restaurant companies have grown very quickly and have had no troubles. However, many others grew before they were ready and are now sitting in the restaurant graveyard because of it.

Take the necessary time to analyze your situation and determine the best course of action. You never know for sure what the right thing to do is until you analyze. You may decide that one well-running, highly profitable restaurant is fine for now. Or you may think things through and decide that growing fast is the best way to reach your goals.

Don't rush into the decision. A few extra weeks of thinking things through won't be detrimental to your growth either way. Relax. Enjoy your situation. You have a great restaurant that is operationally sound and well staffed with a highly trained team. Plus you are growing sales and controlling expenses and putting a fair share of profits in your pocket. Right? You'd better be!

Some Things to Consider

Chapter 2, "Everybody Eats: The State of the Industry," listed the main reasons why so many restaurants fail:

➤ Lack of knowledge

➤ Lack of planning

➤ Poor execution

➤ Lack of funding

Restaurant companies that expand beyond one restaurant still must worry about those four items, and they have a few more to worry about as well:

➤ **Staffing:** Recruiting, hiring, training, and retaining the right people becomes a much bigger priority and concern the bigger your chain becomes. You also must focus on setting and maintaining staffing levels. Try being short staffed when you are only one person and you have more than one place to be. It gets ugly real quick.

➤ **Concept consistency:** This issue is critical to a chain. Each restaurant in a chain needs to have the same concept execution.

➤ **The daily vision:** Daily calls, weekly meetings, development and training classes, memos, and so on keep the vision for the restaurant in everyone's mind. Because you can't run every detail of every restaurant, you need to rely on others. Painting your vision of the restaurant concept for them is crucial.

➤ **Consistent results:** Financial, operational, and sales growth results in each restaurant must be managed, maintained, and increased individually while reaching the goals of the chain.

The Evolutionary Process

There is an evolution (a growth process) that must take place if you expect to be successful in making your single restaurant into a multiple restaurant company. In fact, every time you add another restaurant this evolution happens again. Yes, every time—whether going from one to two restaurants or from eighteen to nineteen restaurants.

Missing any one of the steps in this process could be the end of your beautiful restaurant dream. Certainly, many of these things are very important whether you run one or one hundred restaurants. But many restaurant owners fail to properly evaluate where they stand in these critical categories. That's when opening a second restaurant becomes the end of their beautiful dream. The basics of restaurant growth are as follows:

➤ A well-conceived and tactically planned-out concept and new restaurant plan. Sure, you can copy from the original, but each new restaurant is going to be a little different.

➤ Strong people led by solid training sitting on the bench, so to speak, in your current restaurant(s), so you can funnel them to your new restaurant so you aren't starting from scratch.

➤ Strong operations and unwavering systems execution. This is important with one restaurant, but it becomes life and death with multiple restaurants. The easy to duplicate systems are necessary when you are managing multiple sites.

➤ Good-looking, well-maintained facilities (remodel the existing restaurant if necessary). Again, if something breaks and you're there to fix it, then you're in good shape. But when you are operating multiple restaurants, they will be maintained by others.

➤ Positive word of mouth regarding HQSC (hospitality, quality, service, and cleanliness) and restaurant concept. If people aren't saying nice things about your first restaurant, they will be doubly unimpressed with your second.

➤ Effective and efficient advertising. The cost of advertising becomes significantly more expensive when you start adding restaurants to your stable. Make sure your advertising works before trying to duplicate it.

➤ Consistent sales building. Increased sales is the customers' way of telling you they love you and they probably want more of you. I have witnessed many restaurants opening a second and even an 86th site when existing sales are in deep decline. First, increase sales in your existing restaurants and then begin building new locations.

➤ Solid financial controls. Any poor financial controls will be magnified many, many times over if you open a second and third restaurant. You must ensure that you are in clear control of every number before moving forward with growth.

When these basics are in place, you can make changes:

➤ Consider adding day-parts and menu items

➤ Consider opening a second restaurant

➤ Either saturate the market you are in or penetrate a new market with more restaurants

➤ Be systematic in every new opening and be sure not to negatively impact your restaurant concept

Wet Floor!

Why do second restaurants fail?

➤ The first restaurant is treated with too much priority. You can't lose focus on your first restaurant, but the new one is also important. Or else why did you open it?

➤ Standards are lowered for the second restaurant. When success seems easy, some owners slack off and let someone else take care of meeting standards. Empowerment is great at the right time, but this is not the right time.

Then ride the momentum:

➤ Continue to increase advertising

➤ Learn to execute in your new restaurants

➤ Continue with more market saturation or penetration by continuing to add new restaurants

➤ Continue to increase advertising

➤ Do more of the same. This is not the point to worry about too much of a good thing. Go back to the top of this list and repeat.

What It Takes

Expanding is never easy. It takes the same amount of diligence with each restaurant to get it all right, because if you remember from restaurant number one, there is a lot to get right.

But expansion takes even more of your talent:

➤ **More organization:** You now have one restaurant serving customers every day that still needs your expertise to operate properly and another restaurant in its infancy that needs to be coddled from the moment you begin putting it together. You better be good at time management.

➤ **More systems:** Your systems in your first restaurant may be good, but with two restaurants, they need to be great. Having two restaurants means that you have little time to track down a systems breakdown, so you need to have systems in place and allow no room for slippage.

Tip Jar

The time management required to run different restaurants is similar to that required to raise two kids of different ages. They both need you for different reasons.

➤ **More energy:** Take your vitamins, find time to work out, and eat healthy. The energy it will take to run two restaurants is significantly more than what it takes to run one. Now is not the time to get run down and ill. Stay healthy. It's critical.

You opened one restaurant successfully, and now you are remembering all of the fun and wonderful things that have happened along the way. For some reason, the memory of all of the trials and tribulations has faded. I guess winning sometimes does that to us. But try to recall the hills and the valleys. Doing so is critical to your continued success.

Opening a second restaurant will not be easy. It never is. But if you do it properly and at the right time, two can be twice as nice.

Penetration Versus Saturation

Have you decided to open up restaurant number two in a new city or have you decided to stay close to home and build another restaurant in your current city? Either way is reasonable and acceptable. The choice depends on your restaurant concept and objectives.

If you are building fast-food restaurants, you will probably want to go for *market saturation*. Putting 15 fast-food restaurants in 15 different cities is not wise unless you are opening these restaurants in smaller towns, communities, and suburbs. Even then, keeping close in proximity to the market you are already in is preferable to jumping on a plane everytime you want to go check out one of your restaurants.

On the other hand, having two of the same fine-dining restaurants in the same city is not very common. Therefore new *market penetration* becomes more viable and reasonable.

Recipes Revealed

Market saturation is the concept of building your restaurants in closer proximity within the same city, county, or region to each other, so you gain customer recognition of your concept. With market saturation you may never become as big nationally as Taco Bell, but you can become as big (or bigger) than Taco Bell in your little part of the world.

Concepts for Quicker Growth

There are a lot of different ways to expand a restaurant company more quickly than opening one new restaurant at a time. Building one successful restaurant is not a trend or a track record. If you are successful, keep it simple and basic for a while. Don't risk losing your entire jackpot by being overly aggressive. Nevertheless, consider the following options for longer-term growth:

➤ Acquiring existing restaurants

➤ Building points of distribution

➤ Becoming a franchise system

➤ Merging with another restaurant company

Growth Through Acquisitions

Purchase restaurants that are already going concerns. Sometimes new owners purchase these restaurants and keep them as their current concept; other times they are changed into the concept that the new owner wants to spread. He or she buys an existing restaurant in order to convert it to his or her concept and penetrate the market more quickly.

Growth Through Points of Distribution

Find more places to distribute your food. Selling your menu items in convenience stores, grocery stores, school lunch programs, and more are all ways to add points of distribution.

Larger national chains are selling their salsa, taco shells, desserts, seasonings, and sauces on grocery store shelves across the country. Even smaller restaurants are getting into the act by selling their pizzas to convenience stores—and then the convenience store sells it to their customers by the slice.

There are many options to this growth through points of distribution game, but remember the importance that product quality and image plays in the consumer's mind. If your product does not maintain the same quality and consistency in the new point of distribution, don't do it.

If your products are good, show this potential to a business owner, and he will see how to profit from serving your products. The real challenge is in finding someone who will be as focused on maintaining product quality as you are.

Be prudent, play it safe, and pick people you can trust with your product.

Growth Through Franchising

Take your show on the road and sell franchise rights to others to copy your formula for success. Many restaurant companies every year join these ranks. But many try before they are ready and others start well before the potential franchisees are interested in it.

Yes, becoming a franchisor is a wonderful dream and has an immense amount of upside potential, if you do it right. If you do it wrong, however, it can destroy a perfectly good business.

You cannot just sell franchise rights to your restaurant concept. It has become highly regulated and protected. Franchising restaurants costs a ton of time and money in legal fees and marketing costs, not to mention operational manual design and publication.

I suggest contacting a company that is an expert in franchising to walk you through every step of this process and make sure you have a reputable lawyer who has ton of restaurant franchising experience. Franchising can be a minefield if you do not have an expert who has walked this trail many times before.

If the restaurant is growing sales, growing profits, and has a loyal following of customers, and people are routinely asking you if they can look into purchasing a franchise from you, then you should consider it. But proceed with caution.

Your dream of getting wealthy is sitting right in front of you. Take your time and do it right.

Growth Through Merger

Create a partnership by joining forces with a separate restaurant chain to help each company grow.

Restaurants merge for a variety of reasons. If you have a restaurant that has great breakfast and lunch sales, but no dinner concept, and someone else has a nice dinner concept with not much for lunch or breakfast, you may have a merger match. Sometimes restaurants merge similar and competing concepts to save on overhead expenses. Sometimes the two companies merge to make it look friendly to the customers and the employees, but in reality one of the companies acquired the other one and it was decided for PR reasons to tell the world it was a merger.

These types of transactions should not be attempted alone and you need to rely on a reputable attorney to walk you through the merger processes. No two mergers are alike and therefore rules of thumb get tossed out. There are none.

If merged properly, two companies and even more can be significantly more powerful than one. Ask the folks at Taco Bell, Pizza Hut, and KFC who pulled the three chains together years back and in essence merged them under the PepsiCo umbrella.

Copy the Blueprint

When you started your first restaurant you built a business plan, you devised systems, and you built a blueprint. The blueprint must have been good, or you wouldn't be thinking about opening restaurant number two, number three, and beyond. So copy this blueprint.

Even if your second restaurant happens to be a different restaurant concept in a different city, the blueprint for success is virtually the same. You don't need to reinvent the restaurant wheel. Copy every piece you can and even work to improve on the few things that you feel could have been done better the first go-around.

Food for Thought

Getting the money you need to open your second restaurant will be easier than it was to get the money for your first one. You have a track record now, and because of that track record you become a better risk for the lender or investor. But even though it will be easier, it won't be simple. You will probably still hear "no" a few times.

The Least You Need to Know

➤ Choosing your own future because of success is better than having it chosen for you because of failure.

➤ The basics are always important, whether you are opening your 1st or 101st restaurant.

➤ More restaurants require more organization, systemization, and energy on your part.

➤ Raising restaurants is like raising kids. Each has different needs at different ages.

➤ Whatever worked the first time should be used again and again. Copy your blueprint.

Chapter 24

Restaurant Checklists, Forms, and Guidelines

In This Chapter

➤ What several common restaurant forms look like

➤ Why checklists keep you doing the right thing

➤ How to expand and customize the sample forms to fit your needs

➤ Why making your mark requires that you literally make your mark

Check it out.

No, really, check it all out—on paper.

Go on and use a check mark, many times on many forms, because your restaurant is a complex enterprise that requires many things to run at once in many different areas. The only way to keep track of all these requirements is to use checklists and restaurant forms.

Many different kinds of forms exist to keep track of all that must be tracked. This final chapter shows you some of these forms. I say "some" because a restaurant could use any group out of many dozens of forms. The forms in this chapter provide some outlines of forms you need to build. With these outlines as a guide, you can use a simple computer and a printer to build your own set of restaurant forms personalized to your restaurant and style. This chapter gives you the tools you need to succeed.

Opening Checklist

An opening checklist lists all the tasks that must be completed when the restaurant is opened for the day. As with all checklists, keep opening checklists simple and easy to handle. Any more than one page is a waste of time and effort. If you think you need more than one page to ensure you have the restaurant opened properly, you may have a much bigger issue with your training and follow-up processes. Following is an example of an opening checklist.

Opening Checklist

Comments about opening the restaurant: _____

_____

_____

Check store security upon arrival. _____

Check quality of last night's close. _____

Determine food preparation list. _____

Count daily inventory and note any concerns. _____

Ensure all equipment is properly started. _____

Stock all necessary products. _____

Verify change fund, deposit, and cash drawers. _____

Adjust sales projections if needed. _____

Fill out daily work schedule. _____

Check schedule for proper staffing. _____

Take last night's receipts to deposit in the bank. _____

Pull together paperwork. _____

Assign tasks to employees as needed. _____

Operating the Restaurant

After the restaurant is open, you must keep track of certain tasks to make sure it operates smoothly. Following are two checklists: one for general operation and one for shift changes.

Tip Jar

Make your forms meet your specific needs, but keep all checklists simple and easy to handle. Most well-running restaurants have many checklists that are usually less than one page in length.

Operating Checklist

Ensure that products are ready on time. _____

Coach and direct team members on good service. _____

Correct any procedure violations. _____

Check cleanliness standards. _____

Review and adjust product projection charts. _____

Review labor schedule and adjust it as needed. _____

Place orders as scheduled. _____

Check product availability and quality during shift. _____

Follow proper cash handling procedures. _____

Shift Change

Add up and settle cash drawers. _____

Make bank deposit. _____

Do product inventory over short. _____

Verify change fund. _____

Do product shift change. _____

Date: _____ Checked by: _____

Employment Applications

Some companies have turned their employment applications into a four- to six-page complete personal history that are more painful than a visit to the dentist to fill out. There is no reason for it. Again, keep the application simple and easy to use for both you and the potential employee. Get the basic information you need and move on. Following is an example of an employment application.

Employment Application

Fill this out and return it to this restaurant.

Name: _____

Address: _____

City: _____ State: _____ Zip code: _____

You must be at least 16 years old to work here. Do you meet this requirement? _____ Yes _____ No

You must be at least 18 years old to operate certain kitchen equipment. Do you meet this requirement?

_____ Yes _____ No

Availability

Total hours available per week: _____

Days available to work: _____

School History

Name: _____ Location: _____

Last grade completed: _____ Grade point average: _____

Graduated? ____ Yes ____ No Currently enrolled? ____ Yes ____ No

List any sports or activities that you participate in:

_____

_____

Recent Employment History (If not applicable, list work performed on a volunteer basis.)

Start with your most recent employer:

1. Company name: _____ Address: _____

Phone number: _____

Job title/responsibilities: _____

_____

Supervisor: _____ Dates worked: From _____ To _____

Salary: _____ Reason for leaving: _____

2. Company name: _____ Address: _____

Phone number: _____

Job title/responsibilities: _____

_____

Supervisor: _____ Dates worked: From _____ To _____

Salary: _____ Reason for leaving: _____

3. Company name: _____ Address: _____

Phone number: _____

Job title/responsibilities: _____

_____

Supervisor: _____ Dates worked: From _____ To _____

Salary: _____ Reason for leaving: _____

Wet Floor!

Some states require you to use either a state-approved application form or a local labor board-approved application form. Be sure to contact your local authorities before you use any legal form, including this potential application document.

Reference Check Form

When you call applicants' references, it's helpful to have a reference check form handy to remind you of the bare essentials you need to know and to give you a place to write down the answers you receive. A sample reference check form is provided in this section.

Be sure you have permission to contact the applicant's current employer. Whenever possible, contact the candidate's past supervisors as well. If such contact is not possible, contact the human resources department to verify employment. Make sure you verify the past three to five years of the person's employment.

Reference Check

Applicant's name: _____

Social Security number: _____

Position applied for: _____

Employment History

Name of company: _____ Phone number: _____

Applicant's title: _____

Dates of employment: From _____ To _____

Final salary: _____ Eligible for rehire: Yes ____ No ____

Additional comments: _____

_____

Information from: _____ Title: _____

Name of company: _____ Phone number: _____

Applicant's title: _____

Dates of employment: From _____ To _____

Final salary: _____ Eligible for rehire: Yes ____ No ____

Additional comments: _____

_____

Information from: _____ Title: _____

Name of company: _____ Phone number: _____

Applicant's title: _____

Dates of employment: From _____ To _____

Final salary: _____ Eligible for rehire: Yes _____ No _____

Additional comments: _____

_____

Information from: _____ Title: _____

Comment Card

A comment card is a wonderful opportunity to gain insight into what your customer thinks about your operation. Do not overkill this process by giving the customers a three- or four-page document to fill out (you think I'm joking, but I have seen it many times). The following is an example of a comment card.

Comment Card

Your opinion counts! Please let us know what you think, whether it's good, bad, or indifferent! Thank you.

	Excellent	Good	Fair	Poor
Food quality	_____	_____	_____	_____
Cleanliness of restaurant	_____	_____	_____	_____
Friendliness of staff	_____	_____	_____	_____
Speed of service	_____	_____	_____	_____
Value	_____	_____	_____	_____

Would you visit us again? _____Yes _____ No

Comments: _____

_____

_____

Date of visit: _____ Time of visit: _____

(Mr./Mrs./Ms.) _____

Street: _____

City: _____ State: _____ Zip code: _____

Daytime phone number: _____

Closing Checklist

A closing checklist is critical to the overall execution of the entire operation. Closing time is when all things are moved back to square one, so to speak. Everything is cleaned up and reorganized, and if closing is handled properly, the restaurant is put back in its original order.

Your team members are possibly tired, it is late, and some of them want to get home while others want to go to a friend's house for a game of Go Fish. This checklist helps you hold them to the standard you need to succeed the next day.

The closing checklist should be the most detailed of the checklists and could very well be the only checklist I would allow to be more than a page in length. However, if you can keep it to one page and still get the job done to your standards, by all means do it. Use the following blank form to build your own closing checklist.

Closing Checklist

Kitchen

Dishes washed and put away properly _____

All food stored properly _____

All floors swept and mopped _____

All coolers and freezers organized and doors securely shut _____

_____

_____

Dining room

All tables and chairs cleaned and sanitized _____

All light covers dusted _____

All floors vacuumed and swept _____

_____

_____

Restrooms

Restrooms cleaned and stocked _____

Restroom floors mopped _____

Garbage emptied _____

_____

_____

Wait stations, bus stations

All dishes washed _____

All clean silverware wrapped _____

Wait station stocked _____

Floors mopped _____

_____

_____

Storage areas

Inventory re-organized _____

Garbage tossed out _____

Lights turned off _____

_____

_____

Register areas

Register drawers cashed out _____

Restock mints and toothpicks _____

Wipe down register and POP material _____

_____

_____

Final walk-through and check _____

Money and safe secured _____

All employees clocked out _____

All doors locked, alarm set, and lights set per manual _____

The Daily Business Review

The daily business review can be set up any way you like to help you keep an eye on the items that are most important to the success of your restaurant. Don't try to keep track of everything because the tracking form will become so detailed that you won't be able to keep track of anything. Stick with the critical few versus the menial many. The critical few that have the biggest impact on the success of your business are Sales, Sales vs. Last Year, Food Cost, Labor Cost, Cash, and Customer counts, but you can adjust it to anything you personally want. You may think something else is more important to you.

The following form is an example of a daily business review.

Daily Business Review

Month: _____

Date	Total Sales $	Total Sales Last Year (LY)	Total Sales $ +/− LY	Total Sales % +/− LY	Food Cost %	Labor Cost %	Cash +/−	Customer Counts
Mon								
Tues								
Wed								
Thurs								
Fri								
Sat								
Sun								
Week Total								
Mon								
Tues								
Wed								
Thurs								
Fri								
Sat								
Sun								
Week Total								
Mon								
Tues								
Wed								
Thurs								
Fri								
Sat								
Sun								
Week Total								
Mon								
Tues								
Wed								
Thurs								
Fri								
Sat								
Sun								
Week Total								

Shift Schedule

A shift schedule is used much like a complete restaurant schedule to help the person running the shift know who is coming in and what time each person is scheduled to leave. This working document has notes written on it throughout the shift, such as when people are projected to take their breaks and if someone has a thought to give to the scheduler about a training deficiency or a cross-training need. The following is a sample shift schedule.

Shift Schedule

Day_____ Date _____

Name:	Shift	3:00	4:00	5:00	6:00	7:00	8:00	9:00	10:00	Ttl. Hrs.
# of people scheduled										
Hours scheduled										

Tip Jar

A shift schedule is a great tool to help you control labor costs. If someone is scheduled for six hours and you keep that person for seven, that will cost you more in labor than what was projected. If sales volumes are not higher than projected, that extra labor cost would be a mistake.

Interview Guide

An interview guide is a simple one-page form to help keep the interviewer focused on proper interviewing skills and techniques. This tool is handy and helps make your interviews more productive. The following is an example of an interview guide.

Interview Guide

➤ Do immediate interviews if possible. If a great applicant comes in during a peak revenue period, ask him or her to come back immediately after the peak revenue period.

➤ Be available for interviews at varying times of the day and week.

➤ Offer applicants a beverage and a place to sit to fill out an application; make them feel welcome.

➤ Treat applicants as you would treat your guests. This kind of treatment helps your restaurant maintain a positive reputation as well as communicates your values and expectations.

➤ Conduct the interview in an area where you will not be interrupted.

➤ Get the applicant talking as much as possible. Now is not the time to tell your life story; it is time for applicants to tell theirs.

➤ When choosing your interview questions, consider what the new employee will be asked to do.

➤ Ask open-ended questions (questions that cannot be answered with yes or no).

➤ Don't ask leading questions (questions which give away the preferred answer).

➤ Follow the ADA and EEOC guidelines for interview questions; only ask questions that directly relate to the job.

Successful team member candidate absolutes:

➤ Smiles easily

➤ Maintains eye contact

➤ Good image/neat appearance

➤ On time for interview

Look for S.I.D.E. +1+1 (as discussed in Chapter 9, "Whoever Gets the Best People Wins: It's a People Game"):

Smart

Integrity

Drive

Enthusiasm

+1 Image

+1 Service Orientation

Wet Floor!

If the following things come up during an interview, you probably do not want to hire this applicant:

➤ Left previous job(s) without adequate notice

➤ No verifiable references

➤ Must travel too far to work

➤ Badmouths previous employer

➤ Inappropriate attire

➤ No smiles or eye contact

Secret Shopper Form

A secret shopper form allows you to use friends, family, neighbors, vendors, and even random customers who, for a free meal, will give you valuable information about the performance of your restaurant. Use yes or no questions to keep the form simple and easy for both you and the secret shopper, as shown in the following example.

Secret Shopper Form

Date: _____ Time: _____

Circle Yes or No to answer each of the following questions.

Hospitality

1. Were you greeted with a smile and a friendly introduction?   Yes   No

2. Was the staff hospitable to you during a slow period?   Yes   No

3. Were you thanked and invited back?   Yes   No

4. Did the server suggest additional menu items (suggestive selling)?   Yes   No

5. Were you offered condiment choices?   Yes   No

Comments about hospitality: _____

_____

Quality

6. Was the hot food hot and the cold food cold?   Yes   No

7. Was the restaurant out of any requested items?   Yes   No

8. Was the presentation attractive?   Yes   No

9. Did the food look and taste fresh?   Yes   No

Comments about quality: _____

_____

Service

10. Was the service fast?   Yes   No

11. Was the cashier and/or waiter quick and knowledgeable?   Yes   No

12. Were employees in uniform?   Yes   No

13. Was there sufficient staff to handle business?   Yes   No

Comments about service: _____

_____

Cleanliness

14. Were the restrooms clean and stocked?   Yes   No

15. Was the condiment stand clean and stocked?   Yes   No

16. Was the parking lot area clean and well maintained?   Yes   No

17. Was the entrance and dining room generally clean?   Yes   No

Comments about cleanliness: _____

_____

Accuracy

18. Did you receive what you ordered?   Yes   No

19. Were you charged the correct price and given the correct change? Yes   No

Comments about accuracy: _____

_____

Overall Experience

20. Rank your overall experience: Great   Okay   Poor

Comments about overall experience: _____

_____

Income Statement

Chapter 11, "Basic Accounting: It's More Than Just Counting the Beans," talked about the importance of the income statement. Following is a basic, blank income statement for you to copy and use for your establishment:

Income Statement

For the Period of _____ to _____

	$	Percent of Total Sales
Sales	$	%
Food		
Beverage		
Total Sales		
Cost of Sales		
Food and Beverage Cost		
Paper Cost		
Total Cost of Sales		
Gross Profit		
Controllable Expense		
Direct Payroll		
Indirect Payroll, Taxes, Employee Benefits, etc.		
Misc. Operating Expense		
Repairs/Maint.		
Utilities		
General Admin.		
Advertising		
Total Controllable Expenses		
Profit Before Occupancy Expense		
Rent		
Taxes		
Insurance		
Interest		
Depreciation		
Net Profit	+$	

Product Inventory and Usage Sheet

Use the product inventory and usage sheet to determine how much of a product you have on hand and how much you use of each product each week. Copy this form and build your own form from it.

Product Inventory and Usage Sheet

Date of Inventory _____   *Inventory taken by:* _____

Name of Item	Unit of Mea- sure	Starting Inven- tory (+)	Purchases (+)	Available Inven- tory (=)	# of Units on Hand (–)	Item Usage (=)	Unit Cost $	Item Cost of Usage
Grand Total								

Restaurant Site Analysis Worksheet

When you're looking at possible sites for your restaurant, take lots and lots of notes. Otherwise, you will forget important details and possibly confuse different sites.

Restaurant Site Analysis Worksheet

Address/name of site: _____

Present owner/agent: _____

Contact information: _____

Asking price: _____ Special terms: _____

Date of inspection: _____

Size of space, lot, building: _____

Expansion possibilities: _____

Visibility, accessibility, clearance, zoning, barriers, parking, etc.:

_____

_____

_____

_____

_____

Utilities, soil conditions, water conditions, etc.: _____

_____

_____

_____

Economic data, wage trends, income levels, seasonal features, population makeup, labor supply: _____

_____

_____

_____

_____

_____

Traffic data: _____

_____

Competition: _____

269

Food for Thought

All site selection analysis starts by taking good notes. You will look at many sites (hopefully you won't just take the first thing that comes along), and you won't be able to remember everything about all of them.

Invoice Register

An invoice register helps you keep track of all of your incoming invoices. I have mine on the outside of the invoice envelope with a clasp. I stuff the invoices in the envelope, mark the outside, and get back to serving customers. (That's the restaurant business.) The following is an example of an invoice register.

Invoice Register

Vendor Name	Inv. #	Inv. Date	Food	Paper	Clean Supply	Rest. Supp.	R/M	Off. Supp.	Misc.	Total
Total										

Recipes Revealed

R/M in the preceding form stands for Repairs and Maintenance. Many of the companies providing repairs and maintenance for your restaurant are small businesses with many of the same challenges small restaurants have—not enough time in the day. Often, the entire invoicing and crediting procedures take a back seat to fixing things. This can be a hassle when your invoicing gets messed up. This form will help you track these costs.

Operational Audit Action Plan Form

An operational audit action plan form is a simple but effective form. It works like this: Write down any operational (or for that matter any other kind) issue, concern, or performance letdown you see and then devise an action step or two. Last, assign a follow-up date to ensure the action gets done. The first step to knowing you have a problem is admitting it. The first step to fixing the problem is writing it down.

Operational Audit Action Plan

Deficiency	Corrective Action	Who Is Responsible	Due Date

A Simple Cash Flow Form

A cash flow form helps immensely. Use it.

Besides the obvious of helping you determine your cash flow, it also allows you to easily compare one month to the next and provides an easy analysis on whether your cash flow is improving.

271

Cash Flow Form

	Jan	Feb	Mar	Apr	May	Jun
Income						
Food sales						
Beverage sales						
Sales receivables						
Other income						
Expenses						
Total income						
Cost of food						
Cost of drinks						
Payroll						
Employee benefits						
Direct operating expense						
Advertising and promotion						
Utilities						
Administrative and general						
Repairs and maintenance						
Occupancy costs						
Rent						
Property taxes						
Other taxes						
Insurance						
Interest						
Other deductions						
Total cash disbursements						
Cash flow						
Income						
– Total cash disbursements						
= Net from operations						
Cash on hand						
Opening balance						
+ New loan (debt)						
+ New investment						
+ Sale of fixed assets						
+ Net from operations						
= Total cash available						
– Debt reduction						
– New fixed assets						
– Dividends to stockholders						
– Stock redemption						
– Loans to officers						
= Total cash paid out						
Ending cash balance						

Competitor's Scorecard

You must clearly know how you stack up against your competition. Be honest with yourself. To compete at a high level, you must call it as you see it on a regular basis. The customers do. The following form is an example of a competitor's scorecard.

Competitor's Scorecard

Name of competitor: _____

Date: _____

Customer Seeks:	Competition Offers:	We Offer:
Hospitality		
Quality		
Speed of service		
Cleanliness		
Pricing		
Promotions and discounts		
Menu selection		
Location		
Parking		
Atmosphere/image		
Quality of staff		
Forms of payment		

Comments:

_____

_____

Deposit Verification Log

Use a deposit verification log like the following to keep track of and verify all of your bank deposits.

Deposit Verification Log

Date	Day of Week	Deposit Amount	+/–	Validation Date	Depositor's Signature
	Monday				
	Tuesday				
	Wednesday				
	Thursday				
	Friday				
	Saturday				
	Sunday				
	Monday				
	Tuesday				
	Wednesday				
	Thursday				
	Friday				
	Saturday				
	Sunday				
	Monday				
	Tuesday				
	Wednesday				
	Thursday				
	Friday				
	Saturday				
	Sunday				
	Monday				
	Tuesday				
	Wednesday				
	Thursday				
	Friday				
	Saturday				
	Sunday				
	Monday				
	Tuesday				
	Wednesday				
	Thursday				
	Friday				
	Saturday				
	Sunday				

One Final Checklist

Success is the greatest feeling. Winning is better than losing, and rich is better than broke. Also, giving is better than taking. If you want to succeed in your new restaurant business, you will find that you create your own world.

I am a restaurant guy, and I have clients who come to me needing their restaurants fixed. I am a mechanic, a consultant, a guru, and a purveyor of common sense. Always, I say this:

> Your biggest fear should be the fear of no impact, the fear that you walk through life and no one ever sees that you left your mark, even if some of those marks are stumbles, trips, and falls.

Make your mark. Do things that leave an indelible mark on customers, employees, peers, bosses, friends, and family; things that they can't help but remember and even talk to others about. Be passionate, driven, and unrelenting. Let your heart really pump. Be emotional. Show your feelings; cry when you feel like it and laugh in your belly. Touch people in their hearts and challenge people to be their very best. Make a difference and leave a mark. And be sure to follow this final checklist to guarantee success:

➤ Have great checklists.

➤ Always do everything on your checklists.

Tip Jar

Contact Restaurant Operations Institute via the Web site at www.roiontheweb.com and pick up the complete CD or floppy disk of virtually every restaurant form, checklist, and guideline you could ever need. This CD allows you to download over fifty different forms and provides many different-looking options for the same forms. You can download these and adjust them with a simple click of the mouse to suit your particular needs. Print them and in minutes you're ready to go.

The Least You Need to Know

➤ The forms in this chapter are examples and should be modified as necessary.

➤ Notes help you remember things and accomplish things.

➤ Systems equal success. You must establish systems and keep track of how the systems are working.

➤ The restaurant business requires checklists and forms.

Additional Reference Materials

Books

Bhote, Keki R. *Beyond Customer Satisfaction to Customer Loyalty: The Key to Greater Profitability.* New York: AMA, 1996.

Blanchard, Kenneth, and Robert Lorber. *Putting the One Minute Manager to Work: How to Turn the 3 Secrets into Skills.* New York: Berkley Books, 1985.

Buckingham, Marcus, and Curt Coffman. *First, Break All the Rules: What the World's Greatest Managers Do Differently.* New York: Simon & Schuster, 1999.

Daniels, Aubrey. *Bringing Out the Best in People: How to Apply the Astonishing Power of Positive Reinforcement.* New York: McGraw-Hill, Inc., 1994.

Douglass, Merrill E., and Donna N. Douglass. *Manage Your Time, Your Work, Yourself.* New York: AMA, 1993.

Drucker, Peter. *Managing for Results.* New York: HarperCollins Publishers, 1986.

Freiberg, Kevin and Jackie Freiberg. *Nuts: Southwest Airlines' Crazy Recipe for Business and Personal Success.* Austin: Bard Press, Inc., 1996.

Gedded, Lindsay. *Through the Customers' Eyes: Improving Your Company's Results with the Core Method.* New York: AMA, 1993.

Gross, T. Scott. *Positively Outrageous Service: New & Easy Ways to Win Customers for Life.* New York: Mastermedia Limited, 1991.

Imai, Masaaki. *Kaizen: The Key to Japan's Competitive Success.* New York: McGraw-Hill Publishing Company, 1986.

Karr, Ron, and Don Blohowiak. *The Complete Idiot's Guide to Great Customer Service.* Indianapolis: Simon & Schuster Macmillan Company, 1997.

Kivirist, Lisa. *Kiss Off Corporate America: A Young Professional's Guide to Independence.* Kansas City: Andrews McMeel Publishing, 1998.

Kyne, Peter. *The Go-Getter: A Story That Tells You How to Be One.* New York: Henry Holt Company, Inc., 1921.

Nelson, Bob. *1001 Ways to Reward Employees.* New York: Workman Publishing, 1994.

Paulson, Ed. *The Complete Idiot's Guide to Buying & Selling a Business.* Indianapolis: Simon & Schuster Macmillan Company, 1999.

Sanders, Betsy. *Fabled Service: Ordinary Acts, Extraordinary Outcomes.* San Francisco: Jossey Bass Publishers, 1997.

Slutsky, Jeff. *Streetfighter Marketing.* New York: Simon & Schuster, Inc., 1995.

Sullivan, Jim, Phil Robert, and Andrea Stewart. *Turn the Tables on Turnover: 52 Ways to Find, Hire, and Keep the Best Hospitality Employees.* Denver: Pencom International, 1995.

Thomsett, Michael. *Winning Numbers: How to Use Business Facts & Figures to Make Your Point & Get Ahead.* New York: American Management Association, 1990.

Zemke, Ron, and Kristin Anderson. *Coaching Knock Your Socks Off Service.* New York: AMA, 1996.

Restaurant Publications

Bread & Butter: 202-331-5900

Chain Leader: 847-390-2051

Food Management: 216-696-7000

Hospitality Design: 212-592-6265

Nation's Restaurant News: 1-800-944-4676

Nightclub & Bar: 662-236-5510

Pizza Today: 812-949-0909

QSR: 1-800-662-4834

Restaurant Finance Monitor: 1-800-528-3296

Restaurant Hospitality: 216-696-7000

Restaurant Marketing: 662-236-5510

Restaurants & Institutions: 1-800-446-6551

Web Sites

Internal Revenue Service: www.irs.gov/smallbiz/restaurants/

Restaurant Operations Institute: www.roiontheweb.com

Restaurant Organization: www.restaurant.org

Restaurants & Institutions: www.rimag.com

Why Team-Building Programs Really Work: www.thinksmart.com/articles/teamprograms.html

Catalog of Publications

National Restaurant Association
Department A
1200 Seventeenth Street NW
Washington, DC 20036-3097
Phone: 1-800-482-9122
Fax: 202-331-5971

Broad-Based Industry Consultants and Resources

Restaurant Operations Institute, Inc.
65 Woodbury Drive
Sterrett, AL 35147
Phone: 205-323-5559
E-mail: roi3434@aol.com
Web site: www.roiontheweb.com

Restaurant Associations

Alabama Restaurant Association
61-B Market Place
Montgomery, AL 36117
334-244-1320; Fax: 334-244-9800

Alaska Hotel/Motel Association
P.O. Box 104900
Anchorage, AK 99510
907-272-1229; Fax: 907-272-1819

Arizona Restaurant Association
2400 N. Central #410
Phoenix, AZ 85004
602-307-9134; Fax: 602-307-9139

Arkansas Hospitality Association
P.O. Box 3866
Little Rock, AR 72203
501-376-2323; Fax: 501-376-6517

California Restaurant Association
1011 10th Street
Sacramento, CA 95814
1-800-794-4272; Fax: 916-447-6182

Colorado Restaurant Association
430 East 7th Avenue
Denver, CO 80203
303-830-2972; Fax: 303-830-2973

Connecticut Restaurant Association
731 Hebron Avenue
Glastonbury, CT 06033
860-633-5484; Fax: 860-657-8241

Delaware Restaurant Association
148 Glade Circle West
Rehoboth Beach, DE 19971
302-227-7300

Florida Restaurant Association
230 S. Adams Street
Tallahassee, FL 32301
850-224-2250; Fax: 850-224-9213

Georgia Hospitality Association
600 W. Peachtree Street #1500
Atlanta, GA 30308
404-873-4482; Fax: 404-874-5742

Hawaii Restaurant Association
1164 Bishop Street #905
Honolulu, HI 96813-2810
808-536-9105; Fax: 808-534-0117

Idaho Hospitality and Lodging
1109 Main Street #210
Boise, ID 83702
208-342-1221; Fax: 208-342-0060

Illinois Restaurant Association
200 N. La Salle #880
Chicago, IL 60601
312-787-4000; Fax: 312-787-4792

Indiana Restaurant Association
200 S. Meridian #350
Indianapolis, IN 46225
317-673-4211; Fax: 317-673-4210

Iowa Restaurant Association
8525 Douglas Avenue #47
Des Moines, IA 50322
515-276-1454; Fax: 515-276-3660

Kansas Hospitality Association
359 S. Hydraulic
Wichita, KS 67211
316-267-8383; Fax: 316-267-8400

Kentucky Restaurant Association
512 Executive Park
Louisville, KY 40207
502-896-0464; Fax: 502-896-0465

Louisiana Restaurant Association
2700 N. Arnoult Road
Metairie, LA 70002
504-454-2277; Fax: 504-454-2299

Maine Restaurant Association
Augusta, ME 04332
207-623-2178; Fax: 207-623-8377

Restaurant Association of Maryland
7113 Ambassador Road
Baltimore, MD 21244
410-298-0011; Fax: 410-298-0299

Massachusetts Restaurant Association
95-A Turnpike Road
Westborough, MA 01581
508-366-4144; Fax: 508-366-4614

Michigan Restaurant Association
225 W. Washtenaw
Lansing, MI 48933
517-482-5244; Fax: 517-482-7663

Mississippi Restaurant Association
4506 Office Park Drive
Jackson, MS 39206
601-982-4281; Fax: 601-982-0062

Missouri Restaurant Association
121 Madison
Jefferson City, MO 65101
573-659-8111; Fax: 573-659-7343

Nebraska Restaurant Association
5625 O Street #7
Lincoln, NE 68510
402-483-2630; Fax: 402-483-2746

Nevada Restaurant Association
4820 Alpine Place #F203
Las Vegas, NV 89107
702-878-2313; Fax: 702-878-5009

New Hampshire Restaurant Association
P.O. Box 1175
Concord, NH 03302
603-228-9585; Fax: 603-226-1829

New Jersey Restaurant Association
One Executive Drive #100
Somerset, NJ 08873
732-302-1800; Fax: 732-302-1804

New Mexico Restaurant Association
3700 Osuna NE #603
Albuquerque, NM 87109
1-800-432-0740; Fax: 505-343-9891

New York State Restaurant Association
505 8th Avenue, 7th Floor
New York, NY 10018
212-714-1330; Fax: 212-643-2962

North Carolina Restaurant Association
P.O. Box 6528
Raleigh, NC 27628
919-782-5022; Fax: 919-782-7251

North Dakota Hospitality Association
2718 Gateway Avenue #304
P.O. Box 428
Bismark, ND 58502
701-223-3313; Fax: 701-223-0216

Ohio Restaurant Association
1525 Bethel Road #301
Columbus, OH 43220
614-442-3535; Fax: 614-442-3550

Oklahoma Restaurant Association
3800 N. Portland Street
Oklahoma City, OK 73112
405-942-8181; Fax: 405-942-0541

Oregon Restaurant Association
8565 SW Salish Lane #120
Wilsonville, OR 97070
503-682-4422; Fax: 503-682-4455

Pennsylvania Restaurant Association
100 State Street
Harrisburg, PA 17101
717-232-4433; Fax: 717-236-1202

Restaurant Association Metro Washington
1501 Lee Highway #150
Arlington, VA 22209
703-528-4800; Fax: 703-528-9727

Tennessee Restaurant Association
P.O. Box 681207
Franklin, TN 37068
615-790-2703; Fax: 615-790-2768

Texas Restaurant Association
1400 Lavaca Street
Austin, TX 78701
512-457-4100; Fax: 512-472-2777

Utah Restaurant Association
420 East S. Temple
Salt Lake City, UT 84111
801-322-0123; Fax: 801-322-0122

Vermont Lodging Association
3 Main Street #106
Burlington, VT 05401
802-660-9001; Fax: 802-660-8987

Virginia Hospitality Association
2101 Libbie Avenue
Richmond, VA 23230
804-288-3065; Fax: 804-285-3093

Washington Restaurant Association
2405 Evergreen Park Drive SW #A
Olympia, WA 98502
360-956-7279; Fax: 360-357-9232

West Virginia Association
P.O. Box 2391
Charleston, WV 25328
304-342-6511; Fax: 304-345-1538

Wisconsin Restaurant Association
2801 Fish Hatchery Road
Madison, WI 53713
1-800-589-3211; Fax: 608-270-9960

Glossary

ABCD award   An award (usually a plaque and tickets or a gift certificate) that some restaurants give out to employees who go above and beyond the call of duty (ABCD) in order to reinforce the message that those who provide high levels of hospitality will be rewarded on a continual basis.

backordered   A product that the vendor or warehouse ran out of.

bounce back   A coupon given to the customer after he or she has made their purchase. The idea is to entice them to come back soon. It is usually issued with a seven- to fourteen-day expiration.

casual dining   A restaurant that provides table service, a fun, relaxing environment, and a meal cost between $6 and $15.

company culture   The environment that surrounds and affects every decision made inside your restaurant from how problems are dealt with to how good work is rewarded.

competitive analysis   Detailed information about who your competition is, what your competition provides in the way of products, services, and benefits to the customer, and how well you can compete against the competition.

core menu concept   The main product line of your menu. This concept could be a style of food, such as Italian, Mexican, American, or Japanese, or even a kind of food, such as hamburgers, chicken, or pizza. The rest of the menu (beverages, appetizers, deserts, and so on) is traditionally secondary and is added on to the core menu concept.

corporation (C-Corp)   A legal entity that exists separately from the owners. Legally, a corporation is like a person: It can be sued, own property, or acquire debts. Setting up a corporation is expensive to begin with, but it is usually well worth it if you are going to plan on being in business for a while. Corporations come in many forms and many times offer better tax advantages and liability reduction than other legal structures.

corrective feedback   Giving the employee tips to help improve performance. These tips are given many dozens of times throughout the day.

customer contact point   The point where the customer and the employee come in contact with each other from a service perspective.

day-part   The time of day when a specific type of meal is served. Breakfast, lunch, and dinner are all day-parts.

demographic surveys   Surveys that determine and analyze such characteristics as age, gender, income levels, lifestyles, consumer habits, and more. Restaurant start-ups frequently conduct demographic surveys to collect this type of data to help determine locations, concept types, menu offerings, and prices. A demographic survey helps a restaurateur pinpoint a given market that is appropriate for a given concept.

egress   Ease of exit of the restaurant.

feasibility study   Tests the many components of your business concept to see if it will work.

FIFO   Stands for first in, first out, which means that the product on the shelves should be used before you use the products that are newly coming in.

franchising   A system for expanding a business and distributing goods and services.

full service   A type of restaurant where the emphasis is on waiting on the customer hand and foot and providing a high quality of food and upscale ambience. The cost of a meal in a full-service restaurant is usually above $15.

goodwill   Defined by the Internal Revenue Service as any amount paid for a business that exceeds the fair market value of hard assets. The law allows goodwill to be apportioned to such items as trademarks, patents, copyrights, customer lists, name recognition, concept attributes, the community image, and public perception.

high-impression area   A place that customers frequently see. In these areas, a high number (maybe all) of your customers get their impression about your restaurant's cleanliness.

hold time   The length of time you can hold a product before it must be discarded. If a product has a hold time of ten minutes, then from the time it is done being cooked until it must stopped being served is ten minutes. After that, it is not worthy of serving to your customers.

HQSC   Hospitality, quality, service, and cleanliness. The lifeblood of the business, the common denominator that all restaurant owners must strive to achieve regardless of category, segment, sales volume, or size of company.

ingress   Ease of entrance into a restaurant.

learning organization   One where learning, growing, teaching, mentoring, and continued improvement and education are valued.

limited liability company (LLC)   A company that invests in a business but has no management responsibility and no liability for the business beyond the money invested.

LTO   A limited time offer. This new product or menu item is intended to drive new customer trial or higher customer frequency.

margin markup   The markup above what the distributor paid for the item from the manufacturer. This number is important to know when you are selecting a distributor.

market penetration   Opening a new restaurant in an area where your restaurant concept and name have little to no recognition.

market saturation   Building your restaurants in closer proximity within the same city, county, or region to each other so you gain customer recognition of your concept.

menu mix   The percentage of sales volume each item in your restaurant represents in a given week. This number is calculated by determining the number of each menu item sold in a typical week and then multiplying that number by the menu price and then dividing that number by the total sales. For example, if you sold 868 cheeseburgers at $3.99 each, then cheeseburgers would account for $3,463.32 in sales. If you did $15,000 in sales in the week, then cheeseburgers would account for 23.1 percent of your menu mix.

open-door policy   Refers to the boss' door that is always open so that employees feel free to talk to the boss about any problems, concerns, suggestions, or questions they may have. This policy is more of a theory than actual practice in many restaurants. Usually, a boss allots specific times to discuss issues, or an employee must make an appointment.

outsourcing   When you pay someone who is not an employee of your restaurant to do a project, such as build a food manual. Many times, the person you hire for the project has his or her own business.

partnership   A business relationship between two or more people who agree to share their talents, profits, and losses in specific portions. This business structure is more complex than the sole proprietorship and has some advantages, but many restaurant owners have abandoned it due to tax and liability issues.

pass station   The area where the food is passed from the back of the house to the front of the house. Often it includes a hot hold (on one shelf) and a cold hold (on another shelf). This station provides a place for the kitchen staff to set prepared food until the wait staff picks it up.

perceived value   A fair price as determined by the customers. It is based on a mixture of what they received in the way of products, services, and environment and what they paid for that overall feeling. If the customer was happy with the overall experience, then the perceived value was good.

plate setup   The design of how a product is served.

points of distinction   What makes you different from your competitors. It may be your menu, your decor, your prices, or a host of other things. Your restaurant should have something to make it stand out from the crowd.

Point of purchase   Marketing that is done right at the point where the customer purchases, i.e., near the menu board, in the drive through, or throughout the building. It is intended to persuade the customer to buy the items you're offering at the moment they intend to purchase.

positive mental attitude (PMA) rally   A quick floor meeting that, if executed properly, can significantly improve your hospitality culture. These stand-up rallies should last two to three minutes and should be held at the beginning of every peak revenue period. This rally becomes a great time to bring up new ideas and concepts, but getting two-way communication is paramount. A PMA rally can also instill a higher level of morale.

prime interest rate   The interest rate charged to customers of a bank who have the best credit. It is a reference point for other loan rates given by the bank.

quick service   A restaurant serving low-cost meals (under $7) through counter service. The emphasis is on speed of service and convenience, and the decor is simple and practical.

reprimand   A disciplinary discussion that is held behind closed doors (or at least away from other employees) to deal with a particular performance issue.

Segment   The industry is broken into many segments. Fine dining, casual dining, fast food, and many more. A segment is any business concepts that have like and comparable attributes.

slide deployment   A maneuver when staff move from their main responsibilities to help with a bottleneck. This maneuver shows the power of teamwork and training in helping a customer and a fellow employee in need.

sole proprietorship   A business owned and run by one person. This business structure is a common form for small businesses. This structure is the simplest and cheapest legal structure, but it can cost you tons in lost tax advantages and increased personal liability.

stair-stepping   Bringing people into and out of the shift at different intervals to ensure a smoother transition, higher productivity, and improved labor cost.

table turns   The number of times a given table is occupied per hour. This number determines the average stay and is highly dependent upon your concept, your speed of service, and your service staff's ability to bus, clean, and reset a table. A fast-food establishment may average four table turns per hour (meaning average stays of 15 minutes). Fine-dining restaurants may average less than one table turn per hour.

target market analysis   Profiling your main projected customers to determine their age, income level, and lifestyle. This information greatly affects site selection, the marketing plan and execution, menu design, and virtually every other aspect of your restaurant.

theoretical food cost   The food cost you should run based on your menu mix and your item cost. It does not take into account waste, theft, or spoilage and is an ideal number that gives you an overall food cost in dollars and percentage points that you should achieve.

traffic counts   Figures that indicate the average daily number of cars or pedestrians passing a particular location within a 12- or 24-hour period. These numbers are derived from a traffic survey that can be conducted by a real estate firm, demographic firm, planning commission, highway department, or you. Generally, this survey is done by placing a black rubber hose connected to a digital counter across a traffic artery.

triple-net lease   A lease in which the leasee pays expenses, such as property taxes, insurance, and maintenance.

VIP party   A private party often held the night before a restaurant opening. You invite community leaders, business associates, neighboring business employees, family, friends, the mayor, and the local media to your restaurant to build momentum and a word-of-mouth buzz about your business. Fancy invitations, festive decorations and music, and free trinkets with the restaurant's logo are staples of this kind of party.

waste factor   A percentage added to food cost percentages to account for a small amount of necessary waste. Some products exceed hold time and need to be thrown away, and a small amount of spoilage and mistakes always occur.

what-if situations   Situations that are supposed to be thought out ahead of time, as in "What if such-and-such happens?" Having a ready response helps you to prepare for whatever may come.

yield   The amount of usable product a given item delivers. For example, a 16-ounce cut of meat may produce only 13 ounces of usable product after the fat has been trimmed.

Index

U

V

W

X–Y–Z